CHANGING EMPIRE
Churchill to Nehru
BY ERIC ESTORICK

One of the great events in modern history has been the vast political change in the British Empire, and this has taken place so quietly that most Americans have failed to recognize its far-reaching and hopeful significance. At the 1949 conference of prime ministers, when it was agreed that autonomous republics could enter the Commonwealth, the transformation of the Empire was hailed as a great triumph, particularly for Mr. Attlee, prime minister of one of the oldest nations, and for Mr. Nehru, prime minister of one of the youngest republics. It was a triumph of reason over tradition and prejudice, an affirmation that modern states could hold together in a common purpose and in mutual freedom better than they could unite through the domination of any one power.

Eric Estorick, in this masterful survey, gives a clear, full picture of what has happened to Britain and her Empire. In doing so he has drawn memorable and penetrating portraits of the great statesmen who have played their part in the drama, including Attlee, Mackenzie King, Churchill, Smuts, Nehru, Evatt, and Bevin.

CHANGING EMPIRE

Also by Eric Estorick

STAFFORD CRIPPS: MASTER STATESMAN

CHANGING EMPIRE

CHURCHILL TO NEHRU

Eric Estorick

DUELL, SLOAN AND PEARCE
New York

Copyright, 1950, by
Eric Estorick

FIRST EDITION

For

Salome and Isobel,

in the fond hope that politics can, at this
stage of human development, still advance
the human race

C O N T E N T S

I N T R O D U C T I O N

THIS BOOK IS A STUDY OF THE
driving forces in the history of the *British Empire* which
have distinguished it from its rivals for world power and
transformed it increasingly from a centralized imperial power
into an association of independent nations. I have rejected
what, in some quarters, is an accepted mode of treating the
history of the *British Empire* as if it were a series of empires,
as the *First British Empire,* the *Second,* the *Third,* and so on,
for reasons which appear to me cogent and forceful. At all
stages of its evolution, whatever its vicissitudes and eruptions,
there has been continuous government and authority exercised either by the British monarch or the Imperial British
Government of England over their colonies and dominions,
until the very latest times of its transformation into the Commonwealth. Until the passing of the *Westminster Act* in 1931,
England could, and did, declare war for the Empire as a
whole. That fact alone is sufficient evidence of the power of
the metropolitan center over its dominions and colonies. The
continuity of the *British Empire* from the time England established her first colony overseas is an established fact, but the
form, character, and area of its dominions have changed during its history. With those changes, in form and character,
this book is primarily concerned. For they are most profound
and far-reaching, differing greatly from those of any other
empire, ancient or modern. Whereas other empire states have
sought and succeeded in absorbing nations and undeveloped
territories through conquest, purchase, or creation, as exem-
plified by the United States of America and the Union of
Soviet Socialist Republics, the British Empire has been a
breeder of new nations and a stimulator of nationalism in the

nations it conquered. In the process, its leading statesmen have shown a remarkable capacity for adapting their imperial and national institutions to the new circumstances of the twentieth century. The changes that have taken place in the structure of the *British Empire,* and the adjustment of the power relations of its constituent elements, are sufficiently far-reaching and fundamental in their nature to be described as revolutionary. Nevertheless, they have been made with the minimum of social dislocation. Nor have the statesmen who played the leading roles in steering the nations within the *British Empire* toward *The Commonwealth* been iconoclasts of revolution. In the main, they have been fundamentally conservative, treading cautiously and aiming at the organic continuity of association rather than national separatism or imperial domination.

While the history of the British Empire stretches across centuries, our main concern is with the transformation of the Empire into a Commonwealth and with the statesmen primarily responsible for the transition from the former to the latter stage. Man makes history. He makes it with the materials of history which are his heritage, but in circumstances not of his own choosing. It is a striking fact that in each *crisis* which has marked a decisive change in the evolution toward Commonwealth in the British Empire, some new figure has come forward to epitomize within himself the issue involved in the crisis and the history of the emerging nation. For this reason, on the background of a short analysis of the evolution of the Empire, the story of the emerging Commonwealth has been told in a series of biographical studies of the statesmen who have hammered it into shape. It would be foolish to say that any one of them had set before himself, as a life's purpose or as an ideal scheme, the pattern of human association which has been produced. Indeed, it would be much nearer the truth to say that each has striven to express the national aspirations and the interests, economic, social, and political, of the nation he represented without rupturing their common relation with Britain and to give that relationship a new character and meaning. Naturally, these profiles of the makers of the Commonwealth, while giving due significance to their individual histories, have special regard to the part they have played in the great transition. Their names, indelibly written in the records of these years of rapid transition: Winston Churchill, Clement Attlee, and Ernest Bevin of Great Britain, Mackenzie King of Canada, Jan Christiaan Smuts of South Africa, Jawaharlal Nehru of India, and Herbert Vere Evatt of Australia.

At the same time, it will be readily recognized that the evolution of the *British Empire* into *The Commonwealth* did not end in 1949. The status of 60,000,000 people of the British Empire, scattered in many territories spread across the globe, remains in regard to the British government today what that of the many Commonwealth nations was before they achieved their independence. But they are on the move. The great majority of the Irish people are still dissatisfied at the separation of Ulster from Eire; a number of Indian groups are hostile to Nehru's civil liberties policies: and Bevin's policy in the near East has been severely criticized by Jews and non-Jews. Nor is that all. The new Commonwealth, no less than the old Empire, has been unable to escape the impact of the revolutionary changes in world power and the structure of modern society. Hardly had the Commonwealth emerged from its constitutional inauguration than its very existence was challenged by the trading and financial storms of the Western world and the agitation of *cold war* between East and West.

The Second World War not only hastened the transformation of the British Empire into the Commonwealth but gave birth to the United Nations Organization—the "larger synthesis." All the nation-states which comprise the Commonwealth became members of the larger international association. All became involved in a world crisis which threatens the existence of all nations. It was therefore necessary to carry

forward the discussion of the Commonwealth to the crisis
conditions of the present era. This has been done in the concluding chapter.

The world crisis which has gripped the post-war world and
threatens both the Commonwealth and the United Nations is
twofold—political and economic. The "cold war" is a political term describing the fierce political rivalry within the
world organization—the Eastern and the Western camps. The
economic aspects of the crisis consist fundamentally in reha-
bilitating the economies of the countries broken by the war
and finding new markets for the expanding productive forces
of the Western Hemisphere—with a world cut in half by
political disputation. It may be presented broadly, in another
way, as the problem of whether the nations which have gone
through the storm and stress of social revolution can come to
terms with the nations which have not experienced social revolution, and establish a new political equilibrium in which the
trade of the world can redevelop without political turmoil.
The crisis which has been produced by these conflicting issues
has given rise to a tremendous armaments race. Over the
heads of all nations hovers the most devastating threat to the
very existence of the human race. The Second World War
ended with the explosion of the atom bomb. Today, the
hydrogen bomb, declared to be a thousand times more powerful that the bomb dropped on Hiroshima, is being prepared
by the East and West. The direct consequence of this reality
is that all the perspectives, of Empires and Commonwealths
and United Nations and everything else, are altered.

In spite of the threat of disruption, chaos and disintegration, I have discussed the political and economic problems
confronting the Commonwealth and the United Nations as
matters to be solved, and not obliterated by universal destruction. I have attempted to show that a possible solution
lies in the direction revealed in the history of the Commonwealth, with its future as a "regional association" within the
framework of the United Nations Organization.

There are no other alternatives to a peaceful solution, for Professor Albert Einstein and other scientists have told us that the hydrogen bomb can wipe all life off the face of the earth. This is a prospect which might curb even the exuberant aggression of a Churchill and the fanaticism of a Stalin. For what is the use of conquering a world that will cease to exist at the very moment of victory? To be sure, there is enough destructiveness in man for the hydrogen bomb to be used and the world to perish. But the instinct for survival is also strong. Let us hope it is even stronger. If the ideals of human brotherhood taught by great religious prophets like Moses, Buddha, Confucius, Christ and St. John, and by great secular prophets like Condorcet, Shelley, Marx, Ruskin, Tolstoy and Gandhi will not have the necessary effect, then perhaps the threat of universal destruction by the hydrogen bomb may at last compel the three great empires to follow the path of cooperation.

London
March 7, 1950

CHAPTER I

CRISIS AND CHANGE

WHEN IT WAS ANNOUNCED, IN
September 1949, that Sir Stafford Cripps and Mr. Ernest
Bevin, the British Chancellor of the Exchequer and Britain's
Foreign Secretary, were about to visit Washington and meet
with the statesmen of the U.S.A. and Canada, who held similar positions in their respective countries, the news was
hailed as of momentous significance. That they were to discuss the long-continuing financial and economic crisis that
had overtaken the Western world was, of course, well understood. But speculative interpretation of the significance of
the conference went far beyond the question of the adjustment of the relations between the dollar and the pound,
and trade facilities. They ranged to the future of the British
Empire in dissolution, to the Commonwealth, to a plot on
the part of Sir Stafford Cripps to found a new "sterling"
Empire in flagrant rivalry with the U.S.A., and, alterna-
tively, to the absorption of the British Empire by the U.S.A.

The outcome of the conference, in the devaluation of the
pound, with various measures of accommodation in relation
to trade facilities between all the countries directly concerned, disconcerted most of the political speculators and
caused further consultations with the oracles of history. That
the decisions of the Washington Conference have solved the
crisis no one of the participants has claimed. The most they
have asserted is that they contributed toward a solution. Of
the impact of these decisions upon the future of the British

3

Empire and Commonwealth, and their relations with the U.S.A. and the rest of the world, none of the statesmen in that conference have proclaimed their views. At the time of the Washington Conference, the Assembly of the United Nations was in session in New York. Indeed, when the Washington delegates finished their labors they proceeded to the United Nations Assembly where it was abundantly clear that the problems, discussions, and decisions of the Washington Conference were set in the midst of world-wide changes of the most far-reaching character. However the decisions of the Washington Conference be valued, nothing can obscure the fact that, when placed in relation to the Assembly's *cold war* alignment, the matters with which Washington attempted to deal and the decisions which emerged were inseparable from the world crisis and the power relations of nations, empires, and social strata which have formed the background of the changing world throughout a whole epoch since World War I.

While this book is primarily concerned with the evolution of the British Empire and Commonwealth and the statesmen within it who have played a major role in the decisive stages of its transition, it is no longer possible to separate its fate from that of the world powers who hold the future in their hands. At one time, indeed through the greater part of the nineteenth century, Britain and her empire bestrode the world, supreme in her might, unchallenged by rivals and undisturbed by such a phenomenon as a *World Crisis*. Then, one could write of the evolution of the British Empire and its statesmen without reference to the Commonwealth and with only incidental reference to other nations and potential rivals; then, one could speak of the process of change in measured terms, crises were but relatively minor affairs and largely localized. The twentieth century altered all that. The British Empire became increasingly a Commonwealth. But the Commonwealth itself has evolved in the years of this world crisis. *Crisis* is the most commonplace term used in describing the affairs of the modern world. So commonplace has it become that frequently it is used interchangeably with the word *change*. By *Crisis*, we mean circumstances excepttional and extraordinary. Never before in history has this term, with this definition, been more appropriate to describe the affairs of the world. Hence, in this study of the British Empire in its transition to a Commonwealth, and of the modern statesmen who have effected the transition, our analysis is inevitably linked to the continuing crisis of which it is the product.

There have been no circumstances in history comparable to those of today. Three great empires stand astride the world, looking at each other, jealous, fearful, and suspicious. Emerging victorious from the Second World War they proclaimed themselves the *United Nations*, gathered round them the smaller nations, and created an organization to express their unity. Hardly had the last shot of World War II been fired than the *United Nations* ceased to be united and their international organization appeared to become an umbrella under which the three great empires could line up in disputation, talk freely of a Third World War, begin a new armament race in the name of "preserving peace," and busily wage what is euphemistically called a *cold war*. The peoples of the world, whether they be within the great empires or beyond their frontiers, watch the leaders of these powers anxious and afraid, because they know that upon these powers hangs the fate of all mankind. It is the most remarkable and challenging state of affairs in the history of human society.

These three empires—the U.S.A., the U.S.S.R., and the British Empire and Commonwealth of Nations—arrived at their unique position as unexpected allies in a World War whose final, devastating atom-bombs were so terrible that their crashing still echoes round the earth. No two of these empires are alike. All have their similarities and all are different from each other. The unexpectedness of their coming together applies as much to any two of them as to the three. Indeed, two views dominated the minds of most commentators after the First World War. One held that, however the next war should begin, it would become a war of all the powers and nations adhering to capitalism, against the U.S.S.R. This was a widespread belief in many countries other than Soviet Russia where it was held strongly right up to the day, in June 1941, when Hitler's armies rolled across the Soviet frontiers.

The second point of view affirmed that the principal protagonists would be the U.S.A. and Great Britain, with Soviet Russia looking on gleefully, waiting for the revolution to follow in the track of war. This view was first expounded by Trotsky in 1920, with a forecast of the certainty of an Anglo-American War. For a whole period of years the leaders of the Communist International made this theme the basis of their political forecasts. The Sixth Congress of the Communist International, when Bucharin was at its head in 1927, proclaimed that "the Anglo-American antagonism is the main antagonism in the Imperialist camp." The Congress was certain that it opened up the prospect of a "huge conflict." Stalin agreed with Bucharin on this matter and in *Pravda* of August 18, 1935, he said:

The principal conflict between capitalist rivals is that of the United States and Britain. . . . What is this basic conflict fraught with? It is fraught with war. When two giants collide with each other, when this globe is too small for them, they try to measure their strength, they try to solve the vexing question of world hegemony by means of war.

The Communists were not alone in this matter. Ludwell Denny, a non-Communist, author of *America Conquers Britain,* says in this book written in 1930, "War between America and Britain is more probable than war between America and any other country." The French delegate to the League of Nations, Henri de Jouvenal, predicted in the columns of the

New York Herald Tribune on November 26, 1927, that the next war would be in 1935 and "the United States would not be on the same side as Great Britain." But 1941 came and the United States was on the same side as Britain and the U.S.S.R.

Nor were these Jeremiahs of disaster alone in their mistaken diagnosis. An army of prophets had held the view since 1917 that Soviet Russia was about to dissolve in ruin this day, tomorrow, next week, next month, next year—and even today there are those whose wishful thinking leads them to forecast its collapse in crisis. It has always happened that great changes in human society have been interpreted by interested parties as the harbingers of doom. Ever since the first thirteen colonies of Britain broke away from the centralized power of their mother country and established the United States of America, while Canada set the pace toward the transformation of the British Empire from a closed corporation, directed and controlled from London, into a free association of nations of a Commonwealth, the centrifugal trend of its growth has time and again been announced as evidence of the "break-up of the British Empire," its disintegration and disappearance. Indeed, its historians variously refer to *The First British Empire*, the *Second British Empire*, the *Third*, and so on, and give the impression not of a continuously developing power in a process of transformation but of the life and death of a number of British Empires. Mr. Churchill thought that the granting of independence to India would mean the end of the British Empire. Mahatma Gandhi met Sir Stafford Cripps in 1942 with the declaration that he regarded the proposals which Sir Stafford brought to India on that occasion as "a post-dated check on a crashing bank." He did not think that Britain and the Commonwealth would survive the Second World War. But they have survived the greatest ordeal of their existence and adjusted themselves to the new circumstances. The fact is, there never has been a series of British Empires. There has been one

British Empire, which, born in the Middle Ages, has grown, changed, passed through crises, and emerged revolutionized in its structure and character, transformed from a centralized power dominated by an oligarchy into a free association of nations held together in this freedom by a community of interests and a common purpose of their existence.

This history is as different from the history of the U.S.A. as it is from that of the Soviet Union, although the differences are not the same. The British Empire was born toward the end of the sixteenth century, the American in the eighteenth, and the Soviet Union in the twentieth. The first grew with the expansion of mercantile capitalism, carrying with it a feudal heritage. The second was born in revolution and grew to plenitude and power with the industrial capitalism of the nineteenth century. The third was also born in revolution and has grown to be a great power on the basis of a social-ist economy. These three empires differ not only in the dates of their birth and the nature of their origin; they differ in form and content and mode of development. The Soviet Un-ion, and the countries over which it exercises influence, cover the greatest land-mass of the world, stretching from the mid-dle of Europe to the Pacific Ocean, from beyond the Arctic to sight of the Himalayas and include more than a third of the human race. Its population is geared to a socialist economy and to new forms of political democracy, while its social struc-ture consists primarily of industrial workers and peasants. Its industrial power is second to that of the U.S.A., which stands far ahead in this respect both of the Soviet Union and the British Empire.

The U.S.A. is concentrated in a great stretch of territory on the American continent, reaching from the Atlantic to the Pacific, and occupies a most pivotal and strategic position for exercising its influence over the whole American conti-nent and the two oceans which wash its shores. It is also the richest in developed resources. In one hundred and fifty years of independent growth it has surpassed all empires in the development of its productive powers and its military might. It began as an outcrop of mercantile capitalism and passed quickly into industrial capitalism. None would quarrel with the statement that the U.S.A. is controlled and directed as a capitalist state. Its people are passionate adherents to political democracy. Its development as a world power has been different from that of the other two world powers. Whereas the British Empire grew through territorial conquest and occupation of territory scattered across the earth, the U.S.A. grew from thirteen to forty-eight contiguous states and exercises its world power through economic and financial penetration. Both differed from the Soviet Union in their mode of expansion and development in that Soviet expansion has been effected by means of the growth of social and political affinity among neighboring territories, and the use of an international political arm, of affiliated Communist Parties, to help achieve this affinity.

While these great and outstanding differences between the three dominant world powers mark their evolution, the Soviet Union and the U.S.A. have at least one important similarity peculiar to their history. The territorial expansion of both of them has been in contiguous territory. In this respect too, the Soviet Union has become far vaster in its population and far greater in its territorial possessions. If its technological development and its productive forces were as far advanced as those of America, the U.S.S.R. would be the foremost world power.

Although Britain was fortunate in developing as a nation state in the Middle Ages, on an island separated from Europe by a strip of water, it was singularly "unfortunate" in developing into an empire from such a basis. For this determined that she should be a maritime Empire, on the one hand, and, on the other, that her empire-building should take the form of *giving birth to new nations from its own stock and generating independent nationalism in the populations of the territories it acquired by conquest.* This process which has marked the evolution of the British Empire was the opposite of that which has marked the evolution of the U.S.A. and of the Soviet Union. The growth of America was effected by means of thirteen states adding new neighbor states. Instead of these adding up to forty-eight new nations, the forty-eight states have produced *the American nation* by the growth of its original stock and their absorption of the many immigrants of numerous nationalities from other countries.

A similar process is in operation within the Soviet Union. For while it is true that the Russian Revolution, in its first stages, accentuated nationalism in the nations that were colonials of Czardom, nationalism has become increasingly a cultural variant subordinate to the much more basic common citizenship of the Soviet Union as a whole. Indeed, it is this aspect of its evolution which gives the Soviet Union the appearance of an empire bloc.

Despite these profound differences of origin, history, mode of development, and of economic and social structure, these three world empires, together, conquered all their rivals in the greatest conflict of all time and now stand unchallenged by any external power, face to face only with their own differences.

The differences between the three can be appreciated and understood only in the light of their own history and make-up. In none is this more important than the British Empire, because of the diversity of the elements which have been held together and the manner in which differences between the nations composing it have been resolved.

C H A P T E R   I I

THE BRITISH EMPIRE IN TRANSITION

THE BRITISH EMPIRE IS THE oldest of the modern empires. The first efforts of the English kings to establish a colony aimed at the conquest of Ireland, as early as the middle of the twelfth century when England was feudal England and Ireland was populated by "the tribes" whom the English described as "the wild Irish." These efforts were not very successful until in the dawn of the seventeenth century a colony of Englishmen and Scots settled in Ulster. This became the most permanent settlement and the fate of Ulster to this day remains the bone of contention between the Irish and the British, even after Southern Ireland has at last succeeded in putting an end to the invaders' rule in all but the six counties of the North.

Not until the "Age of Discovery" had fully opened, in the fifteenth century, when the British Isles ceased to be situated at the "edge of civilization" and had become islands at the crossroads of the trade routes that were being formed between the Old World and the newly discovered continent of America, did the ocean empire take shape. Its beginnings grew out of the English participation in the discovery of the New World and the growth of merchant adventurer companies, under the patronage of the Crown, in the age when the Parliament, such as it was, was responsible to the Crown and not the Crown to Parliament. It was then that Henry VII sent the Venetian, John Cabot, to find a new way to the East

Indies; instead, Cabot discovered Newfoundland in the West. Yet another century passed before serious efforts were made to found colonies on the mainland. By then the merchant capitalism of England had become powerful. She had expelled the Hansa merchants and founded the Royal Exchange; the Muscovy Company had established trade with Russia; and the Levant Company set out for the African coast. In 1600 the famous East India Company, the great pioneer of the British Empire in the East was founded. The empire by the seventeenth century was definitely taking shape without the slightest thought of what would be the outcome. Its expansion was taking on two definite forms in two definite directions. In the West, in the newly discovered continent and the islands near its shores, it took the form of the transplantation of English life by means of pushing the native population of American Indians out of the way and establishing English settlements. By the end of the seventeenth century the first thirteen colonies, which were to lead the way in the formation of the United States of America, had been founded and the islands of the Caribbean Sea were mostly in English hands. On the social, economic, political, and religious motivation behind this great adventure and the rivalries that had to be encountered it is not for us to dwell here. Sufficient for our purpose to indicate its principal character, direction, and outcome. One fact should be well kept in mind, however. Those in charge of the settlers were still *liegemen of the King* and were usually heads of trading companies operating under a charter from the King. A committee of the King's Privy Council supervised the whole business, and trade and commerce and settlement were parts of a single process of expansion. A company founded Virginia in 1607. Another company founded Massachusetts in 1629. Between 1624 and 1632 the Barbados, the Leeward Islands, Nevis, Antigua, and Montserrat were occupied by the English. A Dutch trader landed the first cargo of Negro slaves in Virginia in the same year that an

English company landed the Pilgrim Fathers on the shores of New England.

While trading and settlement went hand in hand in the West, the East India Company, or the John Company, sought profit by trade at sea in the East, without the burdens of settlement or responsibility for the government of the countries with which it traded. The Guinea Company, associated with the East India Company in 1631, set up the first factories on the Gold Coast of Africa, and left the slave trade to the Dutch. By 1623 the East India Company was operating with commercial houses at Surat in the west of India, at Fort St. George near Madras in the southeast, and in the northeast near Calcutta. Thus the stage was set for the growth of the empire in *three continents*. But "settlement" was as yet confined to the West, and both the Eastern and African ventures were limited to trading. In the process, England established herself as *the* maritime power, and while her merchant ships were armed she was building rapidly the most powerful of navies. The seventeenth and eighteenth centuries continued what the sixteenth had established with this difference: the commercial penetration of India and Africa was now accompanied by military occupation and *the establishment of British Government over native populations*. Britain, too, became a successful participant in the slave trade.

Along with the growth of the settlement colonies came forms of self-government. The old settlements in the Caribbean Sea—the West Indies—set up representative government among the settlers, and from these emerged an elected federal legislature responsible to the Crown, as the English Parliament was responsible to the Crown until the Cromwellian revolution in Britain reversed their respective positions and the King became responsible to Parliament. In the eighteenth century England's ocean traffic had assumed a definite pattern. England sent her trade goods to West Africa. Then her ships took cargoes of slaves to the West Indies to work the sugar plantations. From the West Indies the ships returned to England with rum and molasses. Farther north the trade route ran from England with manufactured goods to North America. Timber, dried fish, and farm produce came from the mainland to the islands of the Caribbean, and then the ships came home with more molasses and rum. While these things were happening in the West, the East India Company continued each year to make headway in Africa and India. Toward the end of the seventeenth century, confusion spread in India and, with the breakdown of the Mogul Empire, the East India Company reinforced trade with military occupation. The conquest of India by the sword of Britain was begun. In the eighteenth century rapid changes took place in the government of conquered regions. The East India Company still ruled the regions of India which it had conquered but the Company itself was increasingly brought under the more effective control of the central government at home. That was the preliminary to India being governed directly by the British Government and Crown. In Africa the merchant companies were thrust into the background and the African colonies came also under the direct control of the British Government and its Colonial Office.

   In those early days of the growth of the empire the government of the colonies was a simple affair. First, the colonies themselves and trade with them were the King's business and not Parliament's. The colonial administrators received their charters from the King. The King appointed the administrator; his Privy Council supervised the business. Simple principles also governed trade. It was the King's business to insure that English trade should be done in English ships and that English colonies should trade principally with England. Enumerated articles from the colonies had to come to England before they could be exported to other countries; continental goods had to come to England first to be exported to the colonies. Unenumerated goods could be sent to any part of the world, but always *in English ships*. The geographical position of England in relation to the trade routes made this easy. But the growth of the colonies, the difference of their economic life from that of Britain, and the changes within Britain itself broke through the framework of this simple set-up. In England the Cromwellian revolution took power out of the hands of the King and placed it in the hands of Parliament and a hotbed of rival interests proceeded to legislate for the colonies. The West Indies and the southern mainland—colonies with their gentlemen proprietors, slaves, and tropical products—fitted in well with the old scheme. But the middle colonies, and more so the New England colony, had a lack of slaves, had products much the same as those of England, and embarked on manufactures which were England's special preserve. The British Parliament did not like the colonies to become manufacturing countries, for this lessened their dependence upon England, and she vigorously opposed this trend. Government developed into a bargaining business between the colonial administrators and the central authorities, but all the time the English Parliament sought to make bargains benefiting primarily the mother country. In addition the colonials were called upon to pay for the standing army of England which looked after the defense against the Red Indians. Soon the stage was set for great changes. To legislate for people three thousand miles away and to subordinate the interests of the distant people in the new lands to the interests of the peoples of the old country was to ask for trouble. And trouble came. The incidents of the first great rupture are well known. The first shots of the War of American Independence were fired at Lexington on April 19, 1775. On July 4, 1776, the American Congress passed the Declaration of Independence. Thus came the first great breakaway from the British Empire, a landmark in its history. Thirteen colonies broke away. Together they began to found a new empire and new nation. Nevertheless, it was not the end of the British Empire. It was a revolution, the impact of which on the rest of the British Empire was far-reaching. For, from this time onward, began the transformation of the policy of the central government. It now began to recognize the geographical fact that it was too far away from its offspring and its acquisitions to exercise oligarchical authority over them. Significantly enough, this recognition found its first practical expression in Canada, the neighbor of the new states. The British settlers in Canada, reinforced by the Loyalists who had fought against the thirteen were, with the French-Canadians, given colonial constitutions possessing a degree of self-government and calculated to neutralize the influence of the democratic ideas which were surging through the United States.

That was the first effect of the American Revolution and represents the first slackening of the centralized control of the British Parliament over its colonies. But this event also led to the formation of colonies in New South Wales and New Zealand. In 1788, Captain Arthur Phillip with a company of marines and some hundreds of male and female convicts, founded Sydney. A similar cargo and company landed in New Zealand, the land of the Maoris. Nevertheless, the most significant developments of all took place in Canada. Here the "settler colonials" began to grow into a new nation which would become a driving force in the transformation of the British Empire into a Commonwealth of Nations.

It must be observed, too, that the thirteen colonies which founded the United States of America broke away from the British Empire at a most significant time. In England itself a new epoch had opened in which mercantile capitalism was transformed into industrial capitalism. The whole economic, industrial, and social life of England changed with it before even the new nation of America could stabilize its independence and expand its frontiers. Britain became the "Workshop of the World," the foremost industrial power, commanding the ocean highways with her iron-clad navy and the greatest merchant service of the world. But Britain had her surplus population and millions emigrated to the new countries, the

United States and the countries growing out of the colonization settlements of her empire. These carried with them, as
did their forebears, their British traditions, political, religious,
economic. It is important to observe, however, that they were
going from a country now highly industrialized to countries
not industrialized, to occupy wide-open spaces where the
principal interests were predominantly agrarian. This applies especially to all the colonies during the nineteenth
century. It was, therefore, in the very nature of things that
the colonies grew up as widespread, agrarian, raw-material
hinterlands of an industrial metropolis. This, however, was
not the case with the United States. Although the new Americans were of the same origin as the Canadians and the rest of
the British colonists, once they ceased to be colonists subordinate to Britain and had struck the path of independence, it
was in the nature of things that America should develop every
phase of her economy and quickly hasten her own industrial
revolution. But the colonial status of Canada, New Zealand,
South Africa gave these colonies of the British Empire no
impetus toward industrialization. On the contrary, their industrialization was retarded by it. The great attraction of the
British colonies in the temperate zones for emigrants from
the United Kingdom and Europe was in land settlement
and mining, particularly gold mining. The agrarian and
primary products of the colonies were exchanged for the
manufactured goods of the United Kingdom. Hence, industrial development within these colonies followed slowly
in the track of commerce and railway transport. Indeed, it
required two world wars, cutting them off from the supply of
manufactured goods from the United Kingdom, to throw
them onto their own resources in the struggle for existence,
to hasten them toward a development of heavy industries,
which forms the basis of industrialism. It was a striking feature of the development of the British Empire that the metropolitan center of the empire grew as a highly developed
industrial country with a declining agriculture, while the

colonies and self-governing dominions flourished as agrarian communities and producers of primary products with a minimum of industrial development. These developments of the United Kingdom, her colonies, and dominions were not merely complementary to each other; the peculiarities of the one stimulated the peculiarities of the other. Especially was this the case until two world wars cut across this pattern of their development and forced the United Kingdom to begin the redevelopment of her agriculture and the colonies and dominions to forge ahead with industrialization.

The United States developed otherwise. The struggle for independence accelerated her industrialization. While the colonies lingered in agrarian life and served as primary commodity producers, the United States grew into a single *industrial and agrarian empire unit.*

It is one of the greatest ironies of history, and yet how natural, that Britain, having given birth to America, and then having formal ties severed by the American War of Independence, should continue to populate the United States with her emigrants more rapidly than she did the colonies who remained loyal to the Crown. Never did an empire grow less planfully than the British. Like Topsy, it "just growed." Its emigrants went whither they would. Its successive governments adjusted themselves to the pressure of political and economic groups. They reluctantly conceded measures of self-government when faced with revolts and threatened revolts, and made economic bargains which geared the agrarian economies of the colonies to the requirements of the economy of the industrial metropolis. This was not a logically planned affair in which the rulers of the empire conspired to produce an overall development with these principles as keys to the plan. This was the pattern it assumed as the industrial revolution transformed mercantile capitalism into industrial capitalism in the United Kingdom. Instead of a plan there was the rampant individualism of laissez-faire capitalism. The very concept of planned econ-

driving force

omy was not in the currency of the political parties of
the day, although nationalism was growing stronger as the
new centers of civilization became populated and grew in
strength and power.

At the same time the total population of the white dominions, at the dawn of the twentieth century, did not amount
to more than fifteen millions of British stock. To the warmer
zones of the empire there had been no emigration, only the
establishment of military, governing, and administrative
forces. Here was no basis for empire autarchy such as was
growing in America nor even the beginnings of national autarchy. Viewed from the standpoint of the nation-state as a
self-contained unit, the center of the empire was *over*industrialized and every colony *under*-industrialized. Nor did the
empire as a whole show the slightest signs of developing into
an empire economic unit. On the contrary, while it was a
political unit governed by a central oligarchy, the metropolis
was not only dependent on an export trade of manufactured
goods, it was not capable of feeding its own population and
was dependent on imports for considerable amounts of her
raw materials for her manufactures. At the same time every
colony was dependent on a large export of foodstuffs, primary
commodities, and the import of manufactured goods. But the
purchasing capacity of the white colonials, though high per
person, was small in total because of the smallness of the
colonial population. The population of the colonies was too
small to absorb the industrial products of the mother country
and they had, therefore, to seek for their products other cus-
tomers than the United Kingdom, and to trade outside the
empire. So, too, the United Kingdom, for her industrial
products. On the other hand, the colonies with colored populations were too poverty-stricken to buy the balance of the
goods of the United Kingdom not purchased by the white
colonials. The total trade of the United Kingdom with the
empire at the beginning of the twentieth century was not
more than a third of her total external trade. So from

from

every angle, population, economics, trade, industry, geography, historical developments, *there was no basis for a consolidated, centralized, self-sufficing empire.* There was interdependence but not self-sufficiency and every national unit of the empire had to seek independent relations with countries outside the empire, a process quite the contrary of that which marked the evolution of the states which made America.

In the period in which the white population of the colonies which became British Dominions grew to fifteen millions the population of the United States grew to more than twice the size of that of the United Kingdom and more than six times that of the white population of the British colonies. In the process the growth of the thirteen states to forty-eight *produced an empire state and an imperial nation.* Free trade existed between the states, and the millions of immigrants were merging into a single imperial nation. *There grew up a common citizenship of all the American states, a national language, and a national policy which was also an empire policy. Its tariff policy was an empire policy* and not an interstate policy between forty-eight states. Hence American expansionism which, by the time of the First World War, had fully passed the stage of the consolidation of the United States as an empire state, took on the form *not of further territorial acquisitions,* but of the exercise of political influence on *free* nations through economic and financial penetration.

Britain did not and could not evolve on lines parallel to those of America. America advanced along the lines of a centralized empire, consolidated. *The British Empire began as a centralized power and evolved along the path of decentralization. The American nation produced an oligarchical imperial democracy under the banner of liberty while the British Empire dissolved its imperial oligarchy into a Commonwealth of Nations under the banner of political democracy and the independence of nations.* In this process there was no inherent virtue or profound foresight. The makers of these respective empires adapted themselves to circumstances where circumstances were more powerful than men.

Even after the American War of Independence, which should have demonstrated to men of vision the futility of trying to build a maritime empire on the principles of a centralized autarchy, the English government continued to regard the empire as an economic unit until affairs again came to a head in Canada. Papineau, the French Canadian, and William Lyon MacKenzie, grandfather of MacKenzie King, led risings which were put down by the usual methods of violence.

But their suppression, in 1828, was followed immediately by the appointment of Lord Durham, familiarly known as "Radical Jack," as Governor-General of Canada. He produced the Magna Charta of colonial self-government, although his proposals were far from the goal of independent nationhood for the colonials. He recommended that the two Canadas, French and British, established at the termination of the American War of Independence, should be united and that the United Provinces should have self-government. He had four reservations on self-government in the colonies. First, the British Government should retain control of foreign affairs; second, regulate trade; third, administer Crown lands; and fourth, be the sole power to alter the constitution of the colony. Durham, himself, did not live to see his proposals come into operation. Behind them, of course, was the influence of the struggle still going on with the newly formed United States. The proposals were applied to Nova Scotia in March 1849, and a month later in Canada. Under the influence of Earl Grey and Lord Elgin and a group of colonial reformers in the British Parliament, there was a strengthening of local representation and elective assemblies in a number of the colonies of the West Indies, of South Africa, Australia, and New Zealand. Here the real policy of adaptation to the new circumstances really began. The reforms were an outcrop of the Canadian revolt and the American Revolution. By 1852, New Zealand had established representative institutions with a non-racial franchise. Australia and Van Diemen's Land ceased to be convict settlements and responsible ministries were established in Eastern Australia and Van Diemen's Land (Tasmania). By 1860 it can be said that Durham's Magna Charta was generally applied in the regions enumerated. Indeed, by that time two of Durham's reservations were canceled out. Control of "Crown Lands" in the colonies passed to the authority of the colony. So also "control of trade" began to pass to the colonies in 1846 when the representative institutions were permitted to abolish British preferences in their own markets. But, fearful of so radical a trend, the British Parliament passed the Australian Colonies Act of 1850, forbidding the colonies to make trading preferences even with each other. Not until 1873 did the British Parliament give permission to the Australian colonies to offer reciprocity to other colonies. Again the Canadians had exercised pressure. In 1859 Canada *levied substantial duties on goods from Britain*—an unprecedented action on the part of a colony. She claimed that if London dictated fiscal policy then Canada was reduced again to the position of a Crown colony. A novel situation was developing. The United Kingdom had adopted Free Trade while all the colonies adopted a tariff and preference system, without anyone recognizing that Free Trade was the prerogative of a country or an autarchic empire which was in an advanced stage of industrialization, and which possessed a virtual monopoly of the world market. The preoccupation of America with the struggles which followed in the track of its War of Independence delayed the industrial revolution in America as the French revolution and Napoleonic wars delayed it in Europe, and left England free to rush ahead. Besides, England's wars were fought in other people's countries and not on her own territory. Nevertheless, Free Trade notwithstanding, Britain was reluctant to loosen its grip on the control of the trade of its colonies. In 1854 Lord Elgin acted on behalf of a group of North American colonies in negotiating a reciprocity treaty with the United States. But the action of Canada in 1859, when it imposed duties on goods coming from the United Kingdom, created an anomalous position wherein a colony dependent wholly on the mother country for defense paid nothing toward it and yet could levy against her in trade!

Soon only one of the Durham reservations was left, namely that of control of foreign policy. For in 1865, the British Parliament passed the Colonial Laws Validity Act which "empowered any representative colonial legislature to amend its constitution, powers and procedure so long as it did not violate such British Acts, Orders in Council, Letters Patent or Colonial Acts as were still in force." In practice, this meant that the white "settlement" colonies could do what they liked with regard to their internal affairs if they were not vetoed by the central authority directly or through its representative. The power to interfere remained in the hands of the United Kingdom. Actually, it was used less and less in relation to the colonies which became Dominions. There was a striking exception to the Colonial Laws Validity Act and this was provided again by Canada. When the British North America Act was passed in 1867, the French Canadians, fearful that the concessions they had received with regard to religion and certain French ways of life would be lost if Canada had the right to alter its constitution, insisted that the act be unalterable except by the Westminster Parliament.

While these trends in the "settlement" colonies of Britain were the direct sequel to the Canadian revolt, great changes were also taking place in the territories held by such commercial companies as the East India Company. The companies had had the backing of governments, from whom they had received their charters, although the regions occupied were the domains of the companies. The Indian Mutiny, as the British call it, was the first great revolt in the "non-settlement" regions of the British Empire. That revolt ended the reign of the companies and saw political regimes, with a modicum of self-government, established. The regime in India resembled a vast complexity of administration, although the complexity itself was resolved into two simple divisions. The first was a group of states directly governed by representatives from Britain or appointed by Britain and controlled by a government of India responsible to the Viceroy, the King's representative, who was advised by the India Office in Whitehall. This larger part of India, with a population of three hundred millions, was known as British India. The remainder was a great collection of feudal states ruled by princes and governors, swearing allegiance to the British King, whose Parliament was responsible for their foreign policy, through the Viceroy. The violent suppression of the Mutiny was followed by far-reaching administrative reforms; a civil service was created and it became increasingly "Indianized." But it was not until the early years of the twentieth century that movements aiming at Indian independence once more took shape. Until that time the most significant changes in India and the Crown colonies were economic. India became a market for Lancashire cotton goods and a supplier of raw cotton, rice, and other foodstuffs and primary commodities. By 1870, £150,000,000 of British capital had been invested in Indian development, half of it in railways. To India Britain sold her industrial products and India's economy was geared to the requirements of Britain's industrial capitalism. As C. E. Carrington has written in "An Exposition of Empire": "Irrigation of land led to a great increase of population; peace and order enabled a larger number to survive; the railways made it possible for the sahibs to organize famine relief and so to remove the severest check upon natural increases; the Indians multiplied and remained poor."

The industrial revolution in Britain, however, proved to be more than a technological affair. It was an explosive force in human relations. It brought the railway boom which spread from country to country, and linked up continents. It brought the steamship to traverse the oceans with increasing speed, the factory system, mass production, the great industry. But when, with its free-trade economy and cheap "free" labor production, it led to the "abolition of slavery," it hurtled an ancient system of human relations into outer darkness and set millions of feet marching toward new ways of life. By this act, inaugurated by Britain throughout the dominions, it gave an impetus to the clash of the old and the new in the United States of America. It set that newly developing nation head-on toward civil war and created the first great rupture in its imperial development since the formation of the Union, just at the time that America's industrial revolution was getting into its stride.

Whatever else the American Civil War may have accomplished it certainly cleared the way for great developments in the American power. For until then the Southern states had been the world's great reservoir for slave labor for the cultivation of the cotton fields. The outcome of the Civil War was the abolition of slavery and the consolidation of the Union as a centralized empire. But the slavery issue was not so easily resolved in the "settlement" colonies of Britain where the colored populations were in a majority. Especially was this the case in South Africa, invaded first by Dutch settlers in the seventeenth century, and by British settlers in the dawn of the nineteenth century, in which the Dutch saw in any concession to the black man an incitement to the blacks to aspire to equality of rights with the white man. Should that ever be conceded it would put an end to the use of cheap native labor, and make white man's rule untenable. The latter was not the intention of the British in the United Kingdom when they insisted upon the abolition of slavery. It most certainly was not the intention of the British or the Dutch in South Africa. But it did mean a conflict between the British and the Dutch in South Africa concerning the ways and means of maintaining the white man's supremacy while getting rid of slavery. It added fuel to the disputes between the British and the Dutch. After the arrival of the British settlers in South Africa, a large number of the Dutch were pushed back into the interior where they established the Transvaal and Orange Free State Republics. The Dutch were isolated from their original stock just as the French Canadians had been isolated from the support of the French in Europe. Governor George Grey of the Cape Colony in 1859 sought to apply the methods adopted by Durham in Canada and proposed a federation of the Dutch Republics and Cape Colony, but it did not come off. In 1877 the British attempted to annex the Transvaal and this was followed by a successful rising of the Boers under Kruger in 1880. The attempts to unite South African British and Dutch from outside, failed, and it became clear that the fusion of Dutch and British would have to come from within and a new Afrikander nation would have to emerge from the fusion of the Dutch and British settlers. It was Cecil Rhodes, the British imperial prospector, and Hofmeyer, among the Dutch, who remained in Natal and other British provinces, who pioneered the policy of fusing Dutch and British into Afrikander.

Both men represented the nineteenth century invasion of Africa. This applied especially to Rhodes, whose ambitions reached to the extension of the South African British conquest to the whole of Africa. He arrived in South Africa just as the great imperial scramble for Africa had begun. He saw the Germans, the Belgians, the French, the Portuguese, all hastening to grab the continent and was determined that the British should not be among the "secondary powers in Africa." The discovery of gold and diamonds facilitated the invasion of the Europeans and brought the full impact of the modern industrial civilization upon the ancient Dutch, who stood for the old settler's "way of life of the seventeenth century," under Kruger. The fusion of the Dutch and the British became possible only after the war of the British versus the Boer Republics in 1900-02. From that war emerged a new leader of Dutch origin, a disciple of Rhodes who aspired to the founding of the Afrikander nation under the leadership of the Dutch. The man was Jan Christiaan Smuts. From a disciple of Rhodes he became an enemy of the British as a result of the Jameson Raid which precipitated the Second Boer War against the British. He fought against the British under Kruger and Botha. The Boers were defeated, but out of the defeat came the Union of South Africa under the leadership of Smuts who once again wore the mantle of Rhodes. He saw the Union of South Africa as the basis for the new Afrikander nation, carrying the British flag while growing with a Dutch heart. The British flag under Rhodes had gone far beyond the boundaries of the new Union. The British had conquered the Zulus and other natives and stretched their territorial possessions to Rhodesia and beyond. These were essentially military conquests, paving the way for settlements, commerce, and, ultimately, industry.

In the process the pattern of the empire government changed rapidly in all the regions of white settlement from the old centralized control of the mercantile era to that of self-government in local affairs plus consultation in foreign affairs. This latter development was the sequel to the rise of the South African Union, unthinkable when Durham made his famous report on Canada.

By 1907, when Botha and Smuts received "Dominion Status" for South Africa, the British Empire was no longer without modern rivals for world power. It had long ago accepted the domination of the U.S.A. on the American continent and admitted there was no further room for its territorial expansion in that part of the world. The Monroe Doctrine was supreme. In Europe, the German empire was challenging Britain for supremacy among the nations. Hence, it was natural that once again the British rulers of the empire should look over their far-flung possessions as a whole and question

Problem of Imperial Defence (1907)

how they should hold together in unity should war occur. They called together their first imperial conference of representatives of the Dominions and India in 1907. It was attended by General Botha from South Africa, and at this conference were discussed the problems of imperial defense and the part to be played by the colonies now recognized as nations taking independent shape within the empire. The conference itself indicated the fundamental change that had taken place in the structure of the British Empire since the first breakaway of the group which had founded the American nation and the revolt of the Canadians demanding self-government in home affairs. The last of the reservations of "Radical Jack" was slipping away. For once the colonies had been called in to discuss common defense, it was a short step to the discussion of foreign policy. Once the imperial government ceased to have supreme authority in the foreign policy of the empire as a whole, the last step in the transformation of the colonies into independent nations would have been taken, and the British Empire would have evolved into something else. By this time it was generally accepted that the British Empire had changed considerably in its structure, and attempts were made to find a new name to describe that part of the empire whose constituent parts were on the threshold of independence. For it was perfectly clear that not all sections of the British Empire stood in the same relationship to each other or to the British imperial government. Indeed, in the year immediately preceding the First World War, the pattern of self-government within the British Empire had become fairly clear, although the imperial grip was still firm. In all the "settler" colonies, the new white nations, Canadians, Afrikanders, Australians, New Zealanders, had their parliaments patterned on the British Parliament. Although the practice was not yet clearly defined in law, each nation had its independent control over home affairs. All of them, however, still depended wholly upon the central government for defense and the imperial government was responsible for

foreign policy. British India had, by the Morley-Minot reforms of 1911, received its first modicum of an introduction
to British parliamentarism, a step toward self-government.
The "self-government" of the Indian states remained a dic-
tatorship of the rajahs, who accepted the British rule in foreign affairs. The rest of the British Empire consisted of what
were known as Crown colonies, protectorates, and protected
states. All these were widely scattered territories, some large,
some small, some strung along the highways of the oceans as
strategic stations for the British Fleet, others—like the group
of islands in the Caribbean—a heritage of the empire in
the age of mercantilism, and still others consisted of great
stretches of Africa. In all cases the rule was by direct imperial
representation, in the form of a governor, high commissioner, or chief commissioner, directly responsible to the
British Parliament. In all these territories, mainly of the
tropical or subtropical zones, the population is of the colored races, black and brown. After their abolition of slavery
in 1834, the British had evolved adaptations of the principle
of self-government for the native populations; these adaptations varied from country to country, according to the nature
of the native institutions.

The aim of their policy was to leave intact the tribal institutions, customs, religions, and govern through the tribal
leaders. Had the purpose of the penetration of these territories by the British been that of settlement on the land
and acquiring only sufficient land for the newcomers to establish an agrarian life segregated from the natives entirely,
it could have been regarded as a fair liberal policy. But that
was not the purpose of empire-building.

The imperialism of the British meant the introduction of
the natives to new ways of life in production and, therefore,
of social life. It meant the introduction of the native population to the technics of a different kind of civilization based
upon different methods of production. This was destined to
make untenable the political policy of racial segregation and

would sooner or later set the natives in head-on conflict with their rulers. The Boers of South Africa held that the Bible justified slavery and, from the first, fought the "liberal" policy of the British after the latter invaded South Africa. The Afrikanders who emerged from the Anglo-Boer conflicts saw the full implications of the British policy. They abolished slavery but pursued a political policy of segregation and an economic policy of the utilization of native labor in modern production. In the process they were destroying the foundations of the tribal life of the natives and extending to them the economic and social ways of the white population. Tribal life needs its own economy and social life. This the new civilization of the whites destroyed while seeking to retain the political set-up which went with it, leaving the natives without political and social rights they had hitherto enjoyed. Such was the structure and nature of the British Empire in transition when this modern great power was put to the test of war. Hitherto the United Kingdom under its monarchy had waged war on its own account and had automatically used colonial levies as units of England. Those days were gone. Canadians were now Canadians. Afrikanders were Afrikanders. Australians were Aussies.

The imperial government had recognized this process of change in the empire. Since Queen Victoria's Jubilee celebrations in 1897, there had been conferences of the prime ministers of the "self-governing" colonies at intervals, under the auspices of the "Colonial Secretary." At the first conference Mr. Joseph Chamberlain was the Colonial Secretary. He was 'empire conscious' and proposed a "great Council of Empire" and a common defense scheme to be ready for the challenge of the new empires in Europe and the East. The new nationalities did not applaud. They did not want to bear the cost or to share the responsibility implied. They were pulling away from the centralized power and had no desire to accept imperial responsibilities. The year 1907 saw the last of the Colonial Conferences. This was attended by

Botha and Smuts, who had just come to prominence in the Boer War of Independence. In place of the Colonial Conferences appeared the "Imperial General Staff" and Dominion representation on the Committee of Imperial Defence. The Colonial Office no longer handled the affairs of Canada, Australia, New Zealand, and South Africa. They had acquired the new status of "Dominions" and a special department of the British state named the "Dominion Office" was created to deal with them. But the British Government did not consult the Dominions about making its alliance with Japan in 1902, or about the Entente Cordiale with France in 1907, or about British adherence to the two Hague Conventions, or about the signing of the famous Declaration of London. The nearest point to collective decisions in foreign affairs reached before the "lights went out in Europe" was a promise by the British Government to consult the Dominions on the policy to be pursued at peace conferences. Nevertheless, it was clear that the Dominions, which had grown out of the "settler" colonies, were approaching full nationhood.

There was one white man's country still with the status of a colony, and that was on England's doorstep. It was the oldest of the English colonies and, for seven hundred years since the first English invaders of Ireland established themselves there, successive kings and governments of England and the United Kingdom had been unable to make up their minds whether to treat Ireland as a place for English "settlers" and push the Irish out or to recognize the Irish as a nation which could govern itself. Ireland had been conquered by military means. It had been treated as a colony. It had had its own Parliament. It had seen its Parliament dissolved. It had been treated as a Province of England, with its own representatives in the English Parliament. It had been governed by a Lord-Lieutenant, under whose auspices it had a degree of self-government in home affairs. And not a century had passed, since the first conquest of the country, in which the

Irish have not staged an armed revolt to establish their independence. At the approach of World War I, it was on the eve of a rising while the Liberal Government of England was on the point of granting Home Rule, that is, an Irish Parliament, raising Ireland to the level of a Dominion of the British Empire. But it was not yet to be. The war came and the British Empire entered it as a centralized power, the British Government and the King declaring war for Britain, the Dominions, and the colonies at one and the same time, and without consultation with them. That act marked the end of an epoch in the history of the British Empire, the end of oligarchical empire control centered in London.

FROM EMPIRE INTO COMMONWEALTH

WHEN, ON AUGUST 4, 1914, THE British Government, on behalf of the whole British Empire, declared war on Germany without consulting the Dominions and colonies, the whole empire was deemed at war. There was no protest from the Dominions, except in the case of South Africa where the newly formed South African Government had to violently suppress a rising of the Boers before it could effectively implement its confirmation of the British Government's decision. The British Empire, already far on the path of change, now faced decades of war and revolution. Mankind had entered a new epoch. The old order in which Britain had ruled the waves unchallenged for more than a century was gone forever. New powers challenging her supremacy had arisen. *And none of the Dominions and colonies had the means of their own defense.* All were dependent upon the United Kingdom for that purpose. In all cases, too, including the United Kingdom, the armed forces had been recruited on a voluntary basis—a clear indication of the maritime nature of the empire.

The principal challenger to Britain's power in 1914 was the German Empire, with Germany as the metropolitan industrialized country; its main colonies, of similar economic and racial pattern to the British, neighbored those of Britain in the continent of Africa. The empires which aligned themselves with Germany were the Austro-Hungarian, contigu-

ous with Germany, the Ottoman Empire, an essentially feudal empire sprawling across the Dardanelles and the Near
East, and the Italian Empire, jutting south of Europe into
the Mediterranean and penetrating North Africa. On the
side of Britain was the French Empire, with its metropolis
facing Germany in the west of Europe and its imperial possessions spread over North Africa and a part of the Far East;
the Russian feudal empire of the Czars faced Germany from
the east and stretched across half Europe and Asia with the
largest continuous frontier of any empire in the world; the
Japanese Empire, with its foothold on the mainland of Asia,
policed the Pacific coasts and extended its grip on China,
ostensibly in alliance with Britain. The U.S.A., which
emerged from the war the most highly industrialized and
consolidated power in the world, joined the military conflict in its final stages also as an ally of Britain. The outcome
of the war saw the catastrophic collapse of the Austro-Hungarian Empire, the Czarist Empire of Russia, the Ottoman
Empire of Turkey and the drastic rupture of the German
Empire. Italy, switching over from an alliance with Germany
to an alliance with France and Britain, was greatly weakened. In place of the Czarist Empire rose the Soviet Union,
with the loss of Finland and Poland. The Soviet Revolution was a social and political revolution in which state
power passed into the hands of the small industrial working
class in alliance with the peasantry, who after stormy years
of struggle with war and counter-revolution set Russia on
the path of its industrial revolution and a socialist economy.
The German colonies passed under the mandatory control
of Britain and the Union of South Africa. The colonies of
the Ottoman Empire were set free and became the basis of
Arab states under the patronage of Britain. The Pacific islands, which had been part of the German Empire, passed to
Japan's mandatory control, and were annexed by her when
she left the League of Nations.

After the entrance of America into the war in 1917, and

its part in the making of the "Peace System" under the aegis of the League of Nations, America withdrew from the European settlement into temporary isolation from European affairs. The social revolution unleashed in Russia with the collapse of the Czarist regime spread as far west as Germany, until counter-revolution drove it back to the frontiers of the Soviet Union.

The effect of this terrific upheaval upon the British Empire was far-reaching. The United Kingdom had taken the brunt of the clash of power, but *no colony or Dominion had been invaded or threatened with invasion. The war was centered in Europe and the Atlantic Ocean.* Nevertheless, the support of the colonies and the Dominions had been to the limit of capacity. In the outcome the Dominions, in particular, and India, had grown in strength and national consciousness. All of them had been stimulated to accelerate the industrialization of their economy. Britain herself had lost her leading position in international trade to the United States of America. She entered the war as a creditor nation and came out of it a debtor nation. Her National Debt had grown from, £800,000,000 to £8,000,000,000. Her principal foreign creditor was the United States of America. Britain no longer ruled the waves with her naval power, for America's naval strength had become equal to hers. She had lost a million men killed and two million had been injured. Compelled to gear her economy to the requirements of the war she had lost a great proportion of her foreign markets, while Europe's break-up reduced the international market to fifty percent of its pre-war level. Driven off the "Gold Standard" into a period of inflation, her dislocated currency added confusion to the fluctuating exchanges and shattered currencies which cluttered the economies of the countries broken by the war. Britain, a victor in the war, was beset with the problems presented by its victory and by the aftermath of the war, which engendered the spread of revolution in varying forms, not the least significant of which was the fostering of nationalities and the growth of nationalism throughout the British Empire itself.

Promptly on the declaration of war the imperial government called for representatives from the Dominions to serve on the Imperial War Cabinet. The first effect of the war was to strengthen the centripetal tendencies of the empire, that is, to bring the Dominions closer to Britain and give them responsibility in the central direction of the empire. It almost appeared as if Chamberlain's Empire Council was on the point of being established and the empire was about to be transformed into an imperial federation. General Smuts, the one-time intransigent Boer fighter—to whom Mr. Winston Churchill once said, "Did you ever know a conqueror nation to give independence to the conquered nation?" —came from South Africa, and became a friendly adviser to the war leader and Prime Minister of Britain, David Lloyd George. Prime Minister Hughes came from Australia, and other Dominion leaders joined them. But the acceptance of responsibility for the conduct of the war served mainly to inspire the Dominion representatives to step up their demands for the full recognition of their status as independent entities. They demanded and secured not merely the right to be consulted concerning the peace *but the right to be independently represented at the Peace Conference, to have independent representation in the League of Nations when it was formed and independent representation in the International Labor Office when it was established.* This applied also to India in the form of patronage, although the latter was far from being as advanced in parliamentary self-government as the Dominions. The Indian representatives could attend only with the approval of the British Government.

In this period General Smuts gave a name to the new grouping of "Dominions" within the British Empire. He named it "The British Commonwealth of Nations." The British like to apply this euphonious title to the whole empire but it was appropriate only to Canada, Australia, New Zealand, South Africa, and by 1922 to the Irish Free State. The outbreak of war had stopped the British Parliament from proceeding with the Irish Home Rule Bill. In 1916 an Irish insurrectionary movement was crushed and its leaders executed. The end of the war saw an Irish national rising, culminating after two years of fighting in the establishment of the Irish Free State covering all Ireland with the exception of the six most northern counties. This was regarded as a Dominion on a par with the other Dominions. In practice the Dominions were now wholly self-governing. The British Parliament had ceased to function as the overriding authority, and the association was held together by allegiance to the King of England and by mutual interests and traditions. Each Dominion began to send its own ambassadors to other countries and to receive their ambassadors.

Between the two world wars there was a succession of "British Commonwealth Conferences" confined to the white Dominions. The most important was the 1926 meeting. What is known as the Balfour Declaration, defining "Dominion Status," emerged. Balfour, the author of this declaration—which was to be more famous than the Durham report of "Radical Jack," produced after the Canadian risings a century earlier—was a conservative among conservatives and probably the most able one of his generation. He was the nephew of Lord Salisbury, whom he succeeded as Prime Minister in 1902. He was a man of high intellectual capacity, a great debater although no orator, an able administrator but too detached from the multitude ever to be a popular leader. Author of a book on *Philosophic Doubt,* a title which gave rise to the idea that he was a doubter in the realms of metaphysics instead of a defender of orthodoxy, he was at least revealed to be a man with considerable finesse who could express himself lucidly. In his declaration as to the stage of development which had been reached in the evolution of the British Empire he showed his capacity to use words as a means of expressing an idea, with precision and clarity. The declaration stated that the "United Kingdom and the Dominions were 'autonomous' communities within the British Empire, equal in status, in no way subordinate one to another in any aspect of their domestic or external affairs, though united by a common allegiance to the Crown, and freely associated as members of the British Commonwealth."

There was an equally clear addendum to this declaration, a reminder of the realities of power relations within the new association now taking definite form. It said:

> The principles of equality and similarity, appropriate to status, do not universally extend to function. Here we require something more than immutable dogmas. . . . In the sphere of defence, the major share of the responsibility rests now, and must for some time continue to rest, with His Majesty's Government in Britain. (*The British Empire,* p. 154.)

That sharp reminder revealed the imperial government still conscious of its strength and of the weakness of the young nations now asserting their equality of status but sublimely unconscious of the changing relations of power in the world at large and "the shape of things to come." Nevertheless, in 1931, legal form was given to the Balfour Declaration in the Statute of Westminster, which, if once endorsed by the Dominion Parliaments, legalized their sovereignty as nations and superseded all previous colonial-relations legislation. The strange feature of the situation when the Westminster Parliament passed the act, was that only South Africa, Canada, and Eire immediately passed the Westminster Statute through their own Parliaments. The other Dominions, Australia and New Zealand, ignored the statute until the conditions of the Second World War urged it upon them twenty years later.

There were no further adhesions to the "British Commonwealth of Nations" until after the Second World War, but the ground was being well prepared in the sub-continent of India. The war of 1914-18 gave an impetus to the independence movement in India. Although Britain had declared India at war without consulting anyone about it, the Government of India aided the prosecution of the war and the Indian princes gave it their support. Voluntarily recruited Indian soldiers rallied by the hundred thousand and served on all fronts. Indian representatives signed the peace treaties on India's behalf and India was represented in the League of Nations. Nevertheless India had not the autonomy of a Dominion. The imperial government had reached the stage of recognizing that some day India must have self-government, although it was fairly confident that it would not be in their day and generation. The Montagu-Chelmsford Reforms, embodied in the Government of India Act in 1919, made concessions toward that goal, although not large concessions. By this act the Government of India became a mixture of Crown Colony government, representative institutions, and responsible government.

In this year Gandhi became the leader of the Indian National Congress, which, with the Moslem League led by Jinnah, set the pace in the development of the national independence movement for India. The history of India from then onward is a record of surging waves of agitation, repressions, concessions, imprisonment of leaders and followers, negotiations with Gandhi and the Nehrus and Jinnah, conferences, breakdowns, passive resistance, commissions, legislation, millions of Indians becoming conscious of India, and an imperial government holding back from making the changes which they knew they would one day have to make.

Meanwhile the position of the British Empire as a whole had undergone a complete eclipse, in relation to world power among the nations. The days when the United Kingdom was the "Workshop of the World" were gone, never to return. The days when she could maintain a navy at a ratio of two to one of any other nation's ships were gone. After its retreat from Versailles the United States Government called, in 1922, a conference of the victorious powers in Washington. There, Britain and Japan were forced to abrogate the Anglo-Japanese Treaty on the proposal of the Canadian representative at the conference. On the initiative of the United States, the conference fixed the ratio of the capital ships of the navies of the U.S.A., Great Britain, and Japan at 5:5:3. The conference was euphemistically called a disarmament conference. Nevertheless, the terms of its decisions meant that Britain no longer ruled the waves alone or in grand superiority. Nor had it regained its superiority in the world market. The U.S.A. continued to hold its leading position and the days of its concentration on the home market, well protected with high tariff barriers, were also gone. The eclipse of the British Empire by the U.S.A. was complete. Its population was nearly three times the population of the United Kingdom and its productive power was far greater than that of all the states and colonies of the British Empire combined.

In the East the Russian Revolution had been consolidated and the Soviet Empire was busy with a rapid industrialization of its economic life. Out of the ruins of the Kaiser's Germany a new empire would soon rise up under the leadership of Hitler. A similar phenomenon had arisen in Italy, led by Mussolini. These phenomena of Fascism in Europe were reinforced by an alliance with Japan in the Far East. In 1931 Japan invaded Manchuria as the preliminary to an attempted conquest of China. The League of Nations was in process of dissolution and the Second World War arrived with Britain isolated. Here the test was made as to the validity of the national sovereignty of the nations of the British Commonwealth. This time the United Kingdom did not declare war for the empire as a whole. Each of the Dominions acted through its own Parliament, and Eire declared for neutrality and maintained it through the war.

The validity of independence was demonstrated. But this

did not apply to India or the Crown Colonies. They were declared at war by the imperial Parliament as in 1914. In the early stages the war assumed almost the same pattern as the First World War, in that Europe and the Atlantic Ocean were the storm centers of the conflict. The Commonwealth states rushed to the aid of the United Kingdom, directed their economy to give the maximum of assistance, raised arms and men on an unprecedented scale, while their leading ministers flew to the metropolis to participate in the central direction of the war. The Indian nationalists, however, refused to endorse the war and acted on the assumption that England's difficulties were India's opportunities to force the pace toward independence. Suddenly the whole pattern of the war was changed and, for the first time in their history, the Dominions of the British Commonwealth were threatened with invasion. Japan, following upon her invasion of China, less than six months after Hitler had invaded Soviet Russia, plunged all the Pacific powers into the war, set out to conquer the Pacific archipelago and the south of the Asiatic peninsula. Without having thought of this as a probability, the commonwealth states had rushed their forces to wherever the imperial government thought best, and that had meant Europe, the Near East, the colonial regions, with Singapore as their headquarters. Now the Dominions wished to reverse engines, to draw back their forces and receive the aid of Great Britain in defending their shores and fighting the war in the Pacific, only to discover that the British Navy and Air Force were preoccupied with the European and Atlantic battlegrounds. With irresistible force it was driven in upon them that they were now wholly dependent upon the United States of America and their own resources, that alone they were helpless. Indeed it quickly became apparent that the *whole British Empire and Commonwealth* was dependent as never before upon the U.S.A. The Australians and New Zealanders in particular were shocked out of their traditional insularity. Their independence had really come to them as a by-product of the struggles of other Dominions, especially Canada and South Africa. In loyalty to Great Britain they had been more patriotic than the British. To find themselves isolated and compelled to turn to the U.S.A. for aid was an ordeal from which came significant repercussions. Out of it there emerged a full consciousness of their own strategic position among the Pacific nations and the theory of regionalism within larger international combinations. Much earlier they had wished to make reciprocity trading arrangements between Dominions. Now they wished to go further, to group nations in given regions with pacts for mutual defense and collective political and economic action. It certainly made them more nationally conscious and assertive of their rights and importance within the general strategical set-up of the war. Australia and New Zealand made a treaty of mutual assistance. Both insisted upon representative participation in the Near East Council of war direction, while Evatt of Australia fought tenaciously for the establishment of the Pacific War Council and Australia's right to be represented on it. Churchill, then Prime Minister of Britain, resisted Australia's claims and sought to establish an alternative consultative committee to meet in London, but finally gave way to pressure and the Pacific War Council met in Washington and included Evatt of Australia. Smuts of South Africa developed the idea of regionalism still further. He saw that, while Britain might retain the leadership of the British Commonwealth as a whole, the geographical distribution of groups of Dominions would call for the leadership of the group to be in the hands of one or other of the groups and not necessarily of Great Britain. Decentralization within the British Empire was going on apace.

But the most important changes came at the end of the war and they came from the East. The Indian nationalist movement refused to cooperate in the prosecution of the war until Britain should grant independence to India. During the war, in 1942, the British Government sent Sir Staf-

ford Cripps to negotiate with the Indian leaders. He promised
Dominion Status at the end of the war, the condition being
agreement among the Indians as to the New Constitution
for India and of immediate cooperation in a subordinate
capacity during the war. The Indian leaders refused the
terms, continued their agitation, and were jailed until the
end of the war. In 1945 the newly elected Labor Government in Britain, fearing that the Indian people were advancing to revolution, renewed the offer made in 1942.
After much negotiation this offer was rejected, but after still
further negotiation and many modifications of the proposals,
India was divided into two States, India and Pakistan, and
British forces, military and administrative, were withdrawn.
In the same period Burma was set free and became a republic and Ceylon became a Dominion with the same status
in the Commonwealth of Nations as any other Dominion.

These tremendous changes, wherein the greatest of the
colonial territories and populations broke up the old imperial bonds and stood forth as independent nations, raised
great issues. Did they mean simply a rupture and dissolution of empire or a continuance of the process of transformation indicated in the evolution of the British Commonwealth
of Nations from the "settlement" colonies of the beginning
of the nineteenth century? The change had occurred in most
extraordinary circumstances. Indeed, the face of the whole
world was changed. The Fascist empires of Germany, Italy,
and Japan had been shattered. Once again Britain and her
allies had emerged from the greatest conflict of all time as
one of the victorious powers. Europe was in ruins. The countries that had been overrun by the Nazis were again standing on their own feet but in sore distress. The French and
Dutch Empires were striving to pick up their broken threads
of empire. The social revolution which burst upon the world
with the collapse of Czardom in 1917 had spread half across
Europe and deep into China and was stirring all the nations
of the East. Britain itself was exhausted and severely bat-

tered. She had suffered great losses in material strength. Her industries were outdated and her people tired. Her foreign trade had been reduced to a minimum and her indebtedness to America had assumed colossal dimensions while she had become a debtor country to India and the other members of the commonwealth. Britain's foreign investments had shrunk to half their pre-war dimensions and almost half her shipping had been sunk. In the flush of the wartime alliances with the Soviet Union and the U.S.A., she led the way in the establishment of the United Nations Organization as the means of maintaining peace and insuring the world's orderly recovery. The effect of the war upon the countries of the American continent, especially the U.S.A. and Canada, was the opposite of its effect on Britain. The latter had emerged from the war battered and exhausted. America and Canada had come out of the war unscathed internally and had multiplied their power in every direction.

Hardly had the war come to an end than a similar process of realignment of nations began as after the war of 1914-18. Then the alignment soon became governed by the attitude of the nations to the rise of the Fascist powers. This time it was governed by the attitude of the nations to the social, political, and economic system prevailing in each country. The fear of the spread of Communist ideas from the countries in process of social revolution became more influential than the national, imperial, economic and political rivalries which had marked the previous periods. At the same time the national and imperial rivalries of the West were affected enormously by the overwhelming dependence of all of them upon the bounty and abundance of the U.S.A. This applied as much to Britain and her empire as to the countries of Western Europe.

The change in power relations of the nations effected by the war was stupendous. However the comparison be made, it only served to emphasize the overwhelming power of America. With a steel production of ninety million tons a year and a correspondingly enormous industrial apparatus compared with the next largest steel production of twenty million tons of the Soviet Empire, its strength would appear to be unchallengeable.

The fully developed power of America, compacted within a single stretch of territory three thousand miles across, reduced the British Empire to the level of a group of small nations variously bound together and compelled to turn to its successor in world power, as a debtor turns to its creditor, in search of still further credits. On the other hand, America had to face the consequences of her extraordinary wartime development. It now had to find *a new market to replace the war market* which had provided the impetus to the expansion of her economic power. Unless the U.S.A. could find such an alternative market, it would be plunged into an overproduction crisis of great dimensions. This problem was made more acute by the fact that the export of private capital investment in Europe and the Far East could not be renewed after the war in the same way as previously because of the complete dislocation of European and Eastern economy and the change in the political climate. When to physical dislocation was added the disturbance and confusion engendered by political and social revolution, only state capital and state guaranteed capital could flow into these regions from whatever source and to whichever destinations. Such were the fundamental features of the economic situation facing the U.S.A. at the end of the war and which could be met only by massive state financial action at home and abroad.

On the other hand the British Empire was deeply involved in the war dislocation and profoundly influenced by the accompanying political and social revolution that had swept across Europe and Asia. In the process it once again demonstrated the fundamental difference in the structure of the British Empire as compared with that of the American empire, namely: the British Empire was an *association of na-*

tions differing in their history and their political and economic structure and each was affected differently by the war. The United States was and is a single unit, a national entity, an economic entity, under a single political state direction. The separate forty-eight states have no economic frontiers corresponding to their political geographic frontiers. They are not *National* states but forty-eight parts of a single American nation; their strictly limited political authority does not incorporate the political and economic relations between the American nation and other nations. This rests with the authority of the "imperial Government," or, to use its more formal title, the Federal Government, which acts for the United States as a whole.

In the varied effects of the war upon the British Empire the United Kingdom was the worst hit. Canada, like the U.S.A., advanced in strength and power and became a creditor of the United Kingdom. Eire remained neutral and undamaged. Australia and New Zealand, while threatened with invasion, were not invaded and the effect of the war was to stimulate and strengthen their economy. South Africa came out of the war stronger than she went in. Indeed she extended her frontiers to include what was previously known as German South West Africa. India was physically undamaged by the war, the main effect of which was to give impetus to the Indian revolution which culminated in the establishment of the independent states of India, Pakistan, Burma, and Ceylon. The United Kingdom, alone of the countries constituting the British Empire, came out of the war badly damaged economically, weakened in her power, and deeply in debt financially to almost all of the nations included in the term British Commonwealth of Nations. The political sequel to the shrinking of the power of the United Kingdom and the severe battering and wear and tear of its economy were to change the political complexion of its government from Conservative to Labor. It was expected that this social and political transformation would lead to equally profound changes in empire relations and foreign policy. Contrary to alarmist views, there has been no fundamental change in foreign policy. The only difference revealed in the course of the years lay not in direction but in speed of adaptation to the pressure of circumstances. The most striking illustration was seen in the British Government's handling of the Indian independence movement, under the direction of Mr. Attlee. All British governments between the two wars were pledged to grant India Dominion Status at some time, which they deemed equivalent to independence. It was Mr. Attlee's government which implemented the pledge, lest the Indian independence movement pass from moral and political pressure into a violent attempt to force the granting of independence.

That all India came under the influence of the revolutionary awakening of Asia is undoubted. That Pandit Nehru, the Prime Minister of the new Indian state, recognized this is clear from his speech to the Constituent Assembly in December 1948. He then expressed the hope

. . . that the new constitution for India will lead India to real freedom, that it will lead also to the freedom of other countries of Asia because, however unworthy, we have become—let us recognize it—leaders of the freedom movement of Asia, and whatever we do we should think of ourselves in these larger terms.

A few months later he was leading an "Asian Conference" saying, "The time had come for us, peoples of Asia to meet together, to hold together and advance together."

Later in the same year there assembled in London under the chairmanship of Mr. Attlee, the most remarkable of Commonwealth Conferences. Composed of Commonwealth prime ministers, the meeting was remarkable because this was the first time that representatives were present from former colonies of colored peoples, which had become free nations. There were present Nehru, the Prime Minister of India, and the prime ministers of Pakistan, Ceylon, and others.

It was remarkable, also, in its decisions on the principal question before the conference, namely, that of the possibility of their continued association within the "British Commonwealth of Nations." The representative of Eire, however, had severed the connection of Eire with the British Commonwealth, as his government considered it incompatible with its standing as an independent republic. The Burmese Prime Minister did likewise and on similar grounds. The problem of the position of a republic in an association which acknowledged the King as the symbol of the unity of the commonwealth provided the issue of the conference. That India and Pakistan would not budge from their republicanism was clear. Ceylon had no problem in this respect. Her Prime Minister identified Ceylon with the commonwealth. The conference finally decided that some formula should be produced which would enable the republicans to be associated. In 1948 the British Prime Minister introduced into his Parliament the British Nationalities Bill and indicated that the British Commonwealth of Nations would henceforth be known as "the Commonwealth" and that the terms "British subject" and "Commonwealth citizen" will be henceforth interchangeable.

The Prime Ministers of India and Pakistan had indicated that should such changes be made they favored adherence to the Commonwealth. A further conference held in 1949 ratified the proposals of 1948. Thus a Commonwealth has grown out of the British Empire. Step by step the nations of the British Empire have untied the knots of centralized power. Today the Commonwealth is a loose association, with flexible methods of cooperation, of nationally independent nations. It is increasingly a conference for consultation, relying on common understanding in friendly association to produce agreement in policy and action. It has no permanent headquarters. It may meet in any Dominion and any Dominion may take the lead on the issues it may wish to be discussed. It does not function as an empire block within the larger international institutions, although it may be called together to discuss in freedom the questions in which the members are interested in without binding its members to vote in unison. The opposing stand taken between the United Kingdom, and the Dominions, on the other hand, in the case of Palestine before the U.N.O. is an illustration. At the same time the Commonwealth can meet as a collective association and act in unison where agreement is reached in friendly conference. The Commonwealth is undoubtedly a remarkable consummation in the evolution of a centralized oligarchical empire into a free association of nations. It is an equally remarkable example of political adaptation to new circumstances and new times. The men who at successive stages of its modern history have contributed decisively to the making of the Commonwealth are known to the world. Outstanding among them are Winston Churchill, Clement Attlee, Ernest Bevin, Mackenzie King, Jan Christiaan Smuts, Herbert Vere Evatt, and Jawaharlal Nehru, whose lives are dealt with in the following pages, especially in relation to the part they have played in the transformation of the British Empire. To suggest that here the story ends would be absurd. For the Commonwealth emerged in an epoch of crises, is living amidst crises, and must adapt itself to meet them.

C H A P T E R   I V

W I N S T O N   C H U R C H I L L

A CRYPTIC ANNOUNCEMENT IN the birth column of the London *Times* of December, 1874 read as follows: "On November 30th at Blenheim Palace, the Lady Randolph Churchill, prematurely of a son."

The son was Winston Spencer Churchill, the grandson of a duke in a line which stretched back to the days of Queen Anne. The first Duke of Marlborough was a famous soldier. Winston's father was Lord Randolph Churchill, one time Chancellor of the Exchequer and the third son of the seventh Duke of Marlborough. His mother was the beautiful Jennie, daughter of Leonard Jerome, of New York, the dynamic, forceful proprietor and editor of the *New York Times*, and famous as one of the fathers of the American Turf.

However demure the arrival of the youngster, who one day would become Prime Minister of Britain in her hour of greatest crisis, there is no doubting the glamor of his ancestry, his aristocratic parentage, or that he came of stock most famous in the annals of the British governing class. He arrived when the British Empire was flourishing in all its plenitude. The epoch of African expansion had not yet dawned and no great powers were challenging her on land or sea. Whatever portent of eclipse might lay on the horizon was no bigger than a man's hand. Germany had recently emerged from her triumph over France and the challenge she would one day offer Britain was yet far off. Only eleven years had elapsed since Lincoln had spoken at Gettysburg, and America had yet to get into her stride in power building after the terrible interruption of her Civil War. The distant possessions of the Crown in India and the Pacific Ocean had just been brought nearer to the metropolis by the cutting of the Suez Canal, but as yet Disraeli had not bought Britain's control of the waterway to the East. The Panama Canal was still a dream and Britain's Navy was supreme on the oceans of the world. Although there had been murmurings among the Colonial populations of the Empire, which might be regarded as precursors of the self-governing Dominions, the British Parliament and Crown held dominion and power over all territories constituting the British Empire. The British Parliament itself rested upon a restricted social basis. The majority of the adult population had no vote and the voting was on a strictly property basis.

Nevertheless, there was peace and prosperity. Even the Crimean War and the Indian Mutiny, or what the Indians call their first "War of Independence," were memories of stormy days. And the scions of the ruling class, anxious for practice in the use of arms, had to be content with "little wars against restless tribes" and to run about the globe in search of a war, lest their arms rust and they become mere decorated darlings of the drawing rooms of Mayfair and the polo fields of Roehampton or Delhi. England, at this time, was indeed "the Workshop of the World." The industrial cities and towns belched their black smoke into the sky. The hammers of her forges thundered night and day. The machinery roared continuously and England's merchant fleet sailed all the seas of the world with her goods while the King's Navy kept guard over the waterways of every ocean. Supreme confidence marked the attitude of England's statesmen under Victoria Regina in 1874. The population was increasing rapidly. The era of railway expansion was in full blast. Cables for telegraphic communication were now laid under every sea. Froude and Macaulay were the most popular historians, glorying in England's prowess as the world's leader in an ever-expanding civilization. Carlyle thundered, and Ruskin moralized, and Dickens wrote his social novels. Tennyson was writing his poems of doubt and hope. Darwin had quietly thrown into the arena of modern thought the disturbing evidence of the evolution of man which was soon to shake the theological foundations of religious faith.

At the opposite end of the social scale, industrial workers and their families filled rows on rows of blackened red brick houses, characteristic habitations of industrial man power as Britain ran into boom and slump in the golden age of lais-sez-faire, full of "muck and money." The First International Workingmen's Association had arisen ten years before Winston Churchill was born, and the "specter of Communism" began to haunt the ruling families of Europe when the Paris Commune of 1871, for one brief hour, had triumphantly flown the banner of the Fourth Estate as a portent of things to come. When Winston was seven years of age, the First International Workingmen's Association died. The economic and social crises of the time were but the growing pains of an expanding economy. The young empire and the vast regions of America could still absorb millions of emigrants from Europe and Britain was riding supreme with a "natural" monopoly in an age of "free competition." The trade unions of the British working class were young and weak. To the old Tory and Liberal Parties which alternated with each other in periods of government, and the rulers of Britain who "crossed the floor of the House" with the equanimity of a man changing his club, there was no Labor party opposition. It was the heyday of "pendulum" politics for the British ruling classes, which had no thought that this age would ever pass away.

Winston's father, Lord Randolph Churchill, was twenty-five years of age when Winston was born. He was a brilliant young man, steeped in the traditions of his family, and had but recently embarked upon his political career. Indeed, it was in the Spring of 1874 that he was first elected to Parliament; on April 15, 1874 that he married Jennie Jerome, and on November 30, 1874, that the premature birth of Winston was announced to the world. These were exceptional parents and dwelt in the highest circles of society, basked in the affability of the Prince of Wales, were hosts to Disraeli, adorned West End Society, went to Blenheim for hunting, Ascot and the other famous courses for racing, and Cowes for yachting. They varied their program with visits to Paris and Philadelphia. There was nothing mediocre about Lord Randolph. He shot across the sky of British politics like a brilliant meteor, touched the heights of political prestige among a galaxy of stars like Disraeli, Gladstone, Rosebery and Salisbury, careened impetuously from their midst as rapidly as he came, to die young. As an orator he could hold his own with the great figures of his day and it is clear that his son, Winston, modeled himself upon his father and drew his inspiration from the same sources. As Philip Guedalla has remarked, "It is not easy to say which is speaking, when an orator proclaimed the path of Britain is upon the ocean, her ways lie upon the deep, and you should avoid as your greatest danger any reliance on transcontinental communications, where, at any time, you may have to encounter gigantic military hosts."

That was Lord Randolph, but if we did not know it we should be forgiven if we called it "Winstonian," so alike and so true in form and style is it to the Gibbon whose *Decline and Fall of the Roman Empire* had been the passion of the Churchills, father and son.

Hardly had Lord Randolph entered Parliament when his father, the Duke of Marlborough, was appointed by the Earl of Beaconsfield to the post of Lord Lieutenant of Ireland, with the friendly intimation that he might find it convenient to have Lord Randolph as his secretary (unpaid). The post itself, the appointment, and the manner of the appointment all tell their story of the nature of empire relations of the time. "Dominion over palm and pine," and over Ireland as well, lay in the hands of the Marlboroughs, Beaconsfields, Salisburys and Gladstones, splendid and serene. The Duke of Marlborough went to Dublin Castle; Lord and Lady Randolph Churchill and their little Anglo-American son, Winston, installed themselves in the Little Lodge of Phoenix Park with its green spaces as yet undisturbed. For four years Lady Randolph dazzled the drawing rooms of Dublin Castle with her dark beauty while her husband hunted, shot, and fished, and wandered about Ireland's countryside. The little fellow, Winston, grew and played soldiers and rode his donkey, listened to the stories of the Fenians, and learned how to deal with them in the language of a soldier when he was four years of age. The spirit of the original Marlborough seemed to be emerging from the blending of Anglo-American stock.

But the father was no mere passer-on of the Marlborough tradition. He was ambitious in his own right and no man's echo. He was born into the Tory Party. Independent by nature, highly individualistic by temperament, he sought to make his own contribution to party policy, embellish the Tory Party with his own radicalism, and become the leader of the *Fourth* Party (a group within the Tory Party). This was not really a rival party, but a Left Wing of the Tory Party, struggling within it against "the old gang"; it was, as Lord Rosebery put it, a means of expression "for anyone who found himself with Radical opinions inside the Tory Party and who did not wish to leave it." Lord Randolph understood, as well as his son learned, how to rise by challenging the dominant authority in Parliament and playing the role of the *enfant terrible* of politics. At the end of four years in Ireland he returned to England, became, naturally, Opposition leader to Gladstone and by the time he was thirty-five he was the rising star of the Tory Party. He played a leading part in bringing about the downfall of Gladstone's government and, when the Tory Party triumphed in the elections, he became the Secretary of State for India.

Now listen to the voice of the father, so like that of the son who would follow in his steps, as he assured Parliament and the world how conscious he was of his responsibility for "that most truly bright and precious gem in the crown of the Queen, the possession of which, more than of all your Colonial dominions, has raised in power, in resource, in wealth and in authority this small island home of ours far above the level of the majority of nations and of States, has placed it on an equality with, perhaps, even in a position of superiority over, every other Empire either of ancient or of modern times."

He was in his element as he basked in the glory of high office and England's imperial prestige, with a London house famous for its modernity, with a wife famous for her beauty and a remarkable flair for fulfilling the role of political hostess. Connaught Place became the center at which gathered the brilliant and the powerful in the contemporary ruling class life of the metropolis. Lord Randolph was to climb still higher in the hierarchy of the State, however, and touch the threshold of the supreme position of the British Parliament. Conscious of the dignity of his office as Secretary of State for India, he would not tolerate the Prime Minister and the Queen appointing a royal prince into the Bombay command without reference to his office. He forced their hands by resigning. They retreated. It was a signal victory for Churchill, for Lord Salisbury dare not lose his greatest orator on the eve of a general election. When the Tories came to power again, after the defeat of Gladstone's Home Rule Bill, Lord Randolph Churchill became Chancellor of the Exchequer and Leader of the House. One more step and the premiership would be in his hands. But when, in 1886, he tried the resignation trick again, it failed. The circumstances were different. The government could dispense with his services.

Down he went never to rise again. His son Winston, writing of him in later years when he himself was a Liberal, said that Lord Randolph should have become a Liberal. Had it not been for the all-important question of imperial relations there would have been nothing to prevent him taking that course. But he was an uncompromising opponent of Home Rule for Ireland, which had become a burning question of the day. The Liberal Party was identified with Home Rule for Ireland, so he could not join that. He fell from the heights of political power with a grievance against the old party. Unable to adjust himself to joining the Liberal Party, he dreamed dreams of a "National Party," then faded from the political scene and died at the age of forty-six.

Meanwhile the little ginger-headed boy had played with his lead soldiers in his nursery, shot down wicked Fenians with his toy guns, and ridden his donkey-steed in a fantastic environment steeped in the tradition of Marlborough. His imagination was fed with the crudities of nurse and govern-ess until he was ready to go to a boarding school which was one "of the most fashionable and expensive in the country." His stay there was brief and he liked neither the ancient grammars nor mathematical subjects nor discipline. From the outset he was a natural individualist "with plenty of pep." He liked outdoor life. He liked poetry. He liked his-tory and French "and, above all, riding and swimming." Then, when he was twelve, he went to Harrow and it be-came perfectly clear to him and everybody else that here was no academician in the making. He was born a soldier with the imagination of a poet and with a nature as romantic as an Elizabethan pirate. He stagnated in the lowest form but won a prize open to the whole school for reciting a hundred lines from Macaulay's *Lays of Ancient Rome* and passed the preliminary examination for the Army. He himself says that his orientation towards a military career "was entirely due to my collection of soldiers." What his collection of soldiers was due to he does not say. Maybe we can link his predilection toward collecting soldiers and organizing armies to the original Marlborough. He would be pleased to think so. But of the soldiers he had collected when a boy he says, "I had ultimately nearly fifteen hundred. They were all of one size, all British, and organised as an infantry division with a cavalry brigade. My brother Jack commanded the hostile army. But by a Treaty for Limitation of Armaments he was only allowed to have coloured troops; and they were not allowed to have artillery. Very important! I could muster myself only eighteen field guns—besides fortress pieces. But all the other services were complete—except one. It is what every army is always short of—transport. . . .

"The day came when my father himself paid a formal visit of inspection. All the troops were arranged in the correct formation of attack. He spent twenty minutes studying the scene—which was really impressive—with a keen eye and captivating smile. At the end he asked me if I would like to go into the army. I thought it would be splendid to command an Army, so I said 'Yes' at once: and immediately I was taken at my word." Humorously he adds: "For years I thought my father with his experience and flair had discerned in me the qualities of military genius. But I was told later that he had only come to the conclusion that I was not clever enough to go to the Bar." (*My Early Life*, pp. 33-34.)

So the way was paved from Harrow to Sandhurst after two unsuccessful efforts to pass the entrance examination. In the third effort he passed only high enough to become a cavalry officer instead of an officer of the infantry, much to the disappointment of his father who had set his heart on his son becoming an officer in the 60th Rifles. Now environment and subjects of study and all the heredity factors combined in happy harmony to produce a successful soldier student. Churchill says: "Instead of creeping at the bottom, almost by charity, I passed out with honours eighth in my batch of a hundred and fifty." But while Sandhurst catered for his military ambitions, home nurtured his political development.

He read every speech his father ever delivered and dreamed
of the day when father and son would stand shoulder to
shoulder and, with majestic utterance and withering phrase,
triumph over their political foes and reach the highest positions in the foremost ranks of Britain's leaders. A twelve
months' convalescence after an accident gave him a great opportunity to meet the leading statesmen of the day who fore-
gathered in his home, to visit the House of Commons, listen
to the great orators of the day, talk with them, and take the
measure of the parliamentary scene. He read what he liked
and, following his father, became enraptured with Gibbon's
Decline and Fall of the Roman Empire, until father and son
spoke alike and both spoke in the language of their master.
Later the son was to modernize himself a little and mix his
Gibbon with Macaulay. He was in his twenty-first year when
his father died. Thus ended the dream of father-and-son com-
radeship in Parliament. "There remained for me," says Winston, "only to pursue his aims and vindicate his memory."

But not yet. First the glory of the cavalry charge against
the foes of empire and the romance of a few "little" wars. Not
yet were known the common shambles of the wars of democracy and science. These were the days when the shambles
were the private property of the dervishes and the dusky-
skinned hordes of fighting tribesmen who hated the pukka
sahibs of the Great White Queen, when cavalry with "a
beautiful intricacy of archaic manoeuvre" could wheel and
charge and slash and "shout in joyous wrath" as they made
"mincemeat" of the more primitively equipped enemies of
the Queen. Winston became an officer in the 4th Hussars in
1895. But England had no "little war" available for his services and, impatient to be "blooded," he dashed off to aid
the Spaniards against the Cuban patriots. That gave him the
chance to go "under fire." Incidentally, too, it gave him the
opportunity, en route, to visit his mother's home in Havana.
Soon other opportunities for military adventure crowded in
upon him. Although the Colonial Conference of 1887, sum-

moned to honor Queen Victoria's fifty years on the throne, had made the most significant change within the fabric of empire by conceding to Canada a wide autonomy in local affairs along the lines of the famous Durham Report of 1836, it was only a harbinger of things to come. The vast centralized imperial power remained intact and the outlook of the rulers of Britain had not got beyond the views of Durham. The empire was still expanding. There was an important expedition in the Sudan; there was "trouble" on the Northwest Frontier of India. There were bright memories of reverses to be avenged—Gordon at Khartoum, Rorke's Drift in South Africa. So it happened that Churchill was in the Charge at Omdurman with Kitchener, played polo on the Indian plains, participated in the Northwest Frontier fighting. After India he went to Africa to fight the Boers.

Buoyant, fearless, indefatigable in everything in which he was interested, he played polo and fought and adventured with all the ardor of a crusader. It was in this period that he blossomed out as a war correspondent and combined soldiering with writing. The soldier journalist grew into the soldier politician. Returning from the Boer War in 1900, with a wonderfully adventurous record as an escaped prisoner of war who had had a price on his head and who had sent vivid despatches to the newspapers, he was rushed by the Tories to Oldham in Lancashire to be their candidate in an election of that year. Oldham was a two-member constituency and he was returned as its junior member. Quickly, on the heels of this triumph he filled the lecture halls of England with the story of his exploits in the Boer War. From England he went to America, secured Mark Twain as his first chairman in New York, told the Americans his story and reminded them he was "half American himself." Then he filled the halls of the cities of Canada, had another turn round Britain, and bounced into the House of Commons as the "son of his father" intent on the vindication of the paternal record.

The moment was propitious, although the circumstances

were so vastly different from those of the day when his father faced the House of Commons for the first time and stirred the ranks of Victorian politicians with his eloquence and the pomp of the Gibbon phrase. The quarter of a century between the occasions had witnessed great changes. Britain still reigned in majesty over her empire and its centralized authority was still supreme. Her Navy ruled the oceans. But in the East and in the West new powers were rising and changing the pattern of world power. New industrial empires were about to put an end to that happy free monopoly which had characterized England's workshop in its relations with the rest of the world for nearly a century. Within the empire the stirrings among the colonial populations calling for Home Rule had become a feature of the times even as the expansionist program in Africa began to unfold. A man named Gandhi was growing up in India and another named Nehru was born and growing to manhood. The Parnell period in Irish history had come and gone and the age-long struggle for Irish self-government was taking on new forms. Western Australia and the colony of Natal had been granted significant measures of responsible government on the lines of those conceded to Canada. Within Britain itself the industrial working class, which had grown with the industrial revolution and which marked the years of the nineteenth century, was becoming conscious of itself, shaping its own organizations, and developing its own loyalties and political leaders. The modern British Socialist movement, with its Fabian societies and socialist federations and parties, was invading the political arena hitherto monopolized by the old parties of imperial splendor and oligarchical "democracy." The International Workingmen's Association, which died when Winston was a boy, had been reborn as the Second International of Labor and Socialist Organizations. The hitherto submerged classes of many lands were on the move, stirred with ideas which were at once portents and warnings.

But not for the young Member for Oldham. He was

twenty-five years of age, a goodly figure of a man, with a good constitution, a buoyant personality, a soldier of fortune, Hussar, Rough Rider, war correspondent, politician, steeped in the traditions of the ruling caste of England's imperial breed, when he rose in the House of Commons from the seat where once Lord Randolph Churchill "of splendid memory" had often risen to assail the mighty. From there he said he would "lift again the tattered flag I found lying on a stricken field" left by his father. In that same first speech, however, he revealed unconsciously the impact of the new circumstances in which the British Empire flourished and sought to endure. The Boer War had not yet ended. It must perforce be the subject of debate when the Queen opened Parliament and the government presented its program to the House of Commons. Winston was fresh from the field of battle and probably was better acquainted with the state of affairs in South Africa than any man in the House. He had been born into the Tory Party as surely as his father before him was steeped in the traditions of his kind who had held the reigns of power in all the centuries of British empire-building. He had and has a remarkable memory, a vivid imagination, a cultured gift of expression, great courage, a sense of power, and unlimited ambition. He was neither an academician nor a theorist. He thought in terms of nations, races, empires, armies, navies and leaders. He instinctively accepted the assumption of his class that its interests and that of the nation and empire were identical. In his opinion, the rise and fall of empires and social systems were not governed by economic and social laws which he would seek to understand in order to transform the world and man. He thought of his heritage and that of his kind as the God-given spoils of victory in the struggle of nations, "glittering prizes" for the fittest in the fray, and he and his kind were of the fittest. His heart and mind responded to the beat of Elgar's "Imperial Hymn," "Mightier still and mightier may thy boundaries be," and the drama of the human conflict filled his soul. If only he had been born when the British Empire was young, instead of in the years when her sun was moving into eclipse! But such a melancholy reflection was not his as he rose to speak, although he was conscious that new imperial powers were rising where once the scene was clear or nations were somnolent in their feudal backwardness. His morals and creed were those of the chivalrous soldier. He had an admiration for the Boers. They had fought well and ably. Note, then, the theme as the soldier politician held forth: Send overwhelming forces to beat them, then offer them self-government within the empire! The young Tory was out of step with the old and in step with "Radical Jack" Durham of 1836, ready to transfer British institutions to those on the outposts of empire as the means of maintaining the power of England in foreign affairs. He had dared, as his father had dared before him, to challenge the "grey beards" in power. But his challenge was not on the same issue. Indeed that issue, of self-government within the empire, when applied to Ireland by a born Tory turned Liberal, by one named Gladstone, had blocked the way to Randolph Churchill's recovery from disaster. It happened, too, that Winston's speech on this occasion was more acceptable to the Liberals than to the Tories of his own party. That did not worry young Churchill. He would pursue his course and it mattered little to him whether his course lay with the Tory Party or the Liberal Party. It led him into friendship with Lloyd George, Asquith, Grey, Morley, Lord Rosebery. Party loyalty was not his strong point and he would not make the same mistake as his father. His very first speech, as a young Tory, standing where his father had stood, thus led him into the camp of the Liberals who had become the exponents of "Home Rule" for the white colonies. In 1904 Winston Churchill joined the Liberal Party. Nevertheless he would re-cross the floor of the House of Commons when it became necessary to suit the exigencies of his career in his far-flung ambition of imperial leadership.

In 1905, the Tory Government fell. The Campbell-Bannerman Government was formed and Winston Churchill became the Under-Secretary for the Colonies. He was riding with the tide. The great political awakening of the working class was on the way. In the 1906 General Election it swept the Tories aside and carried the Liberal Party to power. Twenty-six Labor men were elected to the House of Commons and they laid the foundations of the modern Labor Party. The young imperial Liberal of Tory origin viewed the newly proclaimed Socialism of the rising movement as "a monstrous and imbecile conception" and "the cause of the Liberal Party as the cause of the left-out millions." As the Liberal Under-Secretary for the Colonies he was in charge of the Transvaal Constitution Act of 1906, conceived on the lines of his first speech in Parliament in 1901. It granted "self-government to the Transvaal" *within the empire,* and was a most positive step in the evolution of the empire toward the commonwealth. It followed quickly on his conferences with General Botha and was the sequel to the defeat of the Boers in 1902.

When Asquith succeeded Campbell-Bannerman, Winston Churchill was promoted from the Colonial Office to become President of the Board of Trade. In September 1908, at the age of thirty-three, he married Miss Clementine Hozier and he says they "lived happily ever afterwards." After the elections of 1910, on the great issue of the future of the House of Lords, he became Home Secretary and soon revealed that he was as much the soldier statesman in domestic affairs as he had been in world affairs. The railway strike of 1911 revealed him ready to use all the powers of the state in the class war at home as he was ever ready to use them for imperial purposes abroad. With tremendous vigor he organized troop movements, ready to smash the strike, and was not a little disappointed that a settlement was arrived at without him having the opportunity to "save the State." In this same year the "German Menace" loomed large on the horizon of world affairs. Winston Churchill had already become a member of the Committee for Imperial Defence and had submitted a memorandum to the Prime Minister upon "military aspects of the Continental problem." Although trained as a soldier, he had never departed from the traditional conception of the preeminence of the British Navy in any war in which Britain might be engaged. In his earliest years in Parliament he had declared, opposing thirty million pounds' expenditure on the Army, "The only weapon with which we can expect to cope with the great nations is the Navy . . . without a supreme Navy, whatever military arrangement we may make, whether for foreign expedition or home defence must be utterly vain and futile. With such a Navy we may hold any antagonist at arm's length and feed ourselves in the meantime until, if we find it necessary, we can turn every city in the country into an arsenal, and the whole male population into an army."

Neither he nor any other member of the government had thought in advance on the nature of the coming war and prepared accordingly. But when Churchill submitted his memorandum he anticipated what the Germans would be able to do in the first weeks of the war, what France would be compelled to do, and made proposals as to what Britain should do within *the compass of the traditional strategy and a small British expeditionary force.* As a result of the reluctance of McKenna, the First Lord of the Admiralty, to endorse his plan, which the Cabinet accepted, a new First Lord had to replace McKenna. It was Winston Churchill himself who replaced McKenna. The Navy was found ready and mobilized for action on the fateful day of August 4, 1914.

Although there had been another Colonial Conference in 1907 and a number of significant and important changes had taken place in the direction of self-government in the local affairs of the white colonies, none had yet any power whatever in relation to foreign affairs. The British Parliament was still supreme, and when it declared war on Germany and her allies, at one stroke the whole British Empire was also at war.

From the moment Churchill became First Lord of the Admiralty in 1911 until the outbreak of war he concentrated wholly on the naval aspects of the coming war. Once he had been thrilled with the magnificence of the cavalry charge. Now he thrilled to majestic naval spectacles, the thunder of their mighty guns, to the new kinds of naval craft, and the swift movements of the seaplane. The war came. Most assuredly, Winston Churchill had done his job in masterly fashion and true to Britain's tradition as a sea power. But it must be said also that this was inadequate to the demands of the Armageddon in which the fate of the British Empire was to be decided; such a war demanded of Britain an army as mighty as her navy, an army ready for launching onto the Continent when the first blows were struck. The fact is that not one of the rulers of Britain had ever anticipated a war of the character now thrust upon them, committed though she was to joint action with France and Russia, should Germany invade Belgium. In that contingency nobody had ever deemed it necessary to send to the Continent more than a relatively small expeditionary force; Britain's principal service in the alliance would be by means of the Navy. This war by its nature, magnitude, and scope called for totalitarian organization of the Navy, Army, industry, economy, manpower—centralized direction and deployment of all forces. It was the absence of this which led to Churchill's inspired improvisations of strategy demanding coordinated actions of Army and Navy, at Antwerp and the Dardanelles, and compelled him to operate with inadequate forces. The schemes were brilliant but they broke upon the historical unpreparedness of Britain for the kind of war which history thrust upon her. In the process they cast down Winston Churchill from the heights of Cabinet rank and the threshold of the supreme leadership of the empire at war, to the level of an M.P. without Cabinet office. At first glance it seemed as if he were repeating his father's history. When Winston became First Lord of the Admiralty he appeared to be running neck and neck with Lloyd George as a possible successor to Asquith, although the Asquith Cabinet was a brilliant team. Asquith was himself a great scholar and law- yer who had not been afraid to call to his side other men of high intellectual stature—Grey, John Morley, Haldane, Lloyd George, Churchill. Here was a team such as England had not had in a single Cabinet for generations.

But examine them closer. Asquith, the classical scholar of the later Victorians, in the tradition of Gladstone; Morley, the man of letters at home in the libraries, browsing among books; Grey, the gentleman-diplomat of Edwardian pacifica- tion; Haldane, who sensed what was required of the forces but who, against the dead weight of England's traditional policy as a sea power primarily, could only use his great abil- ity to reshape the Army and make it ready for rapid expan- sion. Lloyd George, of different social origin from all his colleagues, lawyer, orator, a man without military experience but possessing great imaginative qualities and a far better grasp and understanding of the social process of his times than any of his colleagues. He appreciated and understood better than any of them the full significance of the political awakening of the working class. His attitude to Socialism was not that of the iconoclastic warrior of reaction but of the astute political leader who appreciated the struggles and aspirations of the workers and sought to divert them from their great political aims by extracting from Socialism's program the reforms inherent in it. He viewed the conflict between political parties as the reflection of the social strug- gle. He was also "dated" in his ideas on the totalitarian char- acter of the war that was rushing upon Britain and that ac- tually crashed upon her in 1914. But he, like Churchill, was quick to grasp the realities of the new situation when it came. He was fortunate, too, because he was not bogged down with a department which restricted his range of vision as was

Churchill. Winston had concentrated upon the Navy and, in so far as he had viewed the coming war as a whole, had thought of Britain's part in it as a naval contribution, with the British Army having to play an auxiliary role in the Continental fighting. He thought that the major burdens of land warfare would fall upon France and Russia, and that their forces would suffice. Although he appreciated the necessity of combined operations of all arms and the need for singleness of direction, he was up against the fact that the Army, Navy, and Air Force had developed as separate institutions, each with its own vested interests, pride, prejudices, and traditions. When Asquith made Kitchener his Minister for War he could not have appointed a more conservative military chief, a man more rooted in the traditions of nineteenth-century warfare, more mentally ill-equipped to face the problems of Continental warfare and of the total war into which Britain had plunged. When Churchill recalled Fisher to command the Navy he had recalled a supreme naval leader, the complete embodiment of "the Navy First and Supreme." Although Churchill had a brilliant imaginative grasp of circumstances and quickly appraised the new situation, he was brought to grief and put out of the Cabinet after the actions of Antwerp, Dunkirk, and the Dardenelles. But whatever failures there were in these actions conceived by Churchill they were due not to the lack of brilliance in conception. They were due to the absence of single leadership and the conflict of prejudices and departmental claims in their preparation and operation. Churchill was the first casualty in the ranks of Britain's leaders in the war of 1914-1918 because Britain was ready to wage only a naval war instead of the total war which was thrust upon her. The only other man in the Cabinet with a similar imaginative grasp of the situation and the dynamic qualities required was Mr. Lloyd George. Fortunate at the outset in having no direct military responsibility for waging the war, he won out as the successor to Asquith because he fought to transform Britain's "naval war" into total war, to establish a single command in place of a divided command. Had Lloyd George been at the Admiralty and Churchill at the Exchequer at the outbreak of war it would have assuredly been Lloyd George's fate to fall, for the same reasons that Churchill fell, and the latter would have succeeded Asquith to leadership instead of having to wait until 1940 to achieve this commanding height of statesmanship.

Nevertheless, Winston Churchill did not suffer the fate of his father. He fell only to rise again. Quickly, after Lloyd George had superseded Asquith, and the Dardanelles Commission had cleared Churchill from responsibility for the failure of the Dardanelles campaign, Lloyd George called him back to the Cabinet as Minister of Munitions. Here he performed a great work in bringing British industry to its highest pitch of war production. Although there were other able leaders within the War Cabinet, he was regarded as Lloyd George's second in command. He was now in every phase of the centralized direction of the total war, encouraging and often initiating the development of new techniques of warfare, a field which had absorbed much of his time when he was First Lord of the Admiralty. He was in his element. Once he had bewailed the passing of the days of warfare when the cavalry charge provided the greatest of thrills. But the total war in which he now played a leading role gave him greater scope. The cavalry passed from the scene in favor of the tank and motorized transport. Aircraft swept across the skies. New weapons of war multiplied. Everything contributed to give greater scope to his insatiable ambition as he helped to marshal ever greater hosts of men in imperial conflict.

By 1918 Britain had left behind the concept of a naval Britain with a small voluntary Army to police her empire. By that time she had a vast Army and a growing Air Force, and her economy and man-power were geared to the demands of the all-in war. But it was all too late to hold back the eclipse of Britain as the dominant world power. Had the leaders of Britain grasped the full significance of the rise of the German power after Germany's victory over France in 1870, and kept pace with that power in the transformation of her armed forces and her strategy of warfare, the story of 1914-18 would have to be differently written, although it would not have prevented Britain's eclipse by the U.S.A. It was not to be, and from the first days of the war the utmost of which France and Britain together were capable was to hold the line until American industrial and military power had been developed and had swung into the Western Front. From 1917 Britain's economic dependence upon America grew with each passing year. The Allies, with support from America, brought Germany crashing to the ground but also raised America's industry and economic power to the foremost position of all countries. The British Empire had risen in grandeur to defend itself against the threat of eclipse by the Germanic Empire. The irony of history is that in the process it accelerated its eclipse by the U.S.A. In that gigantic conflict none had played a more magnificent role as the defender of the old empire in battle than had Winston Churchill. He was still at the side of Lloyd George as the "Cease Fire" was sounded on the battlefields of Europe.

But another process was at work in the structure of human society, which Winston Churchill has never comprehended. The war had developed the conflict of social classes and roused the national aspirations of peoples who had hitherto been under the domination of imperial governments. The Russian Revolution of 1917 had swept the Czarist ruling classes aside and brought to power a revolutionary government resting on an alliance of the workers and peasants. Such a change in the affairs of any empire was anathema to Winston. When the working-class movement formed its own party and set before itself the goal of Socialism as he leapt into the political arena in the year 1901, it was threatening everything he held dear and violating every tradition which had contributed to shaping the political outlook of his kind. They had ruled for centuries and built the greatest empire the world had seen. They had studded its Crown with the brightest gems. He saw Socialism "as a monstrous and imbecile conception." He preferred "the true evolution of democracy along the golden thread of historical continuity." He would have conceded that the working class should have many reforms in due time and that the conditions of their labor should be improved. Again he would agree to extend the franchise to increasing numbers of them, but these "forgotten millions" should have the sense to vote for the old parties, the Liberal Party when he was in its leadership, and the Tory Party, when he should lead that. But the idea that the working class should seek to change the whole structure of society from its foundations upward was sheer imbecility leading the nation and the empire into the abyss. The working class must know its place as the servant of its rulers and if it did not he was all for using the full power of the state to teach it. Hence when the Russian Revolution burst upon the scene, it was to Churchill the horror of horrors. He poured contumely upon its leaders. For several years he could speak of Soviet Russia and her Bolshevik leaders only as a man in a delirium tormented by the dream figures of millions upon millions of horrible shapes carrying desolation to the ends of the earth. Speaking at Sunderland on January 3, 1920, he said:

No one could tell what would emerge from the immense, horrible catastrophe of Russia, except that it would be something menacing to civilization and very dangerous to the peace of Europe and Asia. The Allies might abandon Russia; Russia would not abandon them. The ghost of the Russian bear now sat outside the Peace Conference in silent reproach; now it ranged over the enormous countries leading to the frontiers of India, disturbing Afghanistan, disturbing Persia, creating far to southward great agitation and unrest among the hundreds of millions of our Indian population.

Then there was Turkey. A junction of Russian Bolshevism

and Turkish Mohammedanism would be full of danger to many
States—to none more than to the British Empire, the greatest of
Mohammedan States. The armies of Kolchak were almost gone;
the armies of Denikin were in serious danger. Were they to disappear—they might—a series of evil consequences, incalculable
in their scope, would immediately be set in motion, and by those
consequences we of all countries in the world would be most
affected. . . . Supposing the Russian loyalists give up the struggle,
what will the likeliest sequel be? Not surely that Bolshevik Russia
will wallow contentedly in the mess until it dies of its own pu-
tridity. To suppose that is to misunderstand the whole spirit of
the Bolshevik movement. The more it decays at the centre, the
more determined will be its pressure outward. It might decide
that China was the best field for its energies. It might seek fresh
air, away from its own miasma, towards Constantinople and the
Straits or in the highlands of the Asiatic steppes. Or, if Germany
were favourably disposed, Poland might be more attractive. What
should we do in that case? We could not abandon Poland, nor
Armenia and the approaches to India or China. We should be
brought up against the same problem that we could not shirk it.
Our lip attachment to peace would have brought us into another
war, and our doctrine of indifference to Russian affairs would
force us to intervene amid every circumstance of disadvantage and
inconvenience to ourselves.

This nightmarish vision, conjured up by his fertile imagination out of the impact of the Bolshevik Revolution on
the old world of Empire which was his glory, has never
left him, although from 1941 when the Hitler Empire sought
to struggle against the British Empire once again, he put it
into storage for the duration of the alliance between Russia
and the British Empire against the common foe. When he,
side by side with Lloyd George in the Coalition Government
of 1918-22, came to terms with the Soviet Government he
was making a soldier's decision to silence the guns for a time.
It was not the end of his war against the Bolsheviks and everything for which they stood.

But the war produced revolutionary changes within the
British Empire as well as outside it. The British Empire went
into the war as an imperial entity. Out of the war came the

"British Commonwealth and Empire." The white colonies had become Dominions. The colored colonies remained colonies of the British Empire, although disturbing developments were taking place within them. Before the outbreak of war concessions had been made in many colonies, granting them control of their internal affairs. The Imperial Conference of 1911 agreed that in future the various parts of the empire should be fully consulted on all matters of imperial foreign policy and defense. Canada, at this conference led the way to a decision, followed by the other white colonies, which gave them the title of Dominions, and the right to develop their own land and sea forces. Nevertheless, it was the British Government which declared them at war with Germany. The Allied declaration in favor of "self-determination of nations" led to a general demand that the Dominions be given more independence. In 1917, Dominion statesmen came into the British War Cabinet as Privy Councillors. At the Imperial Conference of 1917 Prime Minister Borden of Canada put forward a resolution which stressed that the Dominions were not content to have their foreign relations conducted in London and that the Dominions wished to share in the making of imperial policy. The Dominions demanded independent representation at the Peace Conference. This was conceded and at Versailles the Dominions and India were admitted to the League of Nations as "belligerent powers with special interests." At the Imperial Conference of 1926 the position of the Dominions was defined as that of "Autonomous Communities in no way subordinate one to another . . . united by common allegiance to the Crown," and one after another appointed their own ambassadors to foreign countries. In this development Churchill continued the course he had pursued in relation to the Boers, a course consistent with the traditional policy of organic evolutionary adaptation of the empire to changing circumstances, along the lines of Durham, without conceding anything to

independent republicanism which was as abhorrent to him
as Bolshevism was.

It was in this period at the close of the First World War,
Churchill played a notable part in the settlement of the
"Irish Question." From the very first days of his entrance
into politics he had been in favor of Home Rule for Ireland
as a Dominion within the Empire and had fought against
Irish republicanism. When the Sinn Fein Movement of Ireland followed the insurrectionary rising led by James Con-
nolly in 1916, with a national war for an Irish Republic in
1919, Churchill was Minister of War in the Coalition Government and fought the uprising with the notorious Black and
Tans. Nevertheless, there came the time when an offer was
made to the Irish leaders, Griffith and Michael Collins. Winston Churchill tells in his own inimitable way of his meeting
with these two men. He says:

"To Mr. Griffith I said one day: 'I would like us to have
beaten you beyond all question and then to have given you
freely all that we are giving you now.'

" 'I understand that,' he answered, 'but would your countrymen?' "

Again, in the same account of the signing of the
Irish Treaty which brought forth the Irish Free State, he tells
of his meeting with Michael Collins. He says:

"Lord Birkenhead and I were left with Michael Collins
meanwhile. He was in his most difficult mood, full of re-
proaches and defiances and it was easy for everyone to lose
his temper.

" 'You hunted me night and day,' he said. 'You put a price
on my head.'

" 'Wait a minute,' I said, 'You are not the only one.' And
I took from the wall the framed copy of the reward offered
for my recapture by the Boers. 'At any rate, it was a good
price—£5,000. Look at me, £25 dead or alive. How would
you like that?'

"He read the paper, and as he took it in he broke into a hearty laugh. All his irritation vanished. We had a really serviceable conversation, and thereafter—though I must admit that deep in my heart there was a certain gulf between us— we never to the best of my belief lost the basis of a common understanding."

There was the soldier statesman at his best, the warrior who admires a good fighter, the generous nature, the willingness to come to terms if he can do it without giving too much away. In his concessions to Collins and Griffith, even as with the Boers, he demonstrated to all but himself that he was fighting a losing battle. The old empire was changing.

While he was Minister of War in this period he demonstrated how fully he had learned the military significance of total warfare. Thinking that others had learned it too, he advanced a project for amalgamating the War Office, Admiralty, and Air Ministry under a single Minister of Defence. Of course, he had no doubt whatever as to who should occupy that post. But he had to wait twenty years for his plan to mature, when he became the Prime Minister faced with a total war more terrible and complete than the one from which the nations had just emerged. The times were then not propitious for such a proposal and Mr. Lloyd George, who was not so military minded, was too preoccupied with upheaval at home and abroad to accept his colleague's suggestion. Neither the War Office nor the prospect of another war held his attention. In 1921 Winston was transferred to the Colonial Office and he became preoccupied with Britain's position in the Near East and her relation to Palestine, the Arabs, and Egypt. In this position he made his famous partnership with Colonel Lawrence, reshaped the settlement of the dismembered Turkish Empire, and established British hegemony over a checkered pattern of Arabian states. This arrangement remained intact until the Second World conflagration and its aftermath, when the tangled skein passed into Mr. Bevin's inexperienced hands.

Suddenly the bottom dropped out of Churchill's position. The Coalition Government fell to pieces. Churchill was defeated in his constituency of Dundee at the general election. He was unfortunate in that immediately before the election he was stricken with appendicitis and languished in a London nursing home until two days before the poll when he attempted to address a stormy meeting of electors. Popular reaction against his part in the Dardanelles campaign, and especially his attitude toward Soviet Russia, was too much for him. He was defeated by a large majority and for the first time since the year 1900 he was out of office and out of Parliament.

The fall of Lloyd George's Coalition Government was a memorable event for it fully revealed the inner changes within the British body politic since the Liberal landslide of 1906. The Liberal Party had risen to power on the great tide of the political awakening of the working class which had produced the Labor Party. The split of the Liberal Party, with the fall of the Asquith Government in 1916, and the formation of the Coalition Government under the leadership of the Liberal Lloyd George, had hidden from view the full significance of the changes until the end of the Coalition period. It was seen then that the Liberal Party was in ruins— and the Labor Party had grown from strength to strength as the trades unions had multiplied in membership. Great industrial and political storms had followed in the track of the war, and the working class was greatly under the influence of the Russian Revolution. Lloyd George and Churchill had striven vainly to maintain a united front of the Liberals and Tories against the advancing tide of socialism. The conflict of the interests within the old parties, as to Britain's course of recovery from the shock of the war, shattered the coalition and, lo, the Liberal Party was in fragments and the Tory Party in the hands of mediocrity who dreamed the dreams of the year 1900. In the turmoil the devotees of Joseph Chamberlain, who in the last quarter of the nineteenth century sought to change Britain from a free-trade country to a tariff country, came into the leadership of the Tory Party. Although Britain had been forced off the gold standard by the war, the new government thought to reestablish the golden days of yore. It was also scared by the Russian Revolution and completely shared Churchill's phobia about it.

Had the Tory Party not turned completely to an all-in tariff policy it would have been easy for Churchill to have left the Liberal rump and turned again to the party of his origin. But there it was, and it stood as a barrier, just as Home Rule for Ireland had been a barrier to the return of his father to the fold. But he would not repeat his father's mistake. For a year he convalesced, painted pictures—a hobby which fascinated him and in which he displayed considerable talent. He wrote his history of the war under the title, *The World Crisis*. In 1923 another General Election was held in Britain. Churchill fought an anti-Socialist campaign at West Leicester and was again defeated. In a 1924 by-election he fought as an Independent Anti-Socialist, standing much closer to the Tory Party and receiving the support of Balfour, Birkenhead, Austen Chamberlain, and all his friends of the Coalition days. This time he was defeated by forty votes. Then at the General Election of 1924, he found a safe Tory seat in Epping as a "Constitutionalist" and emerged victorious. That brought him back to the Tory Party, as the most brilliant custodian of King, Lords, and Commons against the oncoming tide of Labor.

With re-election and the return to the House of his father, Churchill was appointed Chancellor of the Exchequer by Mr. Baldwin, the new Prime Minister, and the ghost of Lord Randolph walked again in high places. Churchill had no objections to the return to the gold standard. Indeed it was he, as chancellor, who initiated that measure which precipitated the industrial crisis culminating in the General Strike of 1926. Haunted by the specter of revolution he leapt to the forefront of this "national crisis" and became the generalissimo in command to save the state, the empire, the constitution, and all the traditions of England from dissolution. The state won and the empire was saved. It was an easy victory, followed by sensational denouements of a so-called Bolshevik conspiracy and the breaking off of trade relations with Russia. The warrior politician and statesman was in his element until the tide turned again and the Tory Government fell to the hordes of Labor in 1929. Winston Churchill then found himself in the ranks of the Official Opposition.

In the midst of this short interlude of Labor Government Winston Churchill gave a famous lecture known as the Romanes Lecture of 1930. Here he unfolded his view of the times. He said:

These eventful years through which we are passing are not less serious for us than the years of the Great War. They belong to the same period. The grand and victorious summits which the British Empire won in that war are being lost, have indeed largely been lost in the years that followed the Peace. We see our race doubtful of its mission and no longer confident about its principles, infirm of purpose, drifting to and fro with the tides and currents of a deeply disturbed ocean. The compass has been damaged. The charts are out of date. The crew have to take it in turn to be Captain; and every captain before every movement of the helm has to take a ballot not only of the crew but of an ever-increasing number of passengers. Yet within this vessel there abide all the might and fame of the British race and all the treasures of all the peoples in one fifth of the habitable globe. . . .

Looking still further ahead he saw a great problem for which he had no answer. He said:

The root problem of modern world economics was the strange discordance between the consuming and producing power. Who would have thought that cheap and abundant supplies of all the basic commodities should find the science of civilization of the world unable to use them? Had all the triumphs of research and organisation bequeathed to us only a new punishment—the curse of plenty?

This somber view of the eclipse of the British Empire, the revolutionary changes of the age, and its chronic condition of crisis, led him to get out of step with the leaders of the Tory Party as his attention became directed to the course of events in India. In this vast region of the empire with its population of 350,000,000, the past twenty years had witnessed a great political awakening which had given rise to the Indian National Congress and the Moslem League, focusing the aspirations of the Indian peoples toward "self-determination and independence." Certain concessions in the direction of self-government had been conceded in 1919. In 1927, following the continued agitiation of the Indians led by Gandhi, the British Government had appointed an all-party commission under the leadership of Sir John Simon. This commission included Mr. Attlee who was one day to be Prime Minister of Britain and to implement the demands of the Indians. The purpose of the commission in 1927 was to make an extensive survey of India and to make proposals for such changes in the constitution of India as they thought advisable and which would lead in the direction of self-government. Before the new proposals took shape, it fell to the lot of the Labor Government of 1929-31 to put into legal form the famous declaration of 1926 which defined the "British Commonwealth of Nations." That declaration was formulated by Mr. A. J. Balfour, then Foreign Secretary of the Tory Government led by Mr. Baldwin. Winston Churchill was Chancellor of the Exchequer, again on the threshold of the premiership. He had not quarreled with the declaration when it was made. For it left the power relations within the empire and commonwealth intact. He regarded Balfour's statement as a wonderful combination of words which seemed to give everyone what they wanted without changing anything. Now, however, when the government of the day sought to give legal form and content to the declaration it was a different matter. This legal document became famous as the "Westminster Statute of 1931." Here

Churchill called a halt. The defender of the yesterdays was
up in arms. It appeared to him that the Westminster Statute
signified that the empire was in a state of dissolution. Certainly the bill made it clear that "Dominion Status" meant
"independence." Therefore it meant also that Britain had
promised independence to India!

Addressing the House of Commons on November 20,
1931, on the second reading of the bill, he said:

. . . for the first time, we set out in cold legal language what
"Dominion Status" means. Let anyone who reads these clauses
contemplate the frightful disorder which would be brought upon
India if the full "Dominion Status" as set out here became the
law governing India. For India we have inalienable responsibilities and adequate and necessary powers to maintain them. . . .
When we have before us the actual legal proofs of Dominion
Status, is there anyone who does not see the folly and the wrong
of the declarations which have excited the hopes of the Indian
political classes that after a brief period of transition, full Dominion Status would be conferred upon the Indian central legislature? . . .

Churchill was a lonely figure in the Parliament protesting
against the advancing tide of change. He regarded the
changes as "unnecessary abdication." But having made his
protest he did not vote against the Westminster Statute.
Having striven his best to maintain the ancient glory, he
bowed to "Destiny" as it passed him by.

He repeated the process yet again as India moved onward
from bondage to freedom. Following in the track of the Commission of 1927 and the "Round Table Conference" of
1931 came the Government of India Bill in 1935. This time
the MacDonald-Baldwin combination was in power and
Mr. Attlee was the leader of the opposition. Winston Churchill was still plowing his lonely furrow and out of favor with
the Tory Party. The Government of India Bill granted
concessions of responsible government with a promise of
Dominion Status in the future. The Opposition, led by Mr.

Attlee, opposed the 1935 bill for two reasons. First, because it did not go far enough in recognizing explicitly India's right to Dominion Status, and secondly, because it did not provide the constitutional means for the peaceful economic and social emancipation of the workers and peasants of India.

Churchill opposed it on other grounds. Conscious of his isolation, he said: "I speak solely as a member of Parliament of some service in this House, who holds views upon this matter which ought not to go unrepresented in this discussion." He claimed the right to marshal British opinion against a course of action "which would bring, in my judgment, the greatest evils upon the people of India, upon the people of Great Britain and upon the structure of the British Empire itself. . . ." He continued to "hope, once and for all, to kill the idea that the British in India are aliens, moving, with many apologies, out of the country as soon as they have been able to set up any kind of governing organism to take their place. We shall try to inculcate the idea, coming now to be mentioned more and more in many quarters of this House, *that we are there for ever* as honoured partners with our fellow Indian subjects whom we invite in all faithfulness to join with us in the highest functions of Government for their lasting benefit and our own. . . ." His efforts were of no avail.

For the next decade he remained on the back benches of the Tory Party in the House of Commons, carrying out his pledge to fight against every proposal which would loosen the bonds of Empire.

In the middle of this period his attention became concentrated upon the rise of Hitler's imperial Germany and its renewal of challenge to the British Empire. Now the warrior statesman in his maturity took up his station once again in full consciousness of the changed position and condition of Britain and her empire. The years from 1914 to 1918 had driven in upon him the consciousness that the era of Britain as primarily a naval power had gone forever and that twen-

tieth-century war was total war. He knew that the position
of Britain as a world power had changed. Gone were the days
of the two-to-one ratio of her Navy. Gone were the days when
Britain was the "Workshop of the World." There were
greater workshops belonging to other powers and this was
the age of combined services with centralized direction. He
knew that since demobilization in 1919 no major steps had
been taken to bring the armed forces up to the level required
for the renewal of the conflict and that the Air Force was in
its infancy. From the moment that Germany began to re-
arm and set her factories working at full strength, Churchill,
with relentless persistence, sounded the alarm. The challenge of social revolution no longer obsessed him. He si-
lenced his criticisms of the Soviet Union and became the
earnest advocate of Britain, France, and the Soviet Union
using the League of Nations as a basis of collective security
against the threatening Fascist powers. But he was a lonely
figure on the Tory benches. In 1938 he asked anxiously: "Is
the new policy to come to terms with the totalitarian powers
in the hope that by great and far-reaching acts of submission,
not merely in sentiment and pride, but in material factors,
peace may be preserved? . . . I predict that the day will
come when at some point or other, on some issue or other, you
will have to make a stand, and I pray God that when that
day comes we may not find that through an unwise policy we
are left to make that stand alone."

Quickly the drama of the years proceeded. Mussolini pros-
trated Abyssinia, the last remaining independent nation of
Africa. The Spanish Republic fell. Austria was swallowed
in a single gulp. Munich came and Churchill told the House
of Commons: "We have sustained a defeat without a war
. . . the German dictator, instead of snatching the victuals
from the table, has been content to have them served to him
course by course." The sands ran out and the crash came as
Winston Churchill had said it would. And Britain was alone.

Then the "man with the umbrella" had no option but to

bring Churchill from the back benches into the Cabinet. At sixty-four years of age the warrior statesman, defender of the ancient traditions of Britain's empire, on the first day of the war in September 1939 found himself where he had been nearly thirty years earlier, as First Lord of the Admiralty. Although the white Dominions of the British Commonwealth had complete freedom now to stay out of the war if they so willed, only the Irish Free State, intent on asserting her republicanism, stayed out. Eighteen months later, by common consent, Churchill reached the supreme position of his career and became Prime Minister of Britain.

To his leadership of Britain, until the enemy cried enough, there are few men who will not pay tribute. What he felt in that hour, when he became the leader of the British state, he has himself told in most revealing words. In the last paragraph of *Gathering Storm*, the first volume of his story of the Second World War, he says:

During these last crowded days of the political crisis, my pulse had not quickened at any moment. I took it all as it came. But I cannot conceal from the reader of this truthful account that as I went to bed about 3 a.m., I was conscious of a profound sense of relief. At last I had the authority to give directions over the whole scene. I felt as if I were working with Destiny, and that all my past life had been but a preparation for this hour and for this trial. Eleven years in the political wilderness had freed me from ordinary party antagonisms. My warnings over the last six years had been so numerous, so detailed, and were now so terribly vindicated, that no one could gainsay and I could not be reproached either for making the war or with want of preparation for it. I thought I knew a good deal about it all, and I was sure I should not fail. Therefore, although impatient for the morning, I slept soundly and had no need of cheering dreams. Facts are better than dreams.

He had reached the pinnacle of his dreams—an empire of hundreds of millions of people acclaimed him as a generalissimo, waited for his words of command and inspiration. And he gave them unstintingly with all the assurance and confidence of the ancient Marlborough who had never lost a battle. With lion-hearted courage he brought to bear upon the situation all his character, imagination, experience, knowledge, and vision. Although he felt he was "working with Destiny" he never comprehended that Destiny was using him for a dual purpose. He did not conceive of the war as a revolutionary war, shattering far and wide the social foundations which he conceived indestructible and essential to the very existence of all that had made him what he was and which had thrust leadership into his hands. He thought of the war as one more clash of empires, of the Nazi empire as a resurrected Kaiserdom of vaster and more threatening ambitions which could be realized only by the smashing of the British Empire. He welcomed the entrance of the Soviet Union into an alliance against the Germanic power not because he endorsed a single thing for which it stood except the defeat of the common enemy, for he was deeply conscious that Britain had no chance of victory unless allies came to her side. He did not think that the British Empire was in eclipse, that some new form of association between the nations which had comprised it was about to emerge, and he bluntly told the world it was mistaken if it thought he had become the King's principal minister in order to liquidate the empire. His conduct of the war from beginning to end, was governed by his supreme concern to preserve the ancient power and prestige of the British Empire intact. It dominated his strategical conceptions and his relations with Britain's allies. But he did everything in the grand manner. Even his concessions to "Destiny" were superb. No speech that he made in the course of the war was more splendid than the one he delivered when Hitler's hordes swept across the Soviet frontier. He bowed majestically to Destiny, locked up his anti-Soviet speeches for the duration of the war, and stretched out the hand of alliance to Joseph Stalin with all the enthusiasm of his nature, as if they had been blood brothers in a common cause since the dawn of history. The Alliance they made did not mean that Stalin had ceased to be a Bolshevik and Churchill had ceased to be a conservative imperialist. It meant that the interests of British imperialism and Soviet bolshevism poured into a common stream of history to overwhelm the common enemy—the Fascist powers. Each was fighting its own fight. And the gods of "Destiny" looked on with ironic smile while these principal protagonists went their ways.

Hardly had Winston Churchill assumed command of the empire forces than it was brought home to him that all was not well with the "brightest gem within the imperial crown." The forces of Indian nationalism were on the move. From the inception of this great movement, he had been a relentless opponent of its aims. When, following the report of the Simon Commission, after five years of debate in the British House of Parliament in which Churchill and other Tories fought the proposed legislation of the India Act, was finally passed there was no denying the movement for Indian independence. Writing on the scene in 1937, Churchill said:

A gigantic process of gathering votes of an electorate of thirty million Indians spread over an immense sub-continent, many of them dwelling under primitive conditions, has passed off with smoothness and efficiency. The electoral machinery has worked better than many of its designers expected. The results have, however, seriously disconcerted them. Those who said during the passing of the Act that the Congress Party would be supreme, were disbelieved and brushed aside. But now we see that the Congress Party is powerful everywhere, and all-powerful in six of the eleven provinces of India. . . . The Congress has declared its united resolve to make the constitution unworkable and to court, or even in some cases create, an absolute deadlock. . . .

He was alarmed at the course of "Destiny" and so he declared: "But it is to a different England or Britain that these appeals are directed. Here is an England which feels in all conscience that it has done its best for the Indian political classes. It will stand by its word in spirit and in letter; but it will go no farther. It will enter upon no new slippery slope. Britain has done her best. Others now must make their sincere contribution. . . ." So the warrior statesman of empire commanded the tide to stand still. But it did not and, with the coming of the war, it was surging forward to new heights when Winston Churchill took charge of the imperial state. The war spread. In December 1941 Japan struck and, in a few months, was sweeping toward India. India had been declared at war with Japan, not by a self-governing Indian Dominion of the British Commonwealth but by the British Government on behalf of India, the colony.

The Indians resented this imperial act, although they had no desire to exchange British rule for Japanese rule. In December 1939 Sir Stafford Cripps had made a visit to India with a view to securing the consent of the Indian movement for full cooperation with the British Government on condition that the British Government pledge itself to concede Indian independence at a definite date after the cessation of hostilities with Japan. His visit was entirely unofficial and he was in the position of having to convert the British Government to such a course if he could secure the consent of the Indians. 1942 dawned with the situation more tense. The Japanese invader was nearing India and cooperation had not been achieved. On March 11, 1942, Churchill suddenly announced to the House of Commons:

The crisis in the affairs of India arising out of the Japanese advance has made us wish to rally all the forces of Indian life, to guard their land from the menace of the invader. In August 1940, a full statement was made about the aims and policy we are pursuing in India. This amounted, in short, to a promise that, as soon as possible after the war, India should attain Dominion Status, in full freedom and equality with this country and the other Dominions, under a constitution to be framed by the Indians, by agreement among themselves and acceptable to the main elements of Indian national life. This was of course subject to the fulfillment of our obligations for the protection of minorities, including the depressed classes, and of our treaty obligations to the Indian states, and to the settlement of certain lesser matters arising out of our long association with the fortunes of the Indian sub-continent. . . .

Accordingly, we propose to send a member of the War Cabinet to India, to satisfy himself upon the spot, by personal consultation that the conclusions on which we are agreed, and which we believe represent a just and final solution, will achieve their purpose. My right Hon. Friend the Lord Privy Seal and Leader of the House has volunteered to undertake this task. . . .

On April 11 Sir Stafford Cripps announced that Britain's offer to India had been withdrawn after Indian parties had failed to reach agreement. On September 10, 1942, Churchill attacked the Indian National Congress as unrepresentative of India, denounced Gandhi, accused the Congress of coming forward openly as a revolutionary movement intent on paralyzing communications and creating disorder. "In these circumstances," he said, "the Viceroy and Government of India, with the unanimous support of the Viceroy's Council, the great majority of which are Indians, patriotic wise men, have felt it necessary to proclaim and suppress the central and provincial organs of this association which has become committed to hostile and criminal courses. Mr. Gandhi and other principal leaders have been interned under conditions of highest comfort and consideration, and will be kept out of harm's way till the troubles subside. . . ."

There they remained until the end of the war. The warrior of empire had made his position clear. "I have not become the King's First Minister," he said two months later, "in order to preside over the liquidation of the British Empire. For that task, if ever it were prescribed, someone else would have to be found, and, under democracy, I suppose the nation would have to be consulted. I am proud to be a member of that vast commonwealth and society of nations and communities gathered in and around the ancient British monarchy, without which the good cause might well have perished from the face of the earth. Here we are, and here we stand, a veritable rock of salvation in this drifting world. . . ."

The great defender of Britain's yesterdays, ever reluctant to let go, continued his majestic course. His cooperation with President Roosevelt was complete. He had no secret heartburns concerning locked-up speeches or fearful nightmares of revolution waiting to launch itself upon a stricken world from those quarters. The rise of America to the heights of overwhelming power after the end of the First World War had reconciled him to the conception of the British Empire existing under the protecting wings of the American Eagle and he felt happy that he was "half American," although he had fully manifested all the hereditary qualities, form, and tradition of the Marlborough breed. Time and again Churchill met with Stalin, too. He hailed him as "Stalin the Great" while Stalin greeted him with a clearer political definition of their relationship, welcoming "My Wartime Friend." Here they were, two warriors keeping their powder dry amidst the storm and getting along with the job in hand.

Roosevelt, Stalin, Churchill: all three led the host of allies to the greatest military victories of all time. Never were empires so utterly smashed on the fields of battle as those of Germany, Italy, and Japan. And it may be said, never was there in British history a statesman who commanded greater admiration and affection from the people of Britain than Winston Spencer Churchill. When he stood in Whitehall, before vast throngs, to hail the hour of victory in Europe, it was his greatest hour.

But the process in the body politic, which he had never understood, gave him the greatest shock of his career—a shock which hurt him perhaps more than any blow he had ever received. Hardly had the cheers subsided through the land, than there was a General Election. In that election the people of Britain said by their deeds: "Winston Churchill was the man to lead us in war but he is a warrior-statesman

and not the peacemaker." The Tory Party, of which he was
the leader, was overwhelmingly defeated by the Labor Party.
It was a memorable landslide comparable only with the election of 1906, when he, Churchill, then conveniently a Liberal,
rode to power on the tide of the great modern awakening of
the working class to political consciousness. In the intervening forty years labor had built its own party, set forth its own
aims, drawn large sections of the middle class under its
banner and into its ranks, and had overwhelmed its opponents.

Sorely hurt and puzzled by the turn of events, he took his
place as the leader of the Opposition. It seemed as if his
course was run. He was seventy years of age. Should he step
from the stage of politics, retire, paint pictures, write a history of the war, and play the role of Elder Statesman? This
course was rejected. He had missed the right moment for that.
If he ever thought of it he should have done it in his hour of
triumph on V-E Day. To do it immediately following so
heavy a political defeat would have meant passing into the
shadows. For a man who had been a warrior from his childhood, militant, buoyant, riding every storm with a cheer,
and taking every knock as part of the game of life, to retire
in such circumstances was unthinkable. He gathered together
the sadly depleted forces of His Majesty's Opposition and
stormed against fate and the passing of a way of life for
which throughout his life he had at all times fought. But
the bedraggled army of a Tory Rump in the House of Commons was not large enough for so great a commander. Besides,
for more than four years he had been leading an empire in
martial conflict on a world scale. To see himself reduced to
the level of a company commander was more than he could
bear. Resentful of the defeat which had been thrust upon
him by the Socialists, he leapt on to the stage of world affairs.
Once more he was the field marshal of the forces arrayed
against Socialism of every variety, whether it be in the form

of Bolshevism or respectable Fabianism, and wherever it may
be. He had been a warrior from his childhood. He had recently emerged from leadership of the greatest war of all
time. He would have leapt at the chance to lead the whole
world in a war of worlds, had that been possible. It was not
possible. He could engage, however, in the old political
warfare in which he had played his part as soldier politician,
who always identified his own class as the nation and loathed
the very mention of Socialism. Fortunately, now the world
war was ended, he felt under no obligation to hide his ancient hatred of the Russian Revolution. Now he could let it
be known that even during 1942, while the fate of Stalin-
grad was undecided, he was planning to stop "Russian bar-
barism from overrunning Europe." It would one day be
clear to all that he really shared the view of those who hoped
that Germany and Russia would shatter each other while he
and his kind picked up the glittering prizes of victory. It did
not turn out that way. He launched his world campaign to
replace Hitler in the fear-ridden minds of Europe and
America with the "Spectre of Advancing Communism and
Socialism." By a speech at Fulton, Missouri, he made himself
the ideological leader of the whole Western world from the
Elbe to San Francisco.

Aiming, ostensibly, at the peace of the world, his speech
began to roll the war drums and to lay the blame at the door
of Soviet Russia and Socialism. He interpreted the course of
history in terms of power politics and began to marshal
the West against the East. He said: "The United States stands
at this time at the pinnacle of world power. It is a solemn
moment for the American democracy. With primacy in power
is also joined an awe-inspiring accountability to the future.
. . ." After this somber introduction, he proceeded: "The
United Nations Organization must immediately begin to be
equipped with international armed forces. In such a matter
we can only go step by step, but we must begin now."

Conscious of the existence of the atom bomb, he continued. "It would nevertheless be wrong and imprudent to introduce the secret knowledge or experience of the atomic bomb which the United States, Great Britain and Canada now share, to the world organization while it is in its infancy." Then he expressed his admiration of the Russian people and went straight to the heart of the matter:

It is my duty to place before you certain facts about the present situation in Europe. From Stettin in the Baltic, to Trieste in the Adriatic, an iron curtain has descended across the continent. Behind that line lie all the capitals of the ancient states of northern and eastern Europe—Warsaw, Berlin, Prague, etc. . . . The Russian-dominated Polish Government has been encouraged to make enormous and wrongful inroads upon Germany, and mass expulsions of millions of Germans on a scale grievous and undreamed of are now taking place. . . . Police Governments are prevailing in nearly every case. . . . The outlook is also anxious in the Far East and especially in Manchuria. . . .

All that led up to the main determining strategy:

From what I have seen of our Russian friends and allies during the war I am convinced that there is nothing they admire so much as strength, and there is nothing for which they have less respect than for military weakness. For this reason the old doctrine of balance of power is unsound.

The balance of power being unsound he went on to urge that the Western powers should organize overwhelming power to maintain the peace and keep the Russians in their place. He put it thus:

If the Western democracies stand together in strict adherence to the United Nations Charter, their influence for furthering those principles will be immense and no one likely to molest them. If, however, they become divided or falter in their duty, if these important years are allowed to slip by, then indeed catastrophe may overwhelm us all.

He cried aloud: "The last time I saw it coming and cried aloud to my own fellow countrymen and the world but no one paid attention. . . ."

Having launched his great campaign in the American continent he returned to London and there staged the formation of an all-party committee to propagate the Union of Europe. The high-sounding title of "The Union of Europe" in practice led to the formation of the Western Union which was less than half of Europe. The Union of Western Europe, however, aimed not merely at the countries of Europe but also at linking up the French and Belgium and Dutch Empires in Africa and the Far East with the British Commonwealth of Nations. Great events were happening in the British Empire, however, which disturbed Churchill. When Mr. Attlee, in December 1946 announced the decision to recognize the independence of Burma, Churchill said in the House of Commons:

It was said in the days of that great administrator Lord Chatham that you had to get up very early in the morning not to miss some acquisition of territory which was then characteristic of our fortunes. The not less memorable administration of Mr. Attlee is distinguished for the opposite set of experiences. The British Empire seems to be running off almost as fast as the American loan. The steady and remorseless process of divesting ourselves of what has been gained by so many generations of toil, administration and sacrifice continues. . . .

That lament was as nothing compared to his anguish when the Attlee government implemented the decision to hasten the independence of India. The date was March 5, 1947. Sir Stafford Cripps opened the debate in the House of Commons with a statement for the government announcing a date for the withdrawal from India of all British authority and troops and the appointment of a new Viceroy, Lord Mountbatten, to implement the decision. Churchill turned in fury on the government and accused it of every sin of omission and commission. Winding up in sadder vein, he said:

It is with deep grief that I have watched the clattering down of the British Empire with all its glories and all the service it has rendered mankind. I am sure that in the hour of victory not long ago we had the power or could have had the power, to make a solution of our difficulties which would have been honourable and lasting. Many have defended Britain against her foes; none have defended her against herself. We must face the evils that are coming to us and are powerless to avert. We must do our best in all these circumstances and neglect no expedient that may help to mitigate the ruin and disaster which will follow from the disappearance of Great Britain as a Power in the East. But at least let us not add by a shameful flight or by a premature and hurried scuttle, to the pangs and sorrows. Many of us feel the taint and sneer of shame.

His sadness and shame were mitigated somewhat, when to his surprise, at the Conference of Commonwealth Prime Ministers in 1949, India and Pakistan, now completely freed from British control, decided to remain within the commonwealth as the latter adjusted itself to the admission of republics to the association. But could the old imperialist retract or in any way admit that at any time he had been wrong? Not in the least. Speaking in the House of Commons after the declaration of the Conference of Commonwealth Prime Ministers on April 28, 1949, he said:

I do not in any way retract or regret the views I have expressed over so many years, and I am very glad not to be responsible for much that has been done in the past, but we are all of us governed by events which we cannot control and by the action of majorities elected to the House of Commons. . . . I am unfeignedly glad that an impassable gulf has not opened between the new India and the Commonwealth, or between our famous past in India and our anxious present all over the world. . . .

I feel that the tides of the world are favourable to our voyage. The pressure of dangers and duties that are shared in common by all of us in these days may well make new harmony with India, and indeed with large parts of Asia. We may also see coming into view an even wider synthesis of states and nations comprising both the United States and a United Europe, which may perhaps one day, and perhaps not a distant day, bring to harassed and struggling humanity real security for peace and freedom for hearth and home.

His efforts for the "larger synthesis" continued taking on ever more militaristic formations. General Marshall of the United States followed in his Fulton tracks and the President of the United States announced a policy for America identical with the one that he had suggested for the nations of the West, and Congress and Senate implemented the policy with financial and military support, military and economic pacts. Mr. Bevin, although the Foreign Secretary of a Labor Government, implemented the Fulton policy so completely that the old Tory warrior could say in 1948: "I am pleased to see that what I expressed at Fulton two years ago has now been adopted to a very large extent by the British and American governments. In many ways they have gone far beyond it. What I then urged has now become the policy of the English speaking world. . . ."

In 1949 he was shocked to discover that the monopolistic basis of atomic destructive power no longer lay in the hands of America. Indeed, the monopoly had vanished much earlier than he had ever deemed possible. Though it was suddenly announced that Russia also had the atom bomb and the 'know-how' of its production, the Fulton theme was not discarded. Scientists were ordered to make the hydrogen bomb, possessing a thousand times the destructive power of the atom bomb.

Meanwhile a general election was held in Britain on February 23rd, 1950. It is a significant and striking fact that Churchill did not raise the question of the Labor Government's policy in relation to the transformation of the Empire into Commonwealth. It appeared, in the first stages of the election, that the issues would be confined to domestic questions and that there was a tacit agreement between the major parties on Empire and Foreign affairs. Suddenly, however, Mr. Churchill introduced the discussion of the atom and the hydrogen bombs, and appeared so alarmed that he pressed for an appeal for discussion with the Russians, at the highest level, to secure agreement to prevent atomic warfare. He said:

When you look at the picture as a whole you see two worlds ranged against one another on a larger scale than history has ever seen before. The Soviet Communist world has by far the greatest military force, but the United States have the atom bomb, and now we are told that they have a thousandfold manifestation of this awful power. When all is said and done, it is my belief that the superiority in the atom bomb, if not indeed almost the monopoly of this frightful weapon in American hands, is the surest guarantee of world peace. . . .

Still I cannot help coming back to this idea of another talk with Soviet Russia upon the highest level. The idea appeals to me, of a supreme effort to bridge the gulf between the two worlds, so that each can live their life, if not in friendship, at least without the hatreds and manoeuvres of the cold war. . . .

His opponents in the election sidestepped Churchill's proposal and passed the discussion over to the United Nations Organization where it had previously bogged down. Throughout the electoral campaign, Churchill fought as the aggressive warrior. To the suggestion that he should retire, which for many months had come from Conservative and other quarters, Churchill replied on February 17th, 1950:

I am an old man. All the day-dreams of my youth have been accomplished. I have no personal advantage to gain from undertaking once more the hard and grim duty of leading Britain and her Empire through and out of her new and formidable crisis. But while God gives me strength and the people show me their good will, it is my duty to try and try I will. . . .

At the General Election, the Labor Government was returned to office by the barest of majorities. Though the Conservative Party was in a far stronger position in Parliament than at any time since 1945 it appeared that Mr. Churchill would have to round off his career as Leader of His Majesty's Loyal Opposition rather than from 10 Downing Street.

Winston Churchill was born on November 30th, 1874. He was reared in the splendor of an imperial household when the British Empire was at the zenith of its power, nurtured in the traditions of the ruling families of England when the British Empire was young and centuries of expansion seemed to lie before it. He grew up with martial ambition. He had an extraordinary brain, teeming with the grandiose visions of the soldier-statesman. Buoyant of temperament, great in humor, deep in affection, faithful to his friends and those he loved, he surged through life with the elan of the born adventurer, laughing at disappointment, and rising agilely after every fall. With the mantle of his father upon his shoulders, he leapt into the political arena as the valiant soldier, rough rider, journalist, author, orator, just as there loomed on the near horizon the shadows of imperial eclipse. Instead of life calling upon him to reach to the heights of new conquests and fulfilling his grandiose visions of empire, "Destiny" thrust upon him the role of the great warrior, politician and statesman for the *defense* of Britain's imperial yesterdays in the age of her transit through war and revolution to new forms of human association. He never saw the shape of things except through the distorted mirror of an age that had already turned its face away from the changing world. He fought magnificently, spoke magnificently, wrote magnificently, but always in defense of the yesterdays, their traditions, and their vested interests, never for a world set free. Winston Churchill is the last in the line of Pitt, Chatham, Disraeli, Gladstone, Salisbury, but was less fortunate than they in having been born in the wrong age.

C H A P T E R V

C L E M E N T A T T L E E

DURING THE MONTH OF APRIL 1949, a slim bald-headed man of sixty-six years of age and of schoolmasterly appearance, presided at the most propitious conference since first the peoples of the British Empire began to assert their claims to "self-government." The conference ranked in significance with one held over a hundred years earlier which established self-government in Canada. At the end of six days, on April 28, 1949, the following communique was issued:

During the past week the Prime Ministers of the United Kingdom, Australia, New Zealand, South Africa, India, Pakistan and Ceylon, and the Canadian Secretary of State for External Affairs have met in London to exchange views upon the important constitutional issues arising from India's decision to adopt a republican form of constitution and her desire to continue her membership of the Commonwealth.

The discussions have been concerned with the effects of such a development upon the existing structure of the Commonwealth and the constitutional relations between its members.

They have been conducted in an atmosphere of good will and natural understanding, and have as their background the traditional capacity of the Commonwealth to strengthen its unity of purpose, while adapting its organisation and procedures to changing circumstances.

After full discussion the representatives of the Governments of all the Commonwealth countries have agreed that the conclusions reached should be placed on record in the following declaration:

"The Governments of the United Kingdom, Canada, Australia, New Zealand, South Africa, India, Pakistan and Ceylon, whose countries are united as Members of the British Commonwealth of Nations and owe a common allegiance to the Crown, which is also the symbol of their free association, have considered the impending constitutional changes in India.

"The Government of India have informed the other Government ments of the Commonwealth of the intention of the Indian people that under the new constitution which is about to be adopted India shall become a sovereign independent republic.

"The Government of India have however declared and affirmed India's desire to continue her full membership of the Commonweath of Nations and her acceptance of the King as the symbol of the free association of its independent member nations, and as such the Head of the Commonwealth.

"The Governments of the other countries of the Commonwealth, the basis of whose membership of the Commonwealth is not hereby changed, accept and recognize India's continuing membership in accordance with the terms of this declaration.

"Accordingly the United Kingdom, Canada, Australia, New Zealand, South Africa, India, Pakistan and Ceylon hereby declare that they remain united as free and equal members of the Commonwealth of Nations, freely co-operating in the pursuit of peace, liberty and progress."

After the meeting which issued this communique and declaration, the Prime Ministers went to Buckingham Palace to inform the King of their decisions. According to constitutional procedure each Prime Minister should have done this separately but on this occasion Mr. Attlee, as chairman of the proceedings of the conference, spoke on behalf of all represented there.

The day this announcement was communicated to Parliament it was recognized that this remarkable declaration which held India in continuous association with the nations of the British Commonwealth of Nations was largely due to the skill and wisdom of Clement Richard Attlee. Labor's Prime Minister of the United Kingdom, Attlee, more than any other British statesman, had outfought and outdistanced Winston Churchill. Throughout his career, Churchill had fought a retreating fight to retain the British Empire that had prevailed in the days of his father. Attlee had superseded him by retaining the substance of empire relations through a liberal adaptation of those relations to the principles of the self-determination of nations and the decentralization of power.

Of all the men who have occupied the position of Britain's leading statesman, it is safe to say that none have been so completely underestimated by friend and foe alike. Because of his quiet, gentlemanly demeanor, a complete absence of the qualities of the demagogue, and a self-effacing mode of cooperation with other people, it has been generally assumed that Attlee became the leader of a political movement by accident and Prime Minister because bigger men could not step out of each other's way. It has also been assumed that he retained the post by virtue of superb qualities as a chairman of meetings and by general administrative abilities without possessing any special capacity for leadership. Whatever truth there is in these statements, it is an indisputable fact that the part played by Attlee in the evolution of the British Empire into a free association of nations has been altogether obscured by the unobtrusive characteristics of the man. So much is this the case that in the various biographies that have been written of him only a passing reference has been made to it.

There is an element of truth in the assertion that the "accidents" of history played an important part in his career and favored him with fortune's smile. It is probable that had Herbert Morrison not been defeated in the great Labor debacle of 1931 he would have become the leader of the Parliamentary Labor Party and, therefore, leader of the National Labor Party. Or had Ernest Bevin been a member of Parliament at that time he, also, would have forestalled Attlee as leader. Again, one may add that after Attlee had succeeded George Lansbury to the leadership of the Parliamentary

Labor Party and then expressed the wish to resign and for Sir Stafford Cripps to take his place, the latter declined and persuaded Attlee to continue. Nevertheless, these "accidents" notwithstanding, Clement Attlee proved himself capable of holding the post of leader by virtue of his own qualities and the confidence he inspired.

Attlee's qualities do not include the ability to stir great crowds in the manner of a Churchill. In many respects these two men are, in personal qualities, abilities and methods of work, the antithesis of each other. In histrionic and oratorical capacities they are not in the same street. Churchill, the man conscious of walking with Destiny, master of the Gibbon phrase and language so characteristic of the great orators of the eighteenth and nineteenth centuries, stands in marked contrast to quiet, almost conversationally speaking Attlee, whose speeches always read better than they sound and lack the grandiloquent turn of phrase of his principal opponent. At the same time it would be a mistake to underestimate this man of the clean-cut phrase, thoughtful demeanor, and schoolmasterly mannerisms. For it is on record that no man has more effectively laid his opponent low in parliamentary and public debate than has Attlee in debate with Winston Churchill. His demolition of the latter in the feature broadcast speech of the general election campaign of 1945 was complete. That was no isolated case. On every occasion in the House of Commons when Churchill has "pulled out the stops" for one of his great monologues, Attlee has replied with devastating effectiveness. Listen to the following, from Attlee, on the occasion that Churchill moved a vote of censure on the Labor Government, after Attlee had been Prime Minister for two years:

"It seems to be a terrible shock quite naturally perhaps for people who remember 1935—that a Government should come in prepared to carry out its policy. The Tory Government led by Baldwin went to the country with a program which Baldwin

afterwards told the House of Commons was prepared for the
election only and which he had no intention, even at the time,
of putting into practice. . . .

"Now we have a wonderful cry which the party opposite are
putting forward—'The People versus the Socialists.' This is right
in line with the Rt. Hon. Gentleman's propaganda at the time
of the election. Then the Tory Party was the nation. They are
now the people. 'Truly ye are the people, and wisdom shall die
with you. . . .' I am quite sure that the Rt. Hon. Gentleman's
mind when he was thinking of 'The People versus the Socialists'
must have gone back to an earlier epoch, to the epoch of the
people's Budget, when he and Mr. Lloyd George were standing
for the people against the Tory Party. . . . Only a few years
back the Rt. Hon. Gentleman was telling us that the Conservative Party was ruining the country.

"As a matter of fact, no one who does not believe in the Rt.
Hon. Gentleman is any part of the people. No one who does not
belong to the party which, for the time being, he has selected for
the honor of supporting him, really belongs to the people.

"We were all of the people for five years but I'm afraid we are
out of it now . . . All those able and experienced front bench-
ers, and those who have fallen by the wayside, were after all,
mere chorus girls: the prima donna held the stage. The very
candidates, hon. gentlemen opposite, were commended to the
electors not on their individual merits but as chosen supporters
of the Rt. Hon. Gentleman. We all remember those in the city
of Oxford who wrote on one of them . . . 'Love me, love my
Hogg'!"

There was no answer to this kind of counter attack. It was
not the oratory of the "immense, horrible catastrophe," "the
rolling deep," and "the golden thread of historical continuity" variety. But it got to its mark, hit his opponent where it
hurt and was easily understood. Nevertheless, great oratory
is not his. Histrionics and dramatic display are not in his
armory. He is too shy and self-effacing, too concerned with
light rather than heat, with being explicit rather than colorful in expression.

Attlee has other qualities which stand him in good stead
and in which he excels, or he would not have been able to

hold the leading position in a great political movement for a longer period than any of his predecessors in the history of the Labor Party. His integrity of character, high purpose, intellectual honesty which recognizes his own limitations, his capacity in administration, and absence of vanity, have inspired a loyalty among his colleagues in leadership which holds him at their head where other men would be the victim of rivals for power. His career has not been so colorful and robust as that of Churchill. His social origin is different. He does not belong to the ducal line of the English aristocracy with its background of palaces and landed estates. He belongs to the lower strata of the middle class who made their careers as solicitors, barristers and parsons, who gathered their ribbons for military adventures in the age of mass production of heroes. His ascendancy in public life began not with a cavalry charge into Parliament to justify and perpetuate the ancient traditions of an oligarchical empire in eclipse, but in the depths of a social class slowly awakening to political consciousness and setting before itself the attainment of new ways of life.

Clement Richard Attlee was born in Putney on January 3, 1883, nearly a decade after Winston Churchill was born at Blenheim Palace. He was the fourth son and the seventh child of Henry Attlee, a solicitor who was also the son of a solicitor. His mother, before marriage, was Ellen Bravery Watson. The Watsons belonged to the same social stratum as the Attlees and there were many doctors among their forebears. Ellen Attlee was born at Kew, not far away from Putney. She was a well-educated woman who spoke French and Italian and was thoroughly acquainted with English literature. Her son, Clement, did not go to school until he was nine years of age and she gave him his first lessons at home. But much of his early training came from governesses, one of whom was a Miss Hutchinson who, years earlier, had also been a governess to Winston Churchill. In a comfortable, Victorian, religious, cultured home, Clement Attlee flourished. In 1892 he went to a small boarding school near Potters Bar in Hertfordshire. In 1896, he went to Haileybury College. This school had a strong sense of "imperial destiny" and was thoroughly Conservative in political complexion. In 1901, Attlee went up to University College, Oxford. There he continued for three years and blossomed forth as a very conventional Christian Conservative Imperialist. In the course of that time he wrote:

"I had decided to go to the Bar. My father's position seemed to show the possibility of support. There were 'glittering prizes' to be won. There was a possibility of entering politics, for which I had a sneaking affection. I was not, however, very keen on a career. I rather thought of some profession in which a living could be made while in my leisure time I could continue my reading in literature and history and learn more of art and the antiquities."

In the same year that Attlee went to Oxford, "Rough Rider" Winston Churchill, Member for Oldham, charged into the House of Commons carrying the banner of his father, and none was more ready to cheer the news of Churchill's exploits than the demure Oxford undergraduate, Clement Attlee.

In 1904 he quietly left Oxford, having read much history and become fond of the poets. He was unambitious, moving with the tide of his social group, conservative, nationalist, conformist Christian, a typical middle-class product of Haileybury College, a self-contained person moving into London chambers to study for the Bar and to follow in his father's footsteps. But there was a tide in the affairs of men as he embarked on his legal career. The tide had been rising in English affairs for some years and was soon to sweep him along. Indeed, in the very year of his birth there was formed in London the Fabian Society, propagating a particular brand of Socialism, which through its leaders would inspire and dominate the Labor Movement. By the time Attlee had

reached manhood, the Fabians, led by Sidney Webb and
G. B. Shaw and a number of other clever intellectuals, were
exercising considerable influence on the developing Trade
Union Movement. Their appeal was not made on principle.
It was a strategic appeal to detach workers from their allegiance to the old Liberal and Tory parties and come under
their banner. The Fabians were making great headway. In
1900, the Labor Representation Committee was formed, composed of a number of trade unions, socialist organizations,
and the Fabian Society. Clement Attlee was shocked out of
his middle-class social complacency by what he saw of the
lives of the working people of Limehouse, in the Stepney
district of London, during his training as a lawyer. He himself says:

"I was . . . a Conservative. The Liberals of the type of Asquith, Runciman and McKenna were always distasteful to me.
The Liberal capitalist of the Devenport style even more so. The
violent nonconformist made no appeal. That 'gentlemanly party'
was to me far preferable. I was perhaps only half-consciously sur-
charged with class feeling. I thought then that quite definitely
only gentlemen were fit to govern. I believed in the legend of the
White Man's burden and all the well-to-do were for the most part
where they were because of their virtues. . . . I remember being
quite surprised when an East End parson said what a good chap
Will Crooks was, while I was shocked at an educated man expressing admiration for Keir Hardie, of all people."

Stepney knocked these valuations to pieces. The Fabian Society led him into new ways of life and drew him into the
arena of political struggle for social changes. But the Fabian
Society was not a political party; it was a society of light and
learning which furnished facts and ideas.

Next he joined the Independent Labor Party, led by Keir
Hardie. The I.L.P. stood in the same relation to the Fabian
Society as the Salvation Army to the Church of England. It
provided the Christian moral and social fervor, beat the big

drum, "raised the Scarlet Banner high" in the highways and byways where the working class crowded together. Attlee's moral conscience secured a new intellectual chart which soon replaced the old habits of thinking with intellectual convictions. All this followed upon his becoming a part of the "Christian Slumming" movement and the "University Settlement" experiments, whereby the intellectuals of the middle class "bridged the gulf between the classes," went to live in "settlements" in working class districts and studied and practiced social reform. From Haileybury House, a Boys Club founded by old members of Haileybury College, he passed to Toynbee Hall, propagandized with the Webbs for the reform of the Poor Law, supported the unemployment and health insurance schemes introduced by Lloyd George and Winston Churchill, campaigned for the I.L.P., lectured at the London School of Economics.

There were no indications then, however, that he was a coming Prime Minister, although as we look back upon his activities, it is clear that in his selfless social work of these years in the Stepney district, he was laying firm foundations for his parliamentary career. The war of 1914-1918 stopped his activities in Stepney and halted his rise in the newly developing Labor Party, which had emerged from the Labor Representation Committee formed in 1900, but it would be too bold an assertion to say that in the years before the outbreak of war Clem Attlee had any ambition to rise to the ranks of national leadership. The war came. He was not a pacifist as was his brother, Tom, also a Socialist. Nor had he chased across the seas in search of a little war in which to be "blooded." Whatever reservations he had about the war before it burst upon Europe were swept away by the German invasion of Belgium. He was thirty-one, unmarried, had held a commission in the Cadets, and by the end of September, 1914, he was a lieutenant of the 6th South Lancashire Regiment, stationed at Tidworth. By June, 1915, he became Captain Attlee of the 13th Infantry Division, on his way to participate in the closing stages of the Gallipoli campaign. After that action he was sent to Mesopotamia. Wounded severely in the fighting at El Hannah he was sent to a hospital in Bombay. After ten days there he was invalided home and was returned via the Suez. He recovered and joined the tank corps. After two visits to the Western Front, in 1916, he returned to the infantry at the close of 1917. Again he was posted to the South Lancashire Regiment. In June, 1918, he was sent to France and was promoted to the rank of major. That autumn, in the midst of an engagement, some heavy timber dislodged by a shell, fell on him. A casualty, again, he was invalided home and on November 11th when the "Cease Fire" sounded he was a patient in Wandsworth Hospital. He remained there until early January, 1919, when he was discharged from the hospital and the Army.

The interlude was over. Back to Stepney and the Labor Movement he went. The war, which in that interlude had shattered much in Europe and changed the power relations of nations, and torn nations apart, had not stemmed the tides of social evolution in Britain. On the contrary the Labor Party, which had been so small and so entangled with Liberalism before the war, emerged from the war as a large party with a Fabian at its head and millions of supporters. The ranks of the Liberal Party had been split wide-open and its old members were running hither and thither. Some went into the Tory Party. Thousands joined the Labor Party. The trade unions had wrested important concessions from the employers of labor. The suffrage movement saw its efforts rewarded by an extension of the franchise to millions of women. The warrior-statesman, Winston Churchill, was thundering on the class-war front as if nothing could be more deplorable than to cease the bloodletting.

When Clement Attlee returned from the war to Stepney he found a strong trades council working closely with a local Labor Party. He was nominated as a candidate for the London County Council and missed being elected by only eighty votes. Shortly afterward he became the prospective parliamentary candidate for the division and took on a number of voluntary posts in local government. He resumed his lecturing at the London School of Economics. His course was set. The lecturing gave him an economic basis upon which he could pursue a political career. In the first year of his return he became Mayor of Stepney. In 1922 he was elected to Parliament as the member for Limehouse, one of the three Stepney divisions. In 1949, he still represented this constituency, and had successfully contested every election in the years between. On his election to Parliament, in 1922, he was appointed parliamentary private secretary to Ramsay MacDonald, the Labor spellbinder. The two men provided a study in contrasts. MacDonald, the dithyrambic orator of magnificent presence, with a remarkable capacity to avoid decisions on anything and, as he got older, an increasing inability to bring his perorations to a stop. Attlee, on the other hand, was a quiet, sincere, pedestrian speaker, precise in utterance and clear in meaning, a lecturer for a study circle rather than a platform man for a large audience. Nevertheless, Clement Attlee has been on the Labor Party's Front Bench in the House of Commons for twenty-seven years. But there was some considerable distance between the posts of parliamentary private secretary and Prime Minister.

How fortunate was his choice of Stepney as a constituency upon which to base his parliamentary career soon became apparent. Its social composition was predominantly working class. Once it had been won for Labor it remained staunch to what it believed to be its own party and, while many of the leaders of the Labor Party came in and went out of Parliament in rapid succession in the period of quick elections which followed the war, Attlee was returned to Parliament by Stepney with unfailing regularity. It is one of the peculiarities of the British parliamentary system that a single parliamentary constituency can decide the fate of a leader irrespective of the position of his party in relation to the total vote of the country. Winston Churchill, for example, was kept out of Parliament by constituency after constituency in many elections in which the Tory Party had a majority, until he finally found a constituency the social composition of which was such that it could be guaranteed to return a Tory whatever the qualities of the candidate. Attlee was fortunate from the outset. He became the representative of a constituency which would be loyal to Labor and that meant much in deciding his fate in the ranks of leadership.

His period of apprenticeship as parliamentary private secretary to MacDonald was short. But it was the prelude to a shorter spell in the ranks of government. In the short-lived Labor Government of 1924 he became Under-Secretary of State for War. In the General Election at the end of 1924 in which the Labor Party was heavily defeated, Attlee was re-elected by his constituency, and by virtue of his period of membership of the Labor Government he found himself a leader on the Front Opposition Bench in the House of Commons.

Although the post-war years were witness to profound changes in international relations and the British Empire was astir with new ideas as to its future, Attlee had until now been largely preoccupied with the great social questions and conflicts which marked the impact of war and revolution upon the domestic life of Britain. Hardly had the war come to an end than great strike movements engulfed British industry. All the great industries, coal, railways, transport, cotton, wool, engineering, and shipbuilding, were involved. Demobilization was accompanied by revolts of the troops and mutiny stirred the Navy. Then unemployment swept millions on to the streets, and the highways to London resounded to the tramping feet of marching men demanding "Work and Bread." General Elections followed each other in quick succession. Normally a Parliament is elected for five years. In this period there were three General Elections in four years. The election of a great Tory majority in 1924 under the panic influence of the forged "Zinoviev Letter" was not the beginning of a new stability. It was the beginning of a new "unrest" culminating in the "General Strike" and the great miners' lockout of 1926.

These affairs preoccupied Attlee but there were others afoot which were to sweep him along into the larger arena of imperial and world affairs. 1926, the year of the General Strike was also the year of the transition for the "settler" colonies. The Balfour Declaration described the status of Canada, Australia, New Zealand, South Africa, the Irish Free State as "autonomous communities within the British Empire, equal in status, in no way subordinate one to another in any respect of their domestic and external affairs. . . ." In the year following the Imperial Conference which produced this declaration, Attlee was called upon to take more than an incidental interest in imperial affairs. Suddenly, and quite unexpectedly, in November 1927, he was appointed a member of the Indian Statutory Commission. Far-reaching changes had taken place in the constitutional structure of the British Empire and Commonwealth since the British Government and Parliament declared on August 4, 1914, for one and all that they were at war with Germany. Never again would that happen. All the white governed Dominions had acquired the complete right to self-government in all their affairs, domestic and foreign. Their independence was fully established by what is known as the Westminster Act, in 1931, and henceforth none could declare either Canada, Australia, New Zealand, South Africa, or Ireland at war, except those countries themselves. But this did not yet apply to India or what were known as the Crown colonies, all consisting of colored peoples. But in 1919, in response to growing pressure from the nationalist movement of India, a pledge was given to the Indians that at the end of ten years the constitution of India would be further altered in the direction of self-government. The intention of the 1927 Indian Statutory Commission was to provide a comprehensive report on India which would provide the basis for the shaping of the new legislation.

It was a strangely composed commission, a mixture of Conservatives, Liberals and Laborites. Sir John Simon was the chairman of the commission. Besides Attlee, the commission included Lord Burnham, the owner of the *Daily Telegraph,* a well-known diehard Tory; thirty-five year old Lord Strathcona, the youngest member of the commission; Colonel Lane Fox; Mr. Edward Cadogan, another Conservative. The other Labor member was Vernon Hartshorn, a Welsh miners' leader. Attlee appears to have agreed to serve on this commission almost as a matter of party loyalty rather than anything else. His official biographer, Roy Jenkins, writes: "When MacDonald, backed by J. H. Thomas, asked him to serve, he replied, most characteristically, by saying that he had always regarded the Indian problem as 'particularly intractable and nearly insoluble,' and that he was certain there would be difficulties in making a report which would square with the facts of the situation and also with the prepossessions of some of our members; but if the party wished it, he would undertake the job!"

The work of the commission extended over several years. It involved two extensive tours of India and Burma and innumerable interviews with representatives of Indian opinion. Its work had to be done in the teeth of Indian Congress opposition led by Gandhi. Congress regarded the commission as an insult, because it was all-British in composition, and as one more device to impose a foreign-made constitution on to the Indian people. Nevertheless, the report of the commission was a great work. It was written mostly by Simon and Attlee. It consists of two large volumes. *Volume One* is descriptive and the other makes recommendations. Whatever else may be said about Attlee's participation in the work of the commission, it gave him a first-hand knowledge of India and its problems which stood him in good stead when he had political responsibility thrust upon him to find a solution to "the nearly insoluble" problem. Of course, the trouble was that both the commission and the British Government were trying to solve the wrong problem, as Attlee was later to discover. They were studying how to integrate the developing constitution of India as an essentially British-controlled Dominion whereas the real problem was that of aiding the Indians to produce their own constitution in conditions free from British domination and, in the process, create a new form of British-Indian association. Attlee did not see this at the time but it is to his credit more than to that of anyone else that he was the first British statesman to grasp it and solve the problem with expedition and without fuss and dramatic display. The report of the commission of which he was joint author was an essentially conservative report. It criticized the Indians for their unseemly haste for independence. It said: "Instead of making the most of the existing constitution and learning to deal with practical problems under existing conditions, those who have to work a temporary constitution constantly endeavour to anticipate the future and to push forward the day for the next instalment of reforms."

But the report was stillborn for, long before it was presented, events had moved ahead of the commissioners. Those in India who had been "anticipating the future" had also been very busy building the future which they anticipated. At the same time a Labor government in Britain replaced the government which had appointed the Simon Commission. The new government under the leadership of MacDonald, who had urged Attlee on to the commission in the first twelve months of the government's existence, did not include him. Why MacDonald had overlooked Attlee in the making of his government is not known. When a government re-shuffle occurred, as a result of a crisis involving the resignation of Sir Oswald Mosley, Attlee was installed as Chancellor of the Duchy of Lancaster. In practice, the person who holds the position regards it as a conveyor on which to sit patiently, waiting for the next job or to function as a man-of-all-work assisting other departments and the Prime Minister. In this period, Attlee was again called to service in imperial affairs, helping MacDonald on matters relating to the Imperial Conference. He also served on a number of important committees, one of the most important of which was the Economic Advisory Committee, assisting Dr. Addison on agricultural matters. The Imperial Conference of 1930 was responsible for giving legal form to the famous Balfour Declaration, what became known as the Westminster Statute. At this time neither the Balfour Declaration, nor the Westminster Statute, applied to India. The latter was still a colony, governed from Whitehall. And the one thing which the Tories, such as Churchill, did not want, was that this Statute be applied to India or for the Indians to be in any way encouraged to think that it would ever apply to them. Indeed, Churchill opposed the Westminster Statute when it came before the British Parliament. In the Imperial Conference and the subsequent debates in the House of Commons, Attlee, by virtue of his position in the government, had to function as a "back-room boy," and the debate on the statute in the House of Commons was led by Mr. J. H. Thomas, who was then the Dominion Secretary of the Labor Government. Not until Attlee was the leader of the Labor Opposition in 1935, when the "National Government" of MacDonald and Baldwin introduced the Government of India Bill, did he step to the forefront as the British leader battling for the application of the Westminster Statute to India, as well as to the countries already forming what had been defined as the "British Commonwealth of Nations" within the British Empire.

Much had happened in the period between the Imperial Conference of 1930 and the introduction of the Government of India Bill of 1935. The great economic crisis of 1931 had not only precipitated the fall of the Second Labor Government in Britain. It had led to a political upheaval in which was formed that strange British phenomenon of a coalition of reaction led by a small group of Labor leaders, who destroyed their own government and deserted their own party to hold office with the consent of the Tory Party which had an overwhelming majority within the House of Commons. In these crisis conditions Attlee became the leader of the Labor Party and of His Majesty's Opposition with the post of Prime Minister a realizable possibility. At the same time in the largest section of the British Empire, the surging movement for Indian independence had in nowise abated. The "bloodless war" led by Gandhi had been answered by repression, imprisonment of Indian leaders, the jailing of supporters in concentration camps behind barbed-wire entanglements when prisons were full, political maneuvering through Round Table Conferences, commissions, reports, and finally the emergence of the Government of India Bill, which outlined the new way in which the British conceived they could continue to govern India. The bill, which finally passed through the British Parliament and became the Government of India Act, propounded a federal scheme of government under the British Crown. There was no semblance of the Dominion Status which had been promised. The bill interfered not at all with the feudal states. What was known as British India, divided into eleven provinces, was conceded provincial autonomy on a severely restricted property franchise which would apply to 35,000,-000 people out of 350,000,000. The head of the executive in each province was to be the governor appointed by the King. In six of the more important provinces there was to be established a second chamber. And the governor was supreme although the provincial government could deal only with local affairs. For India as a whole it was proposed there should be a federal union of the "autonomous states" and the states be governed by the feudal rulers. The executive head would be the Viceroy of India, representative of the King. The federal legislature would consist of two houses, the Council of State and the Federal Assembly. Defense and foreign relations would not come within the sphere of these proposed institutions but rest entirely in the hands of the Viceroy who could veto any of its legislation.

It has been wrongly assumed that because Attlee was a member of the Simon Commission, and he and Sir John Simon were the main drafters of its report, and that neither Attlee nor his Labor colleague, Vernon Hartshorn, presented a minority report, that they were necessarily reactionary in relation to their attitude to India. The fact is that there was nothing in Attlee's attitude, at that time, which was strikingly different from that of his Labor colleagues who were still trying to solve the wrong problem, namely, how to hasten slowly toward Dominion Status within the British Empire and Commonwealth without understanding that Dominion Status and Independence were interchangeable terms and that the Balfour Declaration and the Westminster Statute, in their application to India, really meant what they said. What is to Attlee's supreme credit is that he was the first of the Labor leaders to become explicit on the matter and ultimately, without fuss and dramatic display, implement in practice what he had expounded in principle.

In the great debates on the Government of India Bill in 1935 he set his course. In the House of Commons he moved the rejection of the bill, saying:

"We shall be told that . . . we want to go too fast, that if you hand over to the Indians they will make a mess of it. India is in a terrible mess in any case, so is the rest of the world, and we think that it is quite impossible to get the real changes which are demanded in acquiescing to a certain number of people, which may be organized by a privileged class but which will not be supported by any of the advanced parties in India or any of the people of India who really want change . . . We have done some good things in India, but we have done many bad things. The serious thing we have done is that we have managed the Indian people in a position of irresponsibility. If they were irresponsible we were responsible; and they will never learn responsibility without being given responsibility. Indians must take the responsibility for the future government of their country. The Bill does not do that and cannot do it, and so therefore, we oppose it.

The *Times,* reporting on a broadcast speech by Attlee, early in the year, said:

"True statesmanship demanded a greater approach towards the satisfaction of Indian aspirations. For this reason his Labour colleagues and he had put forward alternative proposals. They considered that there should have been a clear recognition of the goal to be attained—Dominion Status as demanded by Indians. Next the constitution should have contained a path clearly marked out for its attainment. . . ."

It was not yet clear to Attlee that the freedom of India from British control had to precede cooperation and the acceptance of good advice on how to govern India. The "freedom" he conceived at this stage was conditioned by continued membership of the British Commonwealth of Nations. Not until he became Prime Minister in 1945, and had full responsibility for dealing with India, did he see that Indian independence must precede cooperation. The war of 1939-45 had accentuated the movement for Indian independence. Indeed, in the middle of it, Mr. Churchill, with Mr. Attlee as his second in command in the wartime Coalition Government, had been impelled to send Sir Stafford Cripps to India with a promise to the Indians of Dominion Status at the end of the war "on terms"—but terms which the Indians would not accept. The terms to which Attlee himself was party were in keeping with his 1935 attitude. The Cripps mission failed because it laid down the terms of prior agreement on the future structure of the constitution of India and subordinate cooperation in the war against Japan as conditions for Indian Dominion Status, that is, freedom within the British Commonwealth. In 1947, however, he realized that this "conditioned freedom" was not enough. He fixed a date for the withdrawal of the British power from India and announced it to the world. Then he changed the Viceroy, Lord Mountbatten replacing Lord Wavell, to negotiate the transfer of power and the withdrawal of the British from India. Instead of forcing agreement upon the Indian National Congress and the Moslem League, as the prerequisite of withdrawal, he promptly accepted his new emissary's advice to bring forward the date of withdrawal to 1947, hand over power to two constituent assemblies—India and Pakistan—and leave the Indians to resolve their differences and determine the future structure of the government or governments of India without interference from Britain. He took his stand on the principle that membership in the British Commonwealth of Nations should be a voluntary act by nations that were free and independent. It was a bold and daring move which, when implemented, made the most unique change that had ever been made by an imperial power in the history of empires. Britain had conquered India by the sword and held it for several centuries by the sword. Here, in 1947, it fell to Clement Richard Attlee, Prime Minister of His Britannic Majesty's Government, to play the greatest political gambit of all time. He negotiated India to freedom as the means to hold India in continuing association with Britain. It may be argued that he retreated before a revolution. There is an element of truth in that. But the fact remains that he held the reins of power and made the choice to travel "with Destiny" instead of to fight it as his predecessor, Winston Churchill, would undoubtedly have done. He chose to strike for the national freedom of India, confident that it would be followed by friendly cooperation. This he was to consummate in the Commonwealth conference of Prime Ministers of 1949.

This does not mean that Attlee suddenly emerged as a brilliant theoretician of Socialism or any other -ism. The fact is that he is not a theoretician and has never laid claim to be such. He knows a lot and learns as he goes. He is armed with certain moral principles which he thinks should govern human relations and he applies these principles honestly, and with imagination, to the circumstances which life thrusts upon him. This is clear enough for all to see in the pattern of his life's story. At no stage of his career did he see the lineaments of the various crises of history which have pitched him into situations of which he never dreamed and which have given him opportunities to reach his high position. Born with well-balanced faculties and an equable temperament, trained to disciplined methods of thinking, nurtured on Christian morals and English middle-class traditions, associated with the legal fraternity, he was shocked by the social conditions of London's East End into acquiring Socialist ideals and liberal principles of conduct in the affairs of nations and classes. Such was Clement Attlee, the man, when he began his parliamentary career. He intensively acquired a rich experience of parliamentary practice in Opposition, and in Government, before the Second Labor Government fell in 1931.

That fall had its sequel in Labor's debacle in the General Election which followed the desertion of the Labor Party's long-established leaders, MacDonald, Thomas, and Snowden; the desertion, plus the electoral debacle, left the Parliamentary Labor Party with less than fifty members, among whom there were only three people who could be looked upon as possible candidates for the leadership. These were George Lansbury, Clement Attlee, and Sir Stafford Cripps. Arthur Henderson, William Graham, Herbert Morrison, and others who might have been considered as in the running, had been defeated in their constituencies. Ernest Bevin was not a candidate for Parliament. The choice, therefore, was exceedingly limited. Lansbury was the oldest of the three, with a lifetime membership in the party and a rich experience inside and outside of Parliament as a leader of the party. Clement Attlee had a much longer experience in the party, and in Parliament, than had Cripps whose membership of the Labor Party and experience in Parliament was of two years' duration. Hence, despite the brilliance of Cripps in his parliamentary debut and the fact that he could outshine both his colleagues in intellectual and legal capacity, it was a very natural thing that Lansbury should become the leader of the Parliamentary Labor Party and Clement Attlee the deputy leader. There was no rivalry between them. All three were ardent Christians accepting the same moral values, except that Lansbury was a pacifist. The other two had no difficulty in detaching the question of war from personal moral judgment and viewing it in terms of national and liberal principles. It is true that Attlee, after serving throughout the First World War, found his conscience greatly disturbed and had a short spell of pacifism but he quickly recovered when MacDonald made him Under Secretary of State for War in the First Labor Government. Stafford Cripps had not slipped in that way and had nothing of that kind to forget. Lansbury was a business man and journalist. Attlee and Cripps were lawyers, the latter at this time one of the most brilliant of his day, and still practicing to the limit of his capacity. Thus, the shrinkage of the Parliamentary Party squeezed out almost all possible rivals and enabled Attlee to step forward toward the leadership of the Labor Party. An accident to George Lansbury put Attlee on the spot as Leader. Having had "greatness" thrust upon him, he asked himself: Could he hold it? How? And during the days when old leaders and rivals would be back again in Parliament? Their return still lay years ahead. He had time to dig in and he took advantage of the opportunity.

It would almost appear that he tackled his new role, as leader of the party, as a "practical" plan with an eye to holding down his job. He traveled with the moods of the party. When, immediately after the defeat of 1931, the party went "Left," that is, moved to adopt a class-struggle attitude in politics and let the world know that the days of "gradualism" had passed, Attlee moved "Left" with Stafford Cripps and was one of the founders of the Socialist League. He quietly stepped out of that organization when the winds from the "Right" returned and grew stronger. On all the questions of the period, from the rise of Hitler, to the outbreak of the Second World War, he kept his sails trimmed to the majority decisions of the Labor Party. His influence grew, although he could at no time hold a conference by his oratory, in a manner comparable to that of Morrison or Bevin. The test came after the General Election of 1935, when Arthur Greenwood and Herbert Morrison were his rivals in an election for the leadership of the Labor Party by the parliamentary body. He was reelected and, from that time forward, his position has never been seriously challenged. It was inevitable, therefore, when the wartime Coalition Government was formed under Churchill, that Attlee should become Deputy Prime Minister. The student of history could detect irony in this action for, ever since the rise of Hitler, Attlee and his colleagues, who now joined the Coalition Government, had emphatically rejected, on principle, all such combinations of rival parties. But irony and contradiction notwithstanding, Attlee had the Labor Party's full support for his opposition to a coalition against Hitler and in making the coalition when the crash came.

He was fifty-seven years of age, when, at the outbreak of war, he stepped into the foreground as deputy leader to Winston Churchill, who after dwelling on the back benches of the Tory Party had leapt at once into the Cabinet and had now assumed supreme command. There was no doubt about the political maturity of Attlee or the richness of his experience in leadership. There was no doubt, either, among those who knew him, that he would measure up to the high position he had now acquired. Indeed, after the event, all agreed that he grew in political stature as a leader and director of government. His position, as deputy for Churchill in wartime, was no sinecure. The latter was a leader to whom war was the breath of life. He was thrilled with the grandeur of the far-flung drama, to be in office at Armageddon, with the world at war in the air, on land and sea! Nothing could be more terrifically thrilling until the Wellsian vision of the Armageddon of worlds should come. It took him across the Atlantic, to Italy, to Yalta and Moscow, Teheran and Normandy, to Egypt and Morocco. As it did so, increasing responsibilities fell upon the shoulders of his deputy, destined to be his successor. Attlee had now to keep his eyes on all departments of state, answer to Parliament and the people for the Cabinet's leadership of the war. He had no lengthy monologues to give at Cabinet meetings but he got through Cabinet work with a speed and dispatch which contrasted greatly with what happened when the "old man" was at home. On several occasions, too, Attlee himself made journeys. He flew to America, Canada, Bermuda, the Azores.

During this period of deputizing for Churchill he was brought into intimate relation with the problems of the empire and the commonwealth. Although the Westminster Pact of 1931 had established the Dominions as independent and free to make their own decisions with regard to war and peace, all of them, with the exception of Eire, had quickly joined in with Britain in September, 1939. Nevertheless, the evolution of the means of cooperation between the nations of the commonwealth had by no means reached the stage of efficient cooperation of nations of equal status. Now came the time to test the new bonds of free association, to develop the new means of cooperation. In the process, Attlee was the man who, with the leaders from the Dominions, participated in the shaping of things which led to the Conference of Prime Ministers establishing the "Commonwealth" in 1948. The fundamental difference of attitude between Churchill and Attlee arose out of their entirely different approach to the problems before them. Churchill had no ideals at which to aim. He had only the power and glory of an acquired empire which he did not wish to see given up to anyone. He conceded only under the greatest pressure, either as a conqueror generously insuring the future against further revolts or when he could no longer carry forward forces to conquer. Attlee, on the other hand, *conceded to the claims for independence as a policy* which would insure a full transition from imperial domination to a free association of peoples equal in national status.

Mr. Francis Williams in the *Triple Challenge* quotes Attlee as saying: "You cannot build or maintain a commonwealth on a foundation of bitterness and distrust. The only safe foundation is friendship and common interest. . . ." It was not difficult for him to pursue that course with the representatives of the British Commonwealth who had already acquired the status of free nations. But it flowed directly from his whole conception of the future of the British Empire and Commonwealth. In his book *The Labour Party in Perspective,* written in 1937, he set forth more fully what he had in mind about the British Empire and Commonwealth. He said:

The Labour Party is, of course, opposed to Imperialism whether in its old or new form. . . .

The British Empire was built upon sea power. The favorable position of the British Isles, divorced to a large extent from continental quarrels, enabled this great Empire to be established and to be exploited by British capital made available by the exploitation of the workers at home. . . .

The British Empire consists of two sections. The first is composed of those countries which are free and equal partners in the Commonwealth, enjoying complete self-government and remaining within the Empire of their own free will, while the second, which is, from the point of view of population, by far the largest, contains a number of countries which are in various stages of development towards self-government, and some which are still directly ruled by representatives of this country. The Dominions of Canada, Australia, and New Zealand, with the Irish Free State, are almost entirely inhabited by people of European stock, and with Great Britain form an ideal basis for the development of an economic and political federation that may show an example of how such a relationship can be extended to cover all those countries which are prepared to share in collective security and the pooling of economic resources. South Africa, which has not a predominantly white population, offers some problems which must be considered separately, but also forms part of this group. . . ."

While Attlee had grave doubts about the fullest economic cooperation being achieved unless these countries all become Socialist, he made no stipulation that they shall become Socialist before they shall cooperate as free nations. In the war period meetings with Commonwealth ministers were occupied with the creation of effective means of cooperation for the winning of the war. What all this would signify and call for afterward was yet to be seen. But the pattern of what Attlee wanted to see emerge was outlined by him in 1937 and was clearly before him in all his association with the Commonwealth and Empire ministers.

As the war came toward its end, even Mr. Churchill sensed the fact that things were not as they had been previously in the body politic and that the relation of the political forces in the country were not as they were when the Coalition Government was formed at the beginning of the war. He realized, moreover, that this effected Attlee's position and that his stature as a leader was much greater than heretofore. In 1944 he paid him a grudging tribute. He said, "The Rt. Hon. Gentleman is not a self-seeking man and always tries to play the game and do the best he can which is very much to his honor. . . ." and reluctantly took him to the Potsdam Conference.

The General Election of 1945 showed that Churchill had played his electoral cards badly, that the British public had come to the conclusion that, however good he might be as a war leader, he was not the man to make the peace. Churchill tried to run an election campaign as the man who won the war, trooping round the country with an army of yes-men who shouted, "A vote for Me is a vote for Churchill," plus the specter of Professor Harold Laski in the role of leader of

a Socialist Gestapo! The result, after Attlee had spoken on
the wireless deploring that a great man should fall so low,
was astounding. He asked the people in plain and simple
language to "face the future," and in a statesmanlike way advised them on how to face it. The Labor Party returned 393
members to Parliament, the Tories 198, and the Liberals
12. It was a great victory and there was no debate within the
Labor Party itself as to who was its leader or who should be
the Prime Minister *with power to implement the program*
to which it was committed. Attlee was the man by unanimous consent, and all the leaders, any one of whom might
have been in his shoes, had fortune smiled on them in the
election of 1931, came under his leadership in the Cabinet
of his own making. Here were Morrison and Bevin and
Cripps and Dalton, his first lieutenants. Across the floor of
the House of Commons sat the leader of the Opposition,
disappointed and morose, watching the empire move into
forms of human association which he could not comprehend.

When Attlee became Prime Minister he had not to im-
provise a program of action or come to any compromise
arrangements with the party opposite. In 1937 he had declared: "A Labor Government when it is returned to power
will not dissipate its power by dealing only with minor matters. It will proceed at once with major measures while its
mandate is fresh. . . . It will initiate measures in every
department of Government designed to fit in with a general
plan." These major measures had been clearly formulated
in the election program: *Let us Face the Future.* Under Attlee's leadership it fulfilled its domestic program by 1950.
The program consisted of far-reaching economic changes
which brought twenty percent of the economy of the country under national ownership, insured full employment, and
effected the greatest social changes in all departments of
health and social well-being of the community. This work
was proclaimed as the creation of the "Welfare State."

That these changes have been carried through under Attlee's leadership in the most extraordinary and difficult circumstances none can deny. The story of these changes has been told. Simultaneously with these changes in the internal affairs of the country, Attlee led the British state in the most critical period of empire transformation.

Nothing is more clear, from the statements of Attlee in relation to the Labor Party's attitude to the British Empire and Commonwealth, than the fact that when it came to power, with Clement Attlee at the head, it inherited an empire in process of disintegration and was committed to transforming it into an association of free nations. The British Empire and Commonwealth was by no means composed of nations of a uniform pattern either with regard to race, nationality, institutions, or social composition. Even that part designated as the British Commonwealth of Nations was divided into two groups: (1) Britain, Canada, Australia, New Zealand, South Africa, and Eire, which were largely of common stock with a common religious and political background. In South Africa this refers only to the white population, of course. (2) India, Pakistan, Ceylon, and Burma, all containing people of completely different races, religions, and cultures, and varying economic systems.

There remained, in what was still left of the British Empire governed by "Whitehall," a third group, consisting of some sixty million colored peoples, living in more than fifty different territories scattered in tropical and subtropical regions. In none of the countries of any of the three groupings, with the exception—until 1949—of Australia and New Zealand, was there a regime of the same political complexion as that of the British Labor Government.

The three groupings of nations presented entirely different problems, although all of them had been and were subject to the impact of the demand for social and political changes incompatible with the preservation of the British Empire in its old form. The first group of nations—the United Kingdom, Canada, New Zealand, Australia, Eire, and South Africa had reached the stage signaled by the passing of the Westminster Act of 1931 when they were definitely designated as politically independent, entitled to make their own laws and determine their own foreign policy. Nevertheless, a degree of mutual dependence in defense and economic affairs remained, along with the fact that they were, on the whole, people of a common stock. There was a good basis for a continuing association and the problem no longer was one of loosening the central authority's grip but of the evolution of means of cooperation. This largely consisted of decentralizing responsibility, a mutual recognition of disparities, and the acceptance of flexible means of cooperation. The problems of the war had already forced a solution of most of these problems upon this group. But at the time Attlee and his government came to power, the Asiatic group was approaching the position which the first group had reached in 1926, while Eire, of the first group, was on the point of breaking away altogether and asserting her independence as a republic. This question of republicanism was to be brought forward, too, by India, Burma, and Pakistan as soon as their independence was established. The test of statesmanship was at hand for Attlee.

The circumstances in which the Conference of Prime Ministers of the British Commonwealth met with the Prime Ministers of the newly established independent countries of Asia were vastly different from those of any previous conference of the British Commonwealth. As the war ended in 1945, it was suddenly revealed to the world that the war had engineered a tremendous revolution throughout Asia and changed completely the power relations of the states which had hitherto dominated the world. In the three years since the war had ended, a complete reorientation of the policy of the U.S.A. and Great Britain from that which had outwardly marked their policy in the war. The alliances of the war, formed under the pressure of the aggression of Nazi Germany, Italy, and Japan, and not out of any inherent common purpose, proved to be "marriages of convenience." From the moment the common struggle for existence against the Nazi powers ended, the Western powers were faced with the advancing revolution from the East. They regarded the Soviet Union as being responsible for extending the revolutionary process in Europe and Asia, and thus reshaped their policies under the leadership of the United States. This resulted in the *Atlantic Pact* of 1949, a political, economic, military alliance ostensibly aimed at no one, but factually directed against the Soviet Union. The British Labor Movement was as antagonistic to the extension of the revolution by revolutionary means as were the Tories of Britain. Attlee and his Foreign Secretary abandoned the foreign policy they had submitted to the electorate in 1945. Then they had proclaimed their friendship with the Soviet Union and the nations of Eastern Europe. They promised they would apply a Socialist policy to Western Germany and base their policy entirely on the internationalism of the United Nations. Economically dependent on the United States and completely eclipsed by her power, Attlee continued where Churchill left off, geared his foreign policy to that outlined by Churchill in his Fulton speech, and became the second partner of the U.S.A. in the alignment of the Western powers against the Soviet Union and advancing revolution. By the time of the 1948 Commonwealth Conference Britain and the U.S.A. had gathered around them the nations of Western Europe and the British Commonwealth in comprehensive pacts involving military, economic, and political commitments, more precise in form and more binding in their obligations than anything in the association of the British Commonwealth of Nations.

The new states of India, Pakistan, Burma, and Ceylon were not uninfluenced by these circumstances. While anxious not to be involved in an East-versus-West bloc, the representatives of the new states of the Indian sub-continent were deeply sensitive of the changing character of the revolution in the East, lest, as in China, the political revolution should turn into a social revolution. Nehru, the Prime Minister of India with its three hundred million population, understood full well that the independence movement of India was part of the vast revolutionary upheaval that was sweeping all the countries of the East and the Pacific archipelago. He was conscious, too, both of the weakness and the strength of India in her relations with Britain and the world at large. Economically, her ties were strong and Britain stood as a debtor to India to the sum of £2,000,000,000. But India had no navy and, generally speaking, her military forces were weak.

Such was the background of recent history when the Conference of Prime Ministers met in 1948 under Attlee's chairmanship. The latter was as keen as any man that the conference should not end with India isolating herself from the nations of the British Commonwealth. Now would be put to the test the validity of his policy of conceding Indian independence without a fight and of his own ingenuity in unraveling the constitutional complexities involved in holding a republic within a monarchist association. Previously, he had displayed his ingenuity in adjusting Britain to the evolution of the commonwealth idea by changing the name of the Dominion's Department of State to that of "Commonwealth Relations Department." Once again he was equal to the situation. He proposed that the association of states known as the British Commonwealth of Nations should henceforth be known as the "Commonwealth of Nations." But he was not too concerned with titles for the association. Later on, when questioned in the House of Commons as to which was the right title, he explained that people could use whichever title they preferred *British Empire, British Commonwealth of Nations,* or the *Commonwealth of Nations.* He was more concerned about the fact of their association and their common allegiance. In 1949 he called a special conference of the Commonwealth Prime Ministers. At that meeting he succeeded in steering the conference to its final declaration of continued association of India, Pakistan, and Ceylon, within the "Commonwealth of Nations," with the King as the symbolic head of the association. That was a triumph and a confirmation of the course he had pursued.

Neither Burma nor Eire would accept the new position, however, Burma because it was too near a social revolution, Eire because it was continuing its fight against the separation of the northern counties from the rest of Ireland, a separation made in 1922 as part of a compromise settlement in Ireland's war of independence against Britain.

Hardly had the ministers attending the conference returned to their respective countries than the commonwealth was put to a new test, in which they would be forced to reveal how far they had common economic interests and could act together upon them. The "dollar" crisis hit the "sterling area," that is, all the countries whose currency was linked to the English pound. This hit the United Kingdom more severely than any other country. At the same time, the United Kingdom was the custodian of the gold reserves of the whole of the "sterling" countries. The rapid drainage of these gold reserves by the "dollar" countries, particularly the U.S.A., was due to the sterling area's lack of dollars. This was due to the inability of the sterling countries to pay for their necessary imports from the U.S.A. and Canada through the sale of an equivalent amount of exports to these countries. The U.K. was forced to cut down imports from the U.S.A. and Canada. Obviously, all the members of the commonwealth, with the exception of Canada (geared to the American dollar), would be affected by the shortage of dollars. Even Canada, a "dollar" country, was short of American dollars. Attlee acted promptly and called together another Commonwealth Conference in London with a view to concerted action with the U.K. This they did. Each of the commonwealth countries decided on large-scale cuts in their imports from the U.S.A. and planned, at the same time, to increase exports to the

U.S.A. as a means of closing "the gap." This could only mean a considerable contraction of international trading, a shrinkage of the world market. Even before these measures came fully into operation the drainage on the gold reserves of the "sterling" countries became so severe that the U.K. was driven to the point of devaluing the pound by thirty percent in relation to the dollar. Promptly, the countries of the commonwealth, with the exception of Canada (which devalued ten percent) and Pakistan, devalued their currencies in the same ratio. Thus were revealed both the weak and strong features in the economic relations of the British Empire in relation to the U.S.A. and the commonwealth countries to each other. All were weak and dependent upon the U.S.A. and all suffered from the "dollar shortage." That weakness strengthened the Commonwealth in securing common action. But common action meant the opening of a veritable trade war with the U.S.A. in a contracting market. It thus fell to Attlee and his government to steer the Commonwealth to common action in the field of economics and finance, as it had fallen to him to initiate the political and constitutional measures of recent years which had made the Commonwealth into a larger reality within the framework of the changing British Empire.

When Attlee stepped into the foreground of British imperial politics in 1945, the "British Commonwealth of Nations" embraced only the old white "settler" colonies transformed into independent dominions. In the intervening period of the Third Labor Government's five-year tenure of office, Attlee steered the British imperial government to the effective liberation of India and made it possible for the independent, colored nations of this region to join the commonwealth of free nations associated with the British Crown. This achievement will rank in the history of the British Empire as the greatest liberating act of any of its statesmen since first the merchant adventurers went forth to conquer—and to create that same British Empire.

In the British General Election, held on February 23rd, 1950 Attlee was not challenged concerning his steering of the United Kingdom in its Empire-transformation policy. In the outcome, Mr. Attlee and the Labor Party were returned to power by a small majority of Parliamentary seats but they received the largest vote accorded to any party in the history of British politics. Again he formed a Government—the Fourth Labor Government—assured that, however the rival parties may differ on other matters, the course he had pursued, and would pursue, in the transformation of the British Empire, had been confirmed by the people of the United Kingdom.

C H A P T E R   V I

W . L . M A C K E N Z I E   K I N G

MACKENZIE KING JOINS THE GAL-
lery of new commonwealth makers for two reasons. First,
because Canada was the first colony within the British Empire to achieve full independent nationhood. Second, because Mackenzie King was the Prime Minister of Canada in
the crucial and final stages of that transformation which led
to the removal of the bonds of imperialist rule and their
replacement by commonwealth association. A third reason
should be added to these. His family history epitomizes the
story of Canada, its origins, its struggles, and its emergence as
an independent state. In 1867, seven years before Mackenzie
King was born, the Dominion of Canada was established by
the Imperial Parliament through the passage of the British
North America Act. Canada was still a dominion when King
became Prime Minister of Canada in 1921. He retired immediately after the 1948 London Conference of Prime Ministers. He had been at the head of a government longer than
any other Prime Minister or President in the entire world.
The political career of William Lyon Mackenzie King has
been dedicated to maintaining and affirming the unity of
Canada as a nation. His motto throughout the years has been
"As we preserve our national unity, so shall we preserve our
national strength."

Canada was born as a nation out of the American War of
Independence and the defeat of the French in war. After
John Cabot had discovered Newfoundland and the coast of

North America off Labrador, Britain laid claim to North America. Her sons began the process of colonization. But there were other claimants and other settlers. The French came to found a New France and made Quebec their headquarters. The British and the French fought for possession. Wolfe's capture of Quebec gave victory to the British in Canada in 1759. The defeat of the French in Europe completed the triumph and they ceded to Great Britain all their territory in North America except the district and city of New Orleans. There were at this time not more than five hundred English settlers in the colony; the French numbered sixty thousand. The former group was composed chiefly of those colonists who refused to renounce their allegiance to the mother country after the thirteen colonies, under George Washington, established the United States of America; these United Empire Loyalists laid the foundations of English settlement in Canada. And, of course, they were supported by the armed forces of England. The abandonment of the French colonists by France stopped the flow of French immigrants. The establishment of Canada as a British colony led to a continuous immigration by Britishers until they composed a majority of the colony's population. Thus, the people of two nations gave birth to the Canadian nation.

But it was not a united nation. Generous as were the terms of the conqueror, the memories of the fighting, and the fact of conquest, were long and bitter. Had the two peoples who were to grow into one nation been of the same language and religion and traditions of government, the problem of fusion into a common way of life would not have been so difficult. But these differences of national history enhanced the bitterness, and the disproportion in the numbers of settlers from the two countries, Britain and France, did not make things easier. From 1774 to 1791 Canada was governed by the Quebec Act. In 1791, the Constitutional Act divided the colony into Upper Canada and Lower Canada. Upper Canada contained the British settlers, Lower Canada the French. Upper Canada then had a population of 20,000 and Lower Canada 120,000. Each province had its own Governor, Legislative Council and Assembly.

Canada began her forward march.

At this time it was a vast virgin country stretching 2,700 miles from east to west and 1,600 miles from north to south, a land area of 3,150,000 square miles of unchartered regions, peopled exceedingly thinly in parts with a native Indian population and the few scores of thousands of Britishers and Frenchmen. Of vast potential wealth, none knew its extent or its nature. In the homelands from which the invaders had come the industrial revolution, which would one day change the face of Canada itself, was about to burst into flood. It would transform Britain into a new kind of imperial power. In Canada, however, the settlers were more interested in what the soil would give forth and what the hunter could gain from the fur-bearing animals of the north than in the mineral wealth under the soil.

The United States of America was young, too. In all the thirteen newly-united states there were not more than a million settlers: a figure similar to that of Canada. There was, however, this vast difference between them: the colonists of the thirteen states had thrown off the governing power of the country of their origin. The Canadians had not. Indeed, the effect of the American War of Independence on the British imperial power was to make it more sensitive to the grip it exerted over the colonies remaining under its control. Although the American Revolution had taught the English government that she could not impose internal taxation on her colonies the effect, at first, was to increase her political control. To forestall any questioning on the part of the colonies as to who had granted them their charters, all subsequent charters had to be granted by statute and not by the Crown. The terms of the Constitutional Act of 1791 were decided by the British Parliament and not by the Crown. This became standard practice. The relations with the colonies grew closer and the grip became more rigid. Although, in theory, the Canadian Assembly was responsible to the people of Canada, the powers of the Governor and officials chosen by him, in practice, were absolute. Sir Francis Bond Head, Governor of Upper Canada from 1836 to 1838, went so far as to assert that he, as the sole representative of imperial power, must ultimately decide in everything.

And there was the rub. The settlers were not made of the stuff that enjoyed dictators or their methods. They had carried with them the traditions of their native land and were no more prepared to be governed by such methods than were their neighbors who had established the United States. Among the new Canadians of this period was one named William Lyon Mackenzie. He had been born in Scotland in 1795. In 1820 he emigrated to Canada, became a journalist in Queenston and published a journal named *The Colonial Advocate*. From Queenston he moved to Toronto where he became a successful printer, journalist, and man of property. He was a man of great character, deeply religious and of liberal political convictions. He became the mayor of Toronto and was elected to Parliament in 1828 for the County of York. His election address, to be quoted and used by his grandson, William Lyon Mackenzie King, in 1917, said:

I have no end in view but the well-being of the people at large —no ambition to serve but that of contributing to the happiness and prosperity of our common country. The influence and authority with which you may invest me shall always be directed, according to the best of my judgment, for the general good; and it will be my care to uphold your rights to the utmost of my power with that firmness, moderation and perseverance, which become the representative of a free people.

Mackenzie quickly became the custodian of the people's rights, exposing corruption in the ranks of the privileged and fighting tenaciously for self-government. He was elected again in 1830 and 1831. In the latter years he was expelled from Parliament on a pretext of the executive. The people reelected him the following year. He was again expelled. He won office yet again on the following year but he was not permitted to take his seat. He was now on the highroad of sacrifice, risking possessions, health, home, in a struggle to make the people's representatives responsible to the people themselves.

Of the corruption in high places there was no doubt. In Britain, enlightened critics had long been denouncing colonial administration as the repository of posts and patronage for sons of the well-to-do. A mute governed the Barbados. The secretary to the Council of Jamaica drew a salary from the country which he had never even visited. In 1833, Mackenzie, at his own expense, came to England in an endeavor to persuade the British authorities to redress the grievances of the Canadian people. But to no avail. The regime of Sir Francis Bond Head was adamant. So bitter became the feelings of the people that they took up arms in rebellion under the leadership of Mackenzie in Upper Canada and of Louis Papineau in Lower Canada. The rebellion was crushed. A hundred years later, at a centennial dinner, the grandson of Mackenzie spoke of this uprising:

It was the assertion of British rights, and their denial by those in authority, and nothing more, which occasioned the Rebellion. The movement which Mackenzie headed was less a movement against the Crown's authority, than against the abuse and prostitution of it. Until hope of redress was crushed by absolute despair, no public man of his time gave stronger proofs than Mackenzie of his attachment to the British Crown and British Institutions, or laboured more earnestly to preserve all that is implied by British connection.

With a price of a thousand pounds on his head, Mackenzie fled to the United States where he was imprisoned as a political prisoner, for an alleged violation of the neutrality laws.

He was set free later by President Van Buren. It was while living in New York State that his wife gave birth to her thirteenth child, a daughter, who was to become the mother of Canada's future Prime Minister, W. L. Mackenzie King.

Nor was it on the maternal side of his ancestry alone that Mackenzie King was associated with Canada's early struggle. His grandfather, John King, native of Aberdeenshire, Scotland, educated at the Royal Military Academy, Woolwich, author of a work on gunnery and military engineering, a member of the Royal Horse Artillery, served in His Majesty's Forces which crushed the rebellion led by Mackenzie. Of his paternal grandfather Mackenzie King has had little to say. The maternal parentage has always exercised a greater influence on him, especially as his life became identified with the aims and principles of grandfather Mackenzie. His mother, born in exile, was a true daughter of her father and grew up in his faith and beliefs. Of her, Mackenzie King has said:

My mother feared God, and He did not forget nor forsake her; never in my early years can I recollect divine worship was neglected, in our little family, when health permitted; never did she in family prayer forget to implore that He, who doeth all things well, would establish in righteousness the throne of our Monarch, setting wise and able councillors around.

It is obvious that the Mackenzie revolt did not aim at the independence of Canada but at *self-government* under the British Crown. The immediate effect of the rebellion on the affairs of Canada was far-reaching. The rebellion was crushed but it ended the regime of Bond Head. Lord Durham was sent to Canada to investigate. His famous report began a complete change in the governing of the colonies by the imperial government; had this policy been operative before the American War of Independence, that war would probably have been unnecessary. For the outcome of Durham's investigation was to concede what Mackenzie had really fought for: that there should be an identity of will and interest between the governing authorities and the popular assembly. Up to that time the Governor chose his own executive council independently of the Assembly. The Governor could and did give posts to exclusive and corrupt minorities and hereditary office-mongers. Durham proposed to end this practice by giving to the popular chamber real and effective control over the executive, as in England where the House of Commons majority had control over the executive. Of course, he drew a strict line between imperial and internal affairs. The former were to remain the affair of the Imperial Parliament in London. But it meant a fundamental change in British colonial policy with unitarian control of colonies by governors making way for responsible government of internal affairs by the colonials. Had Willian Lyon Mackenzie been offered such terms when he came to London in 1833, his heart would have rejoiced. He achieved victory, however, in that Canada led the way as the first of the colonies of the British Empire to achieve self-government in its domestic affairs.

An early sequel for Canada was the passing of the Act of Union which became operative in 1841. By this act, Upper and Lower Canada were reunited, with one legislative council and one legislative assembly. The Legislative Council consisted of twenty members nominated by the Crown and the Assembly of eighty-four representatives—forty-two for each province—elected by popular suffrage. True, this was not all that Mackenzie stood for but it was a great stride forward. Mackenzie, who, after the passing of the Rebellion Losses Bill in 1849, returned to Canada and was received with acclamation by the people of Toronto, advocated that Canada become a confederation of the colonies north of the United States. He had written to the British Government, in 1824, toward this end and wrote in his journal *The Colonial Advocate* that he believed "a union of the colonies would greatly strengthen the ties of friendship, amity and mutual advantages" and be the means whereby England could retain her possessions on the North American continent. Lord Durham, in his famous report which shattered the autocratic traditions of the English Colonial Office at the beginning of the Victorian era, also favored the principle of confederation.

William Lyon Mackenzie died in 1861, six years before Canada became a confederation of provinces established in self-government under the British Crown—the goal of all his activities. In 1867, seven years before Mackenzie King was born, the Dominion of Canada was established by the Imperial Parliament which passed the British North America Act. This act has served ever since as the Canadian Constitution. It provided that the Lower House should be established on a system of representation by population, while the Upper House was to be an appointee body and representative of the various sections of the new nation. That did not solve all of Canada's problems, by any means; it did not alter the fact that Lower Canada was composed of the French, with their own language and traditions and interests, while Upper Canada was composed primarily of Britishers. But as most of Canada's problems, at this stage of its history, were internal and not external (problems of growth and consolidation into a single nation), the responsibility was their own and they could act freely toward a solution.

In 1867, when the British North America Act was passed, British Columbia was a Crown Colony. In 1871 it became a Province of Canada. In 1867, the Northwest of Canada was the property of the Hudson's Bay Company. In 1870 it became the Province of Manitoba. Between 1871 and 1905 the Provinces of Alberta and Saskatchewan were cut out of the West, and Prince Edward Island, the smallest of the Maritime Provinces, joined the confederation. Newfoundland joined in 1949.

Canada adopted the parliamentary system of responsible government. Every precaution was taken to preserve the special rights of French Canada. Quebec was permitted to keep its own civil laws for private rights in general, while it shared the system of English criminal and federal public law with the other provinces. The right of the Roman Catholic Church to supervise education in Quebec was specifically safeguarded. The Quebec province, too, because of its national composition, was guaranteed against any attempt to swamp her politically by the provision that she should have a fixed number (65) of members in the House of Commons, and that every other province was to calculate its representatives in the same proportion to the population as did Quebec. Along with the parliamentary system there was carried over from the old countries the alignment of the people in terms of the two traditional parties—Conservative and Liberal. The Conservatives held sway, first, from 1867 to 1873. From 1873 to 1878 the Liberals were in power. Then, until 1905, the pendulum swung back to the Conservatives. In that year, the Liberals, under the French-Canadian leader, Sir Wilfrid Laurier, took over the reins of government and under his administration of fifteen years' duration, Canada experienced a remarkable economic development. During that period Canada advanced far along the path of national unity. Toward the end of Sir Wilfrid Laurier's long term of office there appeared by his side a prospective successor by the name of William Lyon Mackenzie King.

The name of King comes, of course, from the paternal side of the family. The remainder of the name is from the maternal side which is really more important in the make-up of the man. "Grandfather" King, who had fought on the side of the British Government against the uprising led by William Mackenzie, belonged to the conservative brand of Scotsman, well-educated, dour, religious; he had settled to the life of the new Canada without playing any outstanding part in the shaping of its history after the rebellion. But his son, John King, grew, prospered, and became a barrister, a K.C. who practiced in Ontario. He did not become a poli-

tician although he was so much of a liberal-minded man as
to be approached by the Liberals to become a candidate on
their behalf. He was highly cultured, distinguished both as
an orator and for his literary attainments. He married Isabel
Grace Mackenzie. He taught young lawyers as a lecturer at
Osgoode Hall, Toronto; he became an elder of St. Andrew's
Presbyterian Church, Toronto, and was for thirty-seven
years a representative of the graduates in Arts on the University of Toronto Senate, and an authority on the law of
Libel and Slander who published several works on the subject. He built a well-to-do home, pursued literature and
academic subjects, and, in addition to his legal activities,
served well in disinterested public service. He was the father of four children, two girls and two boys; one of the boys
was W. L. Mackenzie King.

Here, in this cultured home, Mackenzie King grew and
thrived. The blending of these two families from Scotland,
rich in the traditions of the homeland yet sufficiently trans-
planted to Canadian life to have also a Canadian tradition of
their own making, provided a wonderful environment in
which a boy could grow to manhood. The family was well-
to-do and able to insure him a full education and yet in its
own history it was sufficiently near to poverty and harsh
struggle. Those days of Mackenzie's struggles and exile
remained fresh in the memory of King's mother. Her father, too, was a family hero in the new nation's struggle for
social betterment and political liberty. Such a blending
would be difficult to match. Were we to search Canada from
end to end it would be difficult to find one more calculated
to encourage the shaping of a Canadian statesman bred to
the independent liberalism of the nineteenth century. Physically, Mackenzie King grew in the likeness of the paternal
side of the family. Mentally, he grew with all the fervor of
the Mackenzies, tempered with the cautiousness of his father. All the ardent desire for learning that marked both
sides of the family was his. He had studied the arts and law

at the University of Toronto. Having graduated from there with honors in political science he pursued his studies further at Chicago and Harvard Universities.

Mark the period of maturation in the budding statesman's life. His postgraduate work at the University of Chicago began in the winter of 1896-97. In the course of his student days two men in other lands exercised a great influence upon him. One was Arnold Toynbee, famous as the pioneer of the University Settlement Movement in England—the movement which sought to "bridge the gulf between the classes" through university graduates living and studying in settlements in working-class districts. The other was Louis Pasteur. Throughout his life Mackenzie King has ever been fond of quoting Pasteur's famous declaration, made at the inauguration of the Pasteur Institute in 1888:

Two contrary laws seem to be wrestling with each other nowadays: the one, a law of blood and of death, ever imagining new means of destruction, and forcing nations to be constantly ready for the battlefield—the other, a law of peace, work, and health, ever evolving new means of delivering man from the scourges which beset him. The one seeks violent conquests, the other the relief of humanity. The latter places one human life above any victory; while the former would sacrifice hundreds of thousands of lives to the ambition of one.

That statement inspired the young man to follow the Mackenzie trail for social betterment through reforming the conditions under which men and women labor and live. Toynbee's influence led him to Hull House, Chicago, a settlement of the Toynbee variety, while attending lectures at the university seven miles away. He says of this experience in his book, *Industry and Humanity:*

The settlement, its surrounding and studies, brought me into touch with such concrete problems as those presented by the tendency of the foreign population in large cities to become grouped into 'colonies' representative of different nationalities;

and by the tendency of home life to be transferred from single dwellings into overcrowded tenements, allied too often, through opportunities of social intercourse, with some neighbouring saloon and its light, warmth, music and boon companions. The problem of the sweated trades was another of the problems confronted.

Then he says:

Having observed these tendencies in Chicago, on my return to Canada in the summer of 1897, I wrote a series of articles for the "Mail and Empire," Toronto, on possible similar developments in Canadian cities. Among topics dealt with were, the foreign populations of Toronto, the housing of the working people, and sweating in industry. In visiting the homes of the workers in the garment trades, I came across letter carriers' uniforms being made up under contracts awarded by the Post Office Department of Canada. On questioning one of the workers as to the remuneration she was receiving for sewing machine and hand work, I found that it came to a very few cents an hour. As I visited other homes and shops, I found the condition of this woman's employment to be in no sense isolated, but all too common.

Out of this social investigation came political action. He interviewed the Postmaster General who, as a result of Mackenzie King's revelations, introduced into Parliament the Fair Wages Resolution providing for the payment on government work of the current wages of competent workmen. He then returned to his postgraduate studies and won a fellowship in political economy at Harvard University. There he won a traveling fellowship which took him to Europe in 1899, where he visited France, Germany, and Italy. He was now bent on pursuing his sociological studies, and while abroad was appointed to the position of Instructor in Political Economy at Harvard University. But before he could return and take up this work he received from the Postmaster General, Mr. Mulock, who had been greatly impressed and influenced by his research in labor conditions in Toronto, the news that the government had established a Department of Labor and was offering him the post of editor of *The Labor Gazette*. After first refusing the offer, and subsequent pressure from his homeland, he accepted the post of Deputy Minister of Labor and editor of *The Labor Gazette*. He was twenty-five years of age and his course was now set. He held this post from 1900 to 1908 and filled it with distinction.

Canada was no longer a vast wilderness with scattered farm lands and fur stations. The industrial revolution, which had in the nineteenth century transformed England into the "Workshop of the World," was spreading in Canada also, and producing large-scale industrial problems in relation to factories, mills, mines, transport, timber industries, and every other kind of industry common to the new age of machinery. Cities had grown in the wide-open spaces. The Canadian Pacific Railway stretched across the country from east to west. Labor was pouring into Canada from foreign lands.

King became an expert in the problems of human welfare and labor relations in industry. The address presented to him by the staff of the Ministry of Labor on the occasion of his resignation from that post to become parliamentary candidate in the Liberal cause surveys the range and character of his work in his eight years as Deputy Minister of Labor. He was responsible for the fair-wages policy on contracts paid for by public money, negotiated the settlement of forty industrial disputes, and was responsible for the enactment of such measures as the Railway Disputes Act of 1903, the Industrial Disputes Investigation Act of 1907, and the act to prevent fraudulent representations concerning immigration. He investigated the problems of oriental immigration and was responsible for the act abolishing the opium traffic in Canada. His researches into the cotton-manufacturing industry of Quebec led to an upsurge of public feeling against the use of child labor in cotton mills. He embodied his views on all these problems of human relations in industry in his book, *Industry and Humanity: A study in the principles*

underlying industrial reconstruction. It was published and
subsequently reprinted in many editions in Canada, America,
and England.

Mackenzie King's book is an enunciation and discussion
of principles and reveals the man as of full stature and a mature student of the social problems of his time, especially as
they bear upon industry. Significantly, it is dedicated to his
father and mother and bears on its title page a key sen-
tence from Louis Pasteur—"Science will have tried, by obey-
ing the law of Humanity, to extend the frontiers of Life." By
the law of humanity he means the dignity of human persons
in their relations with each other. He says:

Industry and Nationality exist for the sake of Humanity, not
Humanity for the sake of Industry or Nationality. The production and use of material wealth, and the political organisation of
society can be of enduring value to mankind only in so far as
they serve to advance human well-being.

He recognizes the contradictory elements within the structure of industry and society but these, he contends, should
be subordinated to the human spirit.

Political economy is not an art having as its objective the improvement of society, or the lot of the individuals of which society is composed. In combination with other sciences, it may con-
tribute towards this end but as a science of wealth, it is with
wealth alone, its production, distribution, and exchange, that Political Economy is concerned. . . .
Political economy is not concerned with morals . . . it is non-
moral.

But above everything else, Mackenzie King is a Christian
moralist. He believes man is fundamentally a moral being
created in the image of God Himself. Hence, this theme:

When Labour and Capital, and equally also, nation and nation, agree to set aside abstractions; when all learn to distinguish
between wealth and well-being; when each sees the other sensitive

to that to which it is most sensitive itself; when, beneath the circumstances of fortune, men look no longer to the passions which divide, but rather to the sympathy that unites, recognise the common sway of like impulses and feelings of like endeavours and aspirations, then will the way be opened to a better appreciation by each of the many difficulties of the other, and a long stretch be taken on the road that leads to common understanding, mutual forbearance, and enduring peace.

From these premises he sets out to be the great harmonizer of contradictions, the creator of means of reconciliation and harmony in industrial relations. He classifies the different elements within industry as functionary elements and seeks to harmonize them through all sides having representation in consultative machinery governed by rules of fair play. He summarizes his ideas thus:

Once the principle of Round Table Conference, with adequate representation of all the parties of industry, is made the basis of government in industry, Fear will give way to Faith; the conflict of opposed interests will vanish before an understanding of common interests; the principles which underlie Peace, Work, Health will find application; and Industry itself will gain that spirit of hearty co-operation and constructive good-will which means its highest efficiency both as an instrument of production and as an agency of social service.

His record as Deputy Minister of Labor was that of a man who practiced what he preached. It was a great school of training for the coming statesman, in which he learned the value of equanimity of temperament, great patience, and firmness of purpose, all of which would stand him in good stead as he emerged into the political arena as a national leader.

In the General Election of 1908, the year of his resignation as Deputy Minister of Labor, he was elected to Parliament as member for North Waterloo, Ontario, his native constituency; he was promptly called into the Cabinet of Sir Wilfrid Laurier as Minister of Labor and quickly became Laurier's right-hand man. Up to this time he had concen-

trated on labor problems and would make these his main
concern as Minister of Labor but the problems associated
with the evolution of Canada as a nation and an independent
state would soon attract him. Canada had not remained sta-
tionary pending his arrival at political maturity. The original
disproportion of British stock to the French had long since
been reversed but the people of French origin remained
primarily in the Province of Quebec. Besides the influx of
British settlers other nationals arrived. Canada was evolving as a multinational country, although the British stock
far exceeded all others. The primary division of French
and British made it essentially a bilingual country. At the
time Mackenzie King became a member of the Laurier Cabinet, Canada had a population of approximately six million
people. Already too, its leaders had discovered that Canada,
as a nation, could not escape either the consequences of the
duality of its origin or the fact that it was still a colony of
Britain in relation to external affairs. Nor would it be permitted to forget that it was the neighbor of another great
power.

The Boer War of 1900 gave the first big shock to the pro-
vincialism which had marked the life of the Canadians since
the passing of the British North America Act in 1867. The
British elements, so many of whom had but recently come
from Britain, were keen to support the homeland and had
no quarrel with the British Government's call for Canadian
aid. But not so the French Canadians of Quebec. They
had no interest in the Boer War and refused to aid Britain.
The Government of Canada was forced, in order to retain
the unity of Canada, to make Canadian aid a voluntary matter.

In 1908 an Imperial Conference was held and the question
of active help to Britain by her colonies was discussed. In
consequence, Laurier proposed to the Canadian Parliament
the creation of a navy which in time of peace would be
Canadian, in time of war imperial. Laurier met with fierce

opposition; his bill was not passed. With this and with commercial reciprocity with the United States as major issues, Laurier and his party were heavily defeated in the 1911 elections. The French Canadian "isolationists," as they were called, won the day. Mackenzie King shared in that defeat.

Out of cabinet office and Parliament, he was, from 1911 to 1914, in charge of the Liberal Information Office at Ottawa, editor of the Liberal monthly and President of the Ontario Reform Association. Early in 1914 he became the Director of Industrial Research of the Rockefeller Foundation. From this appointment, and his rich experience of industrial affairs at the Labor Ministry, there came early in the war his appointment as labor negotiator in a number of the great industrial corporations. Mackenzie King was again a candidate under the Liberal banner in the election of 1917 but was once again defeated. Shortly after this election, Sir Wilfrid Laurier died.

Then, in 1919, for the first time in the history of the Canadian Liberal Party, the question of succession in leadership was submitted to a party convention. Mackenzie King was nominated and from the election he emerged victorious in the decisive ballot with 476 votes to 438 votes for his nearest rival. This was followed by a unanimous vote. He held the leadership of his party from that day to his retirement in 1948. In September 1919 he won a parliamentary by-election and became the Leader of the Opposition in the House of Commons. In the 1921 General Election he returned to his old constituency. The tide for the Liberals had turned. He won North York, his party won its majority, and he became the Prime Minister of Canada.

When Mackenzie King took over the reins of government he recognized that great changes had taken place in Canada and in her relations to the rest of the world. The French-Canadian revolt against participating in the Boer War, Laurier's open resentment over the manner in which Britain and the United States had settled the Alaskan boundary dispute, the refusal of the Canadians to accept his old leader's naval bill, which in turn was a sequel to the discussion of dominion leaders at the Imperial Conference of 1911, were the first modern indications that great changes were afoot within the British Empire. Laurier had accepted the view that any share in the determination of foreign policy by the dominions had its corollary of obligation to aid. The dominion representatives at the 1911 conference, including Laurier, had expressed dissatisfaction with their completely subordinate role in external affairs. The Imperial Government had conceded that as the dominions were bound by the treaties which were negotiated they should have something to say in their negotiation. But the most which came out of it was a promise that the dominion governments should be kept informed. It was Laurier who warned the dominions at this conference that if they had a voice in determining imperial policy it would not only involve them in responsibility for implementing it, but would involve them in problems in which they had no interest. He preferred "consultation only" on matters particularly affecting the dominions. It was clear to the imperial ministers that the dominions did not desire to be committed to treaties without their consent, nor did they wish to assume the full obligations of the empire. The voice of independent nationhood was sounding. As a result of Canada's remarkable contribution to the 1914-18 war that note could no longer be ignored.

During the First World War the Conservative Prime Minister of Canada, Sir Robert L. Borden, and other Dominion Prime Ministers met in two different bodies—the Imperial War Cabinet, under the British Prime Minister, and in the Imperial War Conference, with British officials and dominion delegations under the Colonial Secretary. In 1915, the Asquith government informed the dominions that they would be consulted on the peace terms. At the War Conference of 1917 it was agreed that the constitutional position of the dominions within the empire needed redefining and the principles upon which they should be defined were put on record. But they got no further than that the principles were (1) full recognition of dominions as autonomous nations of an imperial commonwealth, (2) the right of the dominions to adequate voice in foreign policy, (3) provision of effective means of continuous consultation on all imperial matters. Although Borden had subscribed to these principles without the reservations made by Laurier, he, along with Smuts of South Africa and Hughes of Australia, demanded independent representation for the dominions as minor states at the Peace Conference. Britain agreed. They also won independent representation at Geneva in the League of Nations and the International Labor Office. Another concession was also won, namely, that the King should ratify the Peace Treaty only after the Dominion Parliaments had approved the treaty. Borden, for Canada, had insisted in 1920 upon a Canadian minister being appointed to the United States. Although he secured this right none was appointed until Mackenzie King became the Premier.

The latter took over where the Conservatives under Borden and Borden's successor, Arthur Meighen, left off. He had learned sufficiently from the development of the Canadian nation, people of mixed cultures, to know that it would be fatal simply to function as an underwriter of British Empire policy as a whole. In any case, his whole history as the representative of the Canadian nation forbade it and Canada was no longer a colonial appendage of the British Empire. Besides, there was on Canada's southern border another great nation, which, during the course of Canada's growth, had become a great nation and emerged from the war of 1914-18 as a leading power in world affairs. There was no mistaking the power and significance of the United States of America when her government called the Washington Conference of 1921-22.

Whatever the historical origins of the two nations they both lived on one continent. The boundary between them was an artificial political creation arising from their political history and not a fact of geography. However much their respective histories had separated them, their geographic contiguity made it inevitable that their economic and national development must draw them together in any attempt to solve their common problems in relation to the world at large. In responding to the American invitation to the Washington Conference, the Imperial Government of Britain blundered or at least revealed that it was slow to respond to the growing nationalism in the dominions.

It appointed an empire delegation. Promptly, Mackenzie King and other dominion leaders protested that they had not been sent independent invitations. This was all the more curious because Canadian pressure under Arthur Meighen at the Imperial Conference of 1921 against the renewal of the Anglo-Japanese alliance, was in fact the prelude to the holding of the Washington Conference. There was no time for the British Government to reverse the procedure but it reverted to the procedure adopted at Versailles and made an arrangement whereby the Dominion Governments authorized members of the empire delegation to act on their behalf. This was the conference that changed the power relations of the navies of the world, brought the U.S. Navy to the level of the British Navy and compelled Great Britain and Japan to dissolve the long-standing treaty between the two powers. It was at this time, too, that Canada under Mackenzie King exchanged ambassadors with the United States. Here was not only an affirmation of Canadian independence but a recognition of the tremendous gravitational pull of Canada toward the United States.

Hardly had the Washington Conference concluded its proceedings than the obviously creaking machinery of the Imperial Government of Britain creaked more loudly than ever. The Turkish Government renounced the Treaty of Sèvres. The British Government proposed to protect Constantinople, Chanak, and the neutral zone specified in the treaty.

Prime Minister Lloyd George sent a query to the dominions concerning dominion forces should they be needed and at the same time informed the press of what he had done. Mackenzie King, Premier of Canada, learned all about it from a newspaper aboard a train bound for Ottawa. His feelings can be imagined. At once, he complained to the Imperial Government concerning its methods and said he must consult the Canadian Parliament before he could answer the inquiry. Fortunately for the British Government matters stopped there. There was no war. It is very doubtful whether the Canadians would have provided a contingent had war come. In 1923, Mackenzie King led the way to the establishment of a new principle both in relation to the Imperial Government and other dominions. He established that a dominion representative, alone, should negotiate and sign a treaty which concerned that dominion alone. This he did by concluding the Canadian-United States Halibut Treaty. It was ratified at the Imperial Conference of 1923 which Mackenzie King attended. There it was formalized that henceforth, when such a treaty was signed, the dominion would convey the terms to other dominions and members of the empire, to enable them to indicate if they had any definite interest in the treaty. After the act of independence came the act of cooperation with the independence intact.

The Imperial Conference of 1923 was but the prelude to the conference of 1926 which crystallized the process of changing empire relations between the dominions and the Imperial Government. What had been taking place in Canada was not peculiar to itself although it had led the way. The Irish Free State, on its establishment as such, had insisted upon the treaty of 1921 being registered with the Secretariat of the League of Nations. In 1924, it had been conceded the right to send a minister to the United States. Australia set up a branch of its External Affairs Department in its High Commissioner's Office in London. When the British Government asked the dominions if they would cooperate in the enforcement of the Lausanne Treaty with Turkey, the dominions objected to taking on obligations without their consent. When Canadian Governor-General Byng refused Mackenzie King's request for a dissolution of Parliament, on the ground that the new government which accepted office could exist only for a very short time, he was overridden. The dissolution had to be granted and Mackenzie King was returned with an overwhelming majority. All these things added up to the fact that the days of imperial domination were over, at least as far as the dominions were concerned. Hence the 1926 Imperial Conference redefined the position of the dominions:

They are autonomous communities within the British Empire equal in status, in no way subordinate one to another in any aspect of their domestic or external affairs, though united by a common allegiance to the Crown, and freely associated as members of the British Commonwealth of Nations.

That was a landmark in the history of the nations constituting the British Commonwealth and in the transformation of the one-time centralized British Empire. The conference had arrived at a point of clarity on a theoretical definition of what was emerging as historical and political reality but was not yet a reality of general practice. A new principle of relationship had arrived. The task before the dominions was to apply the principle, to create a body of precedent. The conference changed the title of the King. It revised the position of the Governor-General. The latter would no longer represent the British Government. He would represent the King and would be advised by the Dominion Parliament as the Parliament of the United Kingdom advised the King. Consultation and communication between any one of the governments of the dominions or the U.K. would be made directly and not necessarily through the government of the United Kingdom. There were other adaptations but the process reached a more definitive stage after the enactment of the Statute of Westminster by the Imperial Parliament in 1931. The dominions coming within the scope of this statute were Canada, the Irish Free State, Australia, New Zealand, and South Africa.

But the dominions were not yet entirely free from imperial control although some, particularly the Irish Free State, went further than others toward complete independence. Canada now directed its own international affairs but the Statute of Westminster did not grant her the power to amend her constitution, and a number of functions under the British North America Act were still affected by the actions of the Crown. But even the last vestiges of imperial subordination, such as appeals to the Privy Council, have since been abolished. Indeed, an anomaly was created by this fact in that the French Canadians, while having been an important driving force toward complete independence, opposed the idea of the transfer of the power of Canadians to alter their own constitution for fear of losing the special privileges which had been conceded to them by the British North America Act and which only the British Parliament could alter.

Nevertheless, Mackenzie King pursued his course of asserting Canadian independence in practice. A Canadian legation was established in Washington in 1926, in Paris in 1928, in Tokio in 1929, and, after the passing of the Westminster Statute, in most of the capitals of the world. But it should not be assumed that in pursuing his path of establishing Canada's independent status Mackenzie King was urging Canada to adopt an isolationist policy. On the contrary, his principles in relation to Canada's foreign policy were (1) the maintenance of Canada's unity as a nation, (2) the priority of dominion relations with other nations, (3) non-intervention in European and Asiatic affairs in time of peace, (4) freedom from obligation to participate in the defense of the Commonwealth, (5) the necessity of obtaining parliamentary approval for military or economic sanctions, or war, (6) willingness to participate in international inquiries into economic grievances.

This policy had its corollary in economic affairs, as is clearly seen in his tariff policy. The Canadian Government was the first dominion government to put a tariff on British goods, although the Laurier government first established British preference. In 1897, the preference given to British goods in the Canadian market was equal to one fourth of the general tariff. In 1900 it was one third. In 1923, the Mackenzie King government increased it by ten percent. In 1930 it declared for a far-reaching extension of the British preference with the double object of diverting large proportions of her imports from the U.S.A. to Britain. Nevertheless, this was not a one-way policy so far as he was concerned, as he revealed in his attitude toward the Ottawa Agreements, made in 1932 by a Conservative government. King denounced the method of effecting reciprocal preferences by the increase of tariffs against non-empire countries because this would impose handicaps upon trade relations with other countries, especially the United States.

King's political policy, however, bore all the marks of immaturity and the cautiousness of the canny Scot, revealing an obvious reluctance to take on the full responsibilities of nationhood in a world of change. The drawing away from the centralized control of the British Imperial Government was certainly an affirmation of growing national consciousness and strength but Canadian silence on European and Asiatic developments and King's reluctance to affirm and support positive action toward other nations was a manifest confession of weakness. Canada certainly was represented in the League of Nations and Mackenzie King was at one time its vice-president. But the Canadian record there is largely a negative and appeasing one. Canada tried to weaken the sanctions obligations of the Covenant by moving an amendment to Article Ten of the Covenant. She opposed the Geneva Protocol of 1924; opposed oil sanctions against

Italy in 1936; supported Sir John Simon in discouraging League action against Japan on the invasion of Manchuria in 1931; in short, while affirming her independent nation-hood in relation to imperial control, her "independent" attitude to the rest of the world was an echo of Britain's ap-peasement policy in relation to the Nazi and Fascist powers. Nor is the record of Canada in the International Labor Or-ganization a bold affirmation of independence. She ranked very low among League members who ratified its conven-tions. Out of approximately sixty, Canada ratified but four. Where she shone in the records was in regard to arbitration machinery. She accepted the optional clause for submitting disputes to the Permanent Court of International Justice. She signed the Kellogg Pact for the outlawing of war and agreed to the General Act for the Pacific Settlement of In-ternational Disputes. But to all these the weakest and most immature of nations could subscribe without feeling any obligation to do much about them. Canada in world affairs was still moving in the orbit of its ancestral traditions.

Mackenzie King, however, was conscious of the growing power of the United States and while it was important for Canada, in the assertion of her independence, to work cor-dially with Britain, it did not follow that Canada must feel enmity for the U.S.A. Such animosity would be unnatural and futile. If war was conceivable between the two countries then Canada would be helpless before her neighbor, for in population, industrial power, and every other element of rivalry Canada would be helpless against so mighty a coun-try. Nor could Canada count on Britain in these matters. Britain was nearly three thousand miles away and she, too, could not face a war with the new giant among the nations; in brief, Canada could no longer be defended by Britain. Thus, it was a matter of rejoicing in Canadian hearts when President Roosevelt at Kingston, in August 1938, made the historic statement that "the United States would not stand idly by at a threat of alien domination of Canadian soil."

Mackenzie King was also conscious of the growing interdependence of Canadian and American economy. While he would resist absorption and economic conquest by America as determinedly as he had fought for the relaxation of the British imperial grip upon Canada, he wished the two countries to work in friendship and cooperation.

The most crucial test of his foreign policy came in 1939. He had been Premier of Canada for over a decade. He had attended Imperial Conferences in London in 1923, 1926, 1937. He had signed the Multilateral Treaty for the Renunciation of War in Paris in 1928, addressed the Assembly of the League of Nations, and been its vice-president in 1936.

How now?

On September 1, 1939, Germany invaded Poland and two days later Germany and Britain were at war. Britain did not automatically declare the dominions at war at the same time as Britain, although, so far as Canada was concerned, some authorities argued that because the Statute of Westminster had not removed or altered the validity of the British North America Act the King's Declaration of war on Germany involved Canada also. Whatever the legal experts might say this did not govern the practice of Mackenzie King and his government. The Canadian Parliament was summoned for September 7th. To that Parliament he said:

The action we are taking today, and such further action as this parliament may authorise, are being taken and will be taken by this country voluntarily, not because of any colonial or inferior status vis-a-vis Great Britain, but because of an equality of status. We are a nation in the fullest sense, a member of the British Commonwealth of Nations, sharing like freedom with Britain herself, a freedom which we believe we must all combine to save.

On September 10, 1939, King George VI declared Canada at war with Germany only after the Canadian Parliament called upon him to do so.

The completeness of Canadian participation in the war is

common knowledge. But possibly the most significant agreement made between any two nations in the period prior to the Japanese onslaught on Pearl Harbor, pointing clearly in the direction of American participation on the side of the Allies even had there been no Pearl Harbor attack, was the agreement concluded by Mackenzie King and President Roosevelt at Ogdensburg in August 1940. Of this agreement for mutual aid in common defense against Nazism, Mackenzie King reported to the Canadian Parliament:

. . . it will be recalled that in August 1938, the President made the open declaration that the people of the United States would not stand idly by if domination of Canadian soil were threatened by any other empire. To this declaration I replied at Woodbridge, Ontario, two days later, that we too had our obligations as a good friendly neighbour.

He then referred to their current meeting and continued:

This is perhaps an appropriate place for me to say that from the beginning, and at the time of each conversation, the President made it perfectly clear that his primary interest in the subject was the defence of the United States. I was equally frank in making it clear that my concern was the effective defence of Canada and the defence of the British Commonwealth of Nations as a whole.

This agreement coincided with the leasing of British bases in the Caribbean to America in exchange for naval craft. Cooperation became even closer after another joint statement was made by Prime Minister King and President Roosevelt on April 20, 1941. This was known as the Hyde Park Declaration. Its basic principle was "that in mobilizing the resources of this continent each country should provide the other with the defence articles it is best able to produce, and produce quickly, and that production should be co-ordinated to that end."

It was quite clear, even at this early stage of the war, that

the fundamental change in the power relations of Britain
and America made so manifest in the outcome of the First
World War, would be accentuated beyond all measure by
the Second World War, and in the process it would profoundly influence the course to be taken by Canada. Up to
the outbreak of war in 1914, all the historical ties of national
history between the peoples of Canada and Britain were reinforced by enconomic and financial bonds of considerable
strength. At that time the capital investments of Britain in
Canada were greater than American capital investments
and the general economic development was geared to British
economy much more than it was to American. The First
World War stopped the flow of British capital investments
into Canada while American and Canadian investments in
Canadian industry grew by leaps and bounds. Britain no
longer ruled the waves. She was forced to share power with
the U.S.A. While the latter had become the great creditor
of the nations, Britain had become a debtor country. Britain
had been severely damaged by the war. The war had accelerated enormously the development of American economy. Canada, itself, in the First World War, received loans
from Britain. After the war Britain's investments in Canada
not only ceased but Canada was more than able to repay all
indebtedness. Indeed, in the Second World War, while Britain's foreign-debt position reached enormous dimensions,
Canada made outright gifts of financial aid to her. On the
other hand, the Roosevelt declaration of 1938, the Ogdensburg Agreement and the Hyde Park Declaration were clear
indicators that geography, economic development, and interests in power relations were all pulling Canada ever more
deeply into the orbit of American policy.

Immediately all the dominions were involved with Britain
in the Second World War all the historic factors worked at
full strength and they were drawn closer than ever to Britain. But when America entered the war as an active military
participant and the war spread over the Pacific as well as the

Atlantic, the geographic position of Canada and the other dominions, in relation to the main theaters of the war, served to emphasize the growing power of the U.S.A. and the declining power of Britain.

In 1914, practically every dominion and colony was located on the periphery of the struggle and the war did not endanger their territory. Britain's power also was at its zenith. When Britain entered the Second World War she was in a relatively weak position. The dominions sprang to her aid and were sending their forces into the fray as they had in the First World War. Then, when the war spread and every dominion was itself threatened by a new foe, from a new direction, the weakness of Britain was revealed in a flash. Britain could not fight the war in the Pacific and the war in Europe at the same time, and all the dominions and Britain herself thanked God that America was an ally. With one accord they turned to America to bear the responsibility for the war in the Pacific, to defend the British dominions which hitherto had looked to Britain to fulfill that purpose. Again, the geographic factor impressed itself upon history. Bombs did not drop on American and Canadian towns; their cities and factories, their buildings and enterprises remained undisturbed. At the same time, the demand for war supplies from every quarter of the globe gave an impetus to the development of America's already unrivaled industrial and economic power. The same process had its parallel in Canada on a smaller scale but with the aid and cooperation of the U.S.A. all competitive factors were overwhelmed by the colossal, external demands of the war.

In between the two wars Canada had increased her population from nearly six million people to eleven millions. Mackenzie King was the Prime Minister of Canada at the outbreak of war, and led Canada into it. He was Prime Minister of Canada when the war ended, with the unconditional surrender of the enemy everywhere, in 1945. In these years of war he had steered the people of Canada through remarkable developments, all of which were geared to the main purpose of strengthening a veritable industrial revolution while at the same time increasing its productive power in agriculture. In 1939, Canada produced 1½ million tons of steel. In 1943 3 million tons. Pig-iron production rose from 846,418 tons in 1939 to 1,758,265 tons in 1943. Her aircraft industry produced 3,811 airplanes in 1942 and 11,390 in 1944. She produced 192,000 units of mechanical transport in 1942 and 593,000 units in 1944, 81 cargo vessels and 117 naval vessels increasing to 249 cargo vessels and 336 naval vessels in the corresponding years. Canada had a Navy, Army and Air Force with a combined personnel of 10,300 in 1939. In 1944, the strength of her armed forces was 765,000. At the beginning of the war the Canadian Navy had six combat ships. In 1944 it had grown to 250 and from seven auxiliary vessels to 450.

This transformed economic and military power was reflected in a completely changed financial position as compared with the position in the First World War. Canada bought out all the British-held securities in Canada, amounting to 800,000,000 dollars. She bought out the United Kingdom's interests in Canadian war plant, amounting to 200,000,000 dollars. Thus, whatever influence British financial holdings might have had passed into Canadian hands. Instead of borrowing from Britain, Canada made an outright grant of 1,000,000,000 dollars to Britain. Instead of acting through the United Kingdom, Canada negotiated directly, and drew up separate agreements, with each country receiving supplies. She received no lend-lease aid from the U.S.A. but paid cash for the supplies she received. All this was remarkable evidence of growing strength and consolidation as a national state.

Mackenzie King did not become so engrossed in the immediate tasks of developing Canada's national effort that he failed to look ahead. In a speech delivered in the Canadian House of Commons, on July 9, 1943, he showed that he was thinking of the future. In so doing he made an important contribution to the shaping of whatever international institutions might emerge from the war. He said:

The time is approaching when even before victory is won the concept of the United Nations will have to be embodied in some form of international organisation. On the one hand, authority in international affairs must not be concentrated exclusively in the largest powers. On the other, authority cannot be divided equally among all the thirty or more sovereign states that comprise the United Nations, or all effective authority will disappear.

A number of new international institutions are likely to be set up as a result of the war. In the view of the Government effective representation on these bodies should neither be restricted to the largest states nor necessarily extended to all states. Representation should be determined on a functional basis which will admit to full membership those countries, large or small, which have the greatest contribution to make to the particular object in question.

In the world there are over sixty sovereign states. If they have a nominally equal voice in international decisions, no effective decisions are likely to be taken. Some compromise must be found between the theoretical equality of states and the practical necessity of limiting representation on international bodies to a workable number. That compromise can be discovered especially in economic matters by the adoption of the functional principle of representation. That principle, in turn, is likely to find many new expressions in the gigantic task of liberation, restoration and reconstruction.

It is clear from this speech that King was not only conscious of the growing strength of Canada but that she had become, in Lionel Gelber's early wartime phrase, a Middle Power. It remained for Mackenzie King, as Canada's leading statesman, to work out and apply Gelber's concept of Middle Power to Canada's status in world affairs. He would have to think out how middle, no less than small powers, were going to maintain their independence as well as cooperate with the big ones.

In May 1944, Mackenzie King went to London for the pur-

pose of attending a conference of British Commonwealth
Prime Ministers. He was accorded a welcome such as few
men have received. He was invited to address a joint session
of both Houses of the British Parliament and received great
tribute. In introducing him to Parliament, Prime Minister
Churchill referred to him as "one who has played an un-
rivalled part in the forward march of Canada." Many others
paid tribute to him, too, and the occasion was undoubtedly
a high point in his career. After this great tribute he attended
the conference of Prime Ministers and there he enjoyed the
unique position of being the one Prime Minister to advance
the view which made clear the future character of the commonwealth association. It can be summed up thus, that he,
speaking on behalf of Canada, was in favor of all the consultation and collaboration necessary but against organizational unification in any form, whether of empire or centralized world organization. Field Marshal Smuts, representing
South Africa, was in favor of some loose regional groupings
among the nations. Prime Minister Curtin of Australia favored an Empire Secretariat. Prime Minister Fraser of New
Zealand looked forward to the organization of the commonwealth as a unit. Curtin spoke again to make clear that he
did not mean merely a London Secretariat but that the commonwealth should have regional centers which would take
the leadership of the commonwealth bloc according to circumstances; as for example, that Australia should be in command of the Pacific group of commonwealth countries. Mackenzie King held the field and stood firmly for no agreement
on any proposals which would strengthen centralization of
authority. The statement issued from the conference declared that unity had been achieved but hid the disunity with
the rhetorical addition: "That unity finds its strength not in
any formal bond but in the hidden springs from which human action flows." The world was left to ponder on the "hidden springs."

All were agreed, however, with reference to the coming

conference at San Francisco, in the Communique issued from the Prime Ministers' Conference on May 17, 1944, "that after the war a world organisation to maintain peace and security should be set up and endowed with the necessary powers and authority to prevent aggression and violence." Mackenzie King returned to Canada and on March 20, 1945, he expounded on the course which the Canadian delegation would follow at the San Francisco Conference in relation to the proposed World Organization. Addressing the Canadian House of Commons, he said:

The contribution of states other than the great powers, to the success of the organisations will vary widely. It would be in the general interest to develop the idea, and to accept as a guiding principle that power and responsibility should, as far as possible, be made to coincide. If this could be done, the result would be to narrow the gap between the great powers and other nations while maintaining the principle of the sovereign equality of all member states. It would mean that the smallest and least powerful members would not nominally be given the same responsibilities as, let us say, Australia, or the Netherlands or Brazil. It is the view of the government that the constitutional position within the organisation of important secondary countries should be clarified, and that the delegation should exert the utmost effort to secure due recognition of their relative standing among the nations of the world.

He then proceeded to criticize the draft proposals for the United Nations Organization and this criticism was carried to the San Francisco Conference. He continued:

As the proposals stand, all states, other than the five great powers would have the same constitutional position in the organisation. No regard would be paid to their international significance, or to their record in resisting aggression, or to their potential contribution to the maintenance of peace. It is surely desirable that among the states which are to be elected members of the security council there should be several countries which can make a valuable contribution to the maintenance of security.

At the same time, there should, of course, be representation in the council of different parts of the world.

From here he advanced from the old position of Canada, when she had avoided international responsibilities, to make a firm declaration of principle for which he had fought consistently in the changing British Commonwealth, namely, there must be prior consultation and national acquiescence before action.

To be effective, nearly all decisions of the Council imposing sanctions would require the assistance of one or more states not represented on the Council. The co-operation of states bordering on the offending states or of states in which operational facilities might be essential, would be particularly needed. In practice, if the enforcement of sanctions required active aid from a country not represented on the Council, its consent would probably be sought. The probable practice might well be made the formal rule.

Combining with other delegations of smaller powers, the Canadian representatives succeeded in effecting many changes to the first draft of the United Nations Organization at the San Francisco Conference. But his work in this direction was by no means at an end. The war had emphasized and developed means of cooperation between all the Allied countries both inside the British Commonwealth and outside it. Indeed, there had developed a great deal of centralized power and direction by the major powers now in the United Nations. It was only with the cessation of hostilities that the full impact of the war on all power relations and political and social institutions stood revealed. Those who had not seen the revolutionary content of the war now saw it in all its fullness. Much more than the smoking ruins of shattered Nazi and Fascist empires stared them in the face. The frontiers of social revolution were no longer the same as when the war began. Nations which had for generations been classified as "colonials" were breaking free from imperial control. In no empire were the changes more profound and far-reaching than in the British Empire itself. The comparatively slow "gentlemanly" evolution of the white men's colonies of the British Empire, through dominion status to independent nationhood voluntarily cooperating in the British Commonwealth, now received an augmentation and acceleration from the most populous and wealthiest region of the empire. The four hundred and fifty million subjects of India and Burma were on the threshold of independence.

That, if it were all, would have been enough to test the statesmanship of the nations involved. But the very efforts of the victorious powers which had involved stupendous achievements of industrial and economic organization under the stimulus of the unlimited war market had created an economic and social dislocation of tremendous dimensions. The states on the periphery of the battlefields, America and Canada in particular, had multiplied their industrial and economic power. The states in the midst of the battlefields had emerged with their economic and industrial power in a crippled condition and most of them were overwhelmed by debt to the powers which had prospered in the war. Rehabilitation meant that they would go even further into debt. The social and political changes were also profound. The 1945 General Election in Britain saw Mr. Churchill and the Conservative Party swept from power, a Social Democratic government installed on the crest of a political landslide, and Mr. Attlee become Prime Minister.

Canada itself had witnessed great changes. Its Navy now ranked third among the navies of the world. It had carried through a veritable industrial revolution and emerged from the war second only to the United States as an exporting nation. It had multiplied its industrial productive power. When Mackenzie King began his political career two parties, Liberal and Tory, alternated each other in periods of government. A new party of workers and farmers, the C.C.F., had arisen and was challenging the old parties for power. But it was far from strong enough to displace Mackenzie King at the end of the war as the British Labor Party had displaced Winston Churchill. He could continue to speak for Canada with the full backing of the Canadian Parliament. In the post-war period, true to the traditional national policy which he had built up, of gearing Canada's foreign policy to that of the United States and Britain, he turned with them away from the main trend outlined in his speeches when first the United Nations Organization project was put forward. With them, he discovered that the United Nations Organization was not enough and swung into line behind the policy outlined by Churchill at his Fulton, Missouri, speech, energetically supporting the formation of a bloc of English-speaking nations plus Western Europe, fortified with military, economic, and political agreements and the exercise of a common pressure within the United Nations Organization against the bloc of nations identified with the Communistic revolution of Russia. The lesser "synthesis" of nations became more important than the greater, and the Liberalism which had guided him in the shaping of foreign and commonwealth policies hitherto now became subordinate to the power politics of a world divided into two camps on the issue of Communism.

Such had been the changes in the post-war period when Mackenzie King made his way again to London, in 1948, to attend another conference of British Commonwealth Prime Ministers. This conference differed from all those that had taken place before. Never, previously, had any representative of a dominion attended a commonwealth conference to declare his country's intention to break away from the commonwealth. That was the first shock of its kind and was delivered by the representative of Eire, which had earlier been known as the Irish Free State. It declared itself an independent republic and declined to be further associated with the symbol of empire unity—the British Crown. That was not the only shock. Since last the Prime Ministers had met together, and decided that they were united "by hidden springs," the British Government had negotiated with the Prime Ministers of India, Pakistan, Burma, and Ceylon that henceforth their countries should be free and independent countries. The only comparable event in the history of the British Empire had been the revolt of the "thirteen settler" colonies which fought their way to the establishment of the United States late in the eighteenth century. But this time the colonies had secured their independence by negotiation and they were now invited to continue their association with the empire through membership of the commonwealth association. But the new states of India and Pakistan were determined that they should be republics. When they ceased to be the "brightest gems in the British Crown," they had no intention of even appearing to bring themselves again under British domination. Burma went the way of Eire and declined an invitation to become a member of the commonwealth. Ceylon, however, agreed to the proposal. Could the conference now make an accommodation in the constitution of the commonwealth which would permit a republic to remain in the association? That was the issue before the conference of Prime Ministers. Once again the position taken consistently by Mackenzie King held good—free association of commonwealth countries whether monarchist or republican, mutual cooperation upon policies on which they could agree, but no formation of a new centralized power bloc in place of the old imperial domination. That was the outcome. Through liberal constitutional adjustments, India and Pakistan, the new independent states, signified their adherence to the commonwealth of nations within the British Empire. On this assumption the conference discussed many subjects, such as mutual defense, post-war reconstruction, and economic cooperation.

Mackenzie King was in London during this conference;

he had traveled to England for the purpose of attending it but was unavoidably absent through illness. He was nearing the end of his political career. Indeed, he had already prepared the way for his retirement from the premiership of Canada and the leadership of the Liberal Party. In 1946, Mr. Louis St. Laurent had been appointed Minister of External Affairs. He attended the London conference and deputized for Mackenzie King during its proceedings. Laurent, a French-Canadian lawyer, had grown up in the traditions of Canadian Liberalism and was ready to tread firmly in the footsteps of Mackenzie King. When, immediately after this conference, King proceeded to give effect to his decision to retire and stepped from the center of the stage of Canadian politics and from his place in the front rank of commonwealth leaders, St. Laurent became Prime Minister of Canada in his stead.

Mackenzie King was seventy-four years of age when he retired from the premiership of Canada in 1948. He performed the act of retirement in the same well-prepared, well-thought-out manner as had characterized his actions throughout life. He chose the moment after he had prepared his successor. He retired quietly. He had never rejoiced in the "cavalry charge" and was unconcerned with dramatic effects. His role through life had been that of the mediator and the reconciler of contradictions. While the storm raged he kept cool, self-composed, somewhat phlegmatic; he never permitted crises to disturb his equilibrium or his capacity to sleep well. At retirement he did not look his years. Of medium height and somewhat heavily built he walked and stood with a slight stoop, as one pondering on the problems of life. Perhaps no man of his time has expressed more fully in himself the blending of two Scottish families—the Mackenzies and the Kings—with their mixture of radicalism and conservatism, independence and loyalism, combined with the deep religious convictions of the Presbyterians.

His opinions and convictions were shaped early in life and rooted in family traditions. Speaking on "Culture and Religion" in 1914, he said:

With the Greek, let us measure our contribution to civilisation in what we give to the humanities. With the Hebrew, let us believe that God continues to work through the centuries and that He may work for continents as well as men. With the founder of our faith, let us believe that all life is sacred and all human life but the reflected image of the Divine.

His mind lingers on his family history. His greatest treasures are a portrait of his mother who trained him in Christian teaching and kept bright the memory of her father, and a framed document—the royal proclamation issued in 1837 offering a reward of one thousand pounds "to anyone who will apprehend and deliver up to Justice, William Lyon Mackenzie." The political principles and convictions of Mackenzie King were derived early from his grandfather Mackenzie and the conservative liberalism of his father John King.

Mackenzie King stepped into the leadership of the Liberal Party and became Prime Minister of Canada in the most formative period of the Canadian nation. Conscious that a new nation was being founded out of the mixing of people of different national stock, he aimed to weld them into a single nation while clinging to the best of their varied traditions. While he approached every new crisis cautiously, he yet firmly untied the knots of imperial control and replaced them with the bonds of fraternal cooperation. Violent ruptures he abhorred, although his pulse beat a little faster and his eyes gleamed a little brighter when he glanced at the thousand-pound offer for the head of "grandfather Mackenzie." Hence his role of mediator and commonwealth builder.

Nor did he stop at that. For the rise of Canada to full nationhood coincided with world-shaking events from which emerged a new correlation of nations in world organization, first in the League of Nations and later in the United Nations. His attitude to both corresponded to the growth of Canada as a nation and its power as a modern state, reaching in the latter the full expression already made manifest in the course he had taken in the shaping of the "Commonwealth." The historian of tomorrow will classify Mackenzie King as Canada's "statesman of independence," who led Canada from the status of a colony to that of an independent nation and substituted "Commonwealth" relations in place of "Imperial" relations.

CHAPTER VII

JAN CHRISTIAAN SMUTS

wrote:
                              IN 1917, WINSTON CHURCHILL

There arrives in England from the outer marches of the Empire a new and altogether extraordinary man. The stormy and hazardous roads he has travelled by would fill the acts and scenes of drama. He has warred against us; well we know it. He has quelled rebellion against our own flag with unswerving loyalty and unfailing shrewdness. He has led raids at desperate odds and conquered provinces by scientific strategy. His astonishing career and his versatile achievements are only the index of a profound sagacity and a cool, far-reaching comprehension.

Thus the old imperial warrior welcomed the new, Jan Christiaan Smuts, from the southern reaches of the black continent of Africa amidst the gloom of the First World War.

It was not the first time this South African mantle-bearer of Rhodes had been to England and met Winston Churchill. They first met during the Boer War when the Boers captured Ladysmith and Churchill was taken prisoner. They next met in London in 1907 when Smuts came to England to ask for responsible self-government for South Africa from the newly elected Liberal government headed by Campbell-Bannerman. Of that occasion Smuts says:

I saw Churchill, Morley, Elgin, Lloyd George, Campbell-Bannerman. The only one I had met before was Churchill. . . . He asked me if I had ever known of a conquered people being al-

170

lowed to govern themselves. I said no, but we did not want to govern ourselves without England's assistance, and that was the truth, we could not. . . . The Boer has fought for independence, the Englishman has fought for empire. All have fought for what they considered highest. Now the highest is Union . . . and there is only one thing the people of South Africa can do—become a united people.

That meeting of Smuts and the British Government marked off South Africa as the second of the white governed colonies of Britain to reach "Dominion Status," and drive the British Empire along the road to "Commonwealth." The Boer War had begun as a classic piece of British imperial brigandage. It finished with a unique act of statesmanship whereby the conquered and the conquerors joined in a common purpose of uniting the white population of South Africa in self-government and establishing new relations of peoples and governments within the British Empire. The first of the white colonies to do this was Canada which emerged as a by-product of the American and French Revolutions. The triumph of Washington and formation of the United States drove the "Loyalists" of England into the expanses of Canada, providing Canada with its basic English population. The defeat of the French in the Napoleonic wars sealed the fate of the French colonists of Quebec and destined them to become French Canadians and integrate them in the Canadian Dominion of the British Empire.

There is a singular parallel to this in the emergence of the Union of South Africa. Smuts is an Afrikander of Dutch origin. He derived from the stock of Dutchmen who had settled in South Africa during the last three hundred years. An outpost of the Dutch East India Company, founding a calling station at the Cape of Good Hope, began the process in 1652. In the course of the following centuries Dutch settlers came and slowly pushed inward into a continent so vast that to this day great stretches of its territory are still unchartered and the surface of its resources has only been scratched.

The Dutch and the few fellow German and Huguenot settlers soon left their past European life behind them and became the pastoral nomads, Boer patriarchs with oxen and trek wagons pushing into the back country, subordinating the primitive black population to their service or driving them into other regions of the vast continent. Far away from the main streams of white civilization in Europe their numbers grew slowly. Meanwhile, they ossified in isolation with the religious and social ideas the pioneers had brought from Europe. The back-country Boers, of whom Paul Kruger became a representative ruler, firmly believed that slavery was sanctioned by the Bible and that white supremacy was as natural as the phenomenon of day and night. At the beginning of the eighteenth century there were approximately five thousand Boers scattered over a wide region of South Africa and their numbers were steadily growing.

They were an outcrop of Dutch imperial expansion during the mercantile period but before the close of the eighteenth century naval supremacy had passed from the Dutch to the British and London had replaced Amsterdam as the financial center of Europe. The English East India Company beat the Dutch East India Company in the markets of the East. When the French armies overran the Netherlands in the Napoleonic wars the British in 1795-96 occupied the Cape as a "strategic necessity" and made their occupation permanent in 1806. Then began the same kind of conflict between British and Dutch in South Africa as that which had marked the history of North America between the British and the French, except that the South African struggle was ever bedeviled by the "black versus white" problem. This problem had baffled the Dutch. It baffled the British and today baffles the Afrikanders. The Dutch had no dubiety about slavery or about pushing their frontiers farther and farther into the continent at the expense of the black man. When the British came to South Africa and annexed Natal they arrived not merely as farmers and trekkers to the North, they came as representatives of the industrial revolution and the new commerce that grew with it. With that industrial revolution had come new ideas about slavery and consequently new ideas about how the white supremacy was to be maintained. The British were at one with the Dutch on the latter issue, but not on ways and means! This clash of ideas about slavery gave the Boers in the Slachters Nek Rebellion of 1815 their "Boston Massacre." The rebellion had its origin in the maltreatment of a slave by a Boer farmer who was consequently brought to court. The rebellion was fiercely suppressed by British troops. It was the growing immigration of the British in the eastern districts of Cape Colony and the new British colony of Natal, bringing with it land hunger and the demand for the abolition of slavery throughout the British Empire, which produced the great trek of the Boers to the north beyond the Orange River. There, the Boers were left to fight the Zulus and ultimately to found the Orange Free State and the Transvaal.

Uneasy decades of Anglo-Boer relations were suddenly electrified in the 1870's by the discovery in Griqualand West and the Witwatersrand of diamonds and of gold in undreamed-of quantities. Griqualand West was the "No Man's Land" between Cape Colony and the Orange Free State. The Witwatersrand was well within the Transvaal. Diamonds and gold were as dynamite amidst human relations. Hordes of adventurers from all parts of the world, chiefly from Britain and America, flocked to the regions of discovery between 1870 and 1890. In this period the nineteenth century really moved in on the seventeenth, for the Boers were still living in the latter century politically, religiously, and economically. The British annexed the diamond fields and there grew up like mushrooms overnight the *Uitlanders* of the Transvaal, the new type of "settlers" of the goldfields. Here began the fierce and relentless fight of Kruger and his burghers to protect their accustomed way of life from being transformed by the newcomers, the intruders scrambling for gold. Out of this attempt to achieve the impossible came war, openly declared in 1877, between the Boers and the British. For four years the Boers waged a stubborn fight and became a formidable military force, achieving military victories at Laing's Nek and Majuba Hill in 1881. The Boers emerged from the fighting with the Transvaal and the Orange Free State intact and independent. But they could not stop the progress of the nineteenth century against the seventeenth. The Rand gold reef began to pay and its industrial population of Uitlanders claimed political rights which Kruger and his burghers could not grant on penalty of losing their own political supremacy and their long-established customs.

Into this arena came Cecil Rhodes, the British empire-builder. He organized a syndicate which secured control of ninety percent of the diamonds of South Africa. This was the first source of great power. But his vision was limited neither by the diamond fields nor by the prospects of great wealth. He was a dreamer of imperial dreams which encompassed all the unclaimed lands north of the Transvaal and a vast African empire. He was convinced too that the time to make his dreams come true had arrived and that nothing should be allowed to stand in the way of their realization. He organized the British South Africa Company to carry railway and telegraph lines from the Cape to Cairo, encourage immigration, promote trade, develop mineral concessions, secure native rights. That, however, was only part of his dream. He wanted the British colonists and the Boer republics to form a customs union as a step toward a political federation with the British flag held high above the republican flags which would wave over local governments controlling local affairs. His vision embraced a whole continent equal to more than a sixth of the land surface of the earth and a British empire that would one day re-absorb the America which had been lost by the stupidities and absence of vision of England's eighteenth-century rulers. Rhodes had vision and power and dynamic energy and was utterly unscrupulous in his haste to conquer. Kruger and the Boers stood in his way, for his eyes were on territory immediately beyond the Transvaal which was one day to be named Rhodesia. The Matabeles, the natives of this territory, also stood in the way. They were dealt with in summary military fashion and the British flag flew over Bulawayo. That was 1893. Two years later, Rhodes was the Premier of Cape Colony, controller of the De Beers Diamond Syndicate at Kimberley, of the Goldfields Company of the Rand, and head of the chartered British South Africa Company. The time had arrived to move once more against Kruger and the Boers. Through his lieutenant, Dr. Jameson, he conspired to aid an "uprising of the Uitlanders of the Witwatersrand" with five hundred armed troopers of Rhodes' British South Africa Company Police. The "rising" was premature and Kruger's government smashed it. But the issue of citizenship for the Uitlanders of the Transvaal remained insoluble. Kruger could not grant citizenship to a mass of foreigners who would soon outnumber his burghers and destroy the old order. What the "uprising" failed to accomplish could only be settled by the arbitrament of war between the British and the Dutch, both remembering Laing's Nek and Majuba Hill. To the Boers they inspired confidence that what they had succeeded in doing in 1881 they could repeat. To the British they were defeats to be avenged. But beyond all that was the Rhodesian vision of the African empire. The war came on October 9, 1899, and raged until May 31, 1902, with the Boers defeated and the British militarily supreme.

It was in this conflict between the British and the Boers that there came to the side of Kruger a new figure who would, out of this war and defeat, take the mantle of Rhodes from the British and step onto the world stage as a statesman whom Winston Churchill would in 1917 hail as "an extraordinary man."

Jan Christiaan Smuts is "extraordinary" not merely because of his participation in many scenes of dramatic incident but because he symbolizes in his checkered career the attempted fusion of the Boers and British of South Africa into a new nation of "Afrikanders." As definitely as Mackenzie King represented the emergence of the Canadian nation out of the British and French stock of Canada, Smuts represents the emergence of the Afrikander nation of the Union of South Africa.

He was born in 1870, the same year as Lenin, though two men could not be more unlike in social origin, training, and purpose in life. There the coincidence ends. Jan Smuts was the son of Jacobus Abraham Smuts, a well-to-do yeoman farmer of Dutch origin, of large girth and ample paunch, the physical proof of standing and prosperity. They lived and prospered on the farm named Bovenplatz outside the village of Riebeck West, between thirty and forty miles north of Cape Town. They belonged to those Dutch settlers, of whom there were many, who had refused to trek farther northward under the pressure of the British. In Jan's earliest years the family moved from Bovenplatz, which was a family farm and wanted by the elder brother of Jacobus Smuts, to another farm known as Stone Fountain, a few miles away. The Smuts family flourished there on primitive baronial lines, in a large house without baths or lavatories, but on rich corn-growing land known as the "Black Land" because the soil at a distance looks black. Jan's mother was an unusual housewife for a Dutch farmer of the Cape. She came from an old French Huguenot family, was very religious and very well educated. She had been to school in Cape Town, had musical talent, could read and write French, and was fond of reading. Perhaps it was from his mother that Jan Smuts inherited a passion for reading, which annoyed his father immensely. The latter would have been content had his son been satisfied to learn the three R's and confined his reading to the Bible.

Stone Fountain was isolated, a speck in the great Zwartland, miles away from the nearest village, and the roads to it were mere tracks of deep dust in summer and quagmires in winter. Transport in the days of Jan's boyhood was by large wooden wagons on wooden wheels hitched to eight or more slow-moving oxen. The contact of the folk of Stone Fountain with their nearest neighbors was made four times a year when the Calvinist pastor came to the nearest church for the Holy Communion.

The boyhood of Jan Smuts was spent on this farm. When he grew big enough he helped to look after the geese and the pigs and the sheep, helped the black men and the half-caste farm hands. An old Hottentot shepherd later taught him to drive the cattle and round them up, and filled him with weird tales of the native people. Jan started life as a sickly babe and grew up thin and rickety, taking little interest in anything, dirty, barefoot, and raggedly dressed. At ten years of age his father decided it was time for him to go to school. The nearest one was at Riebeck West, too far away for Jan to be a day boy. As a result, he was boarded at the house of the headmaster. It was here, in his third term, that this shy frightened boy who hated the discipline of the new social life suddenly developed a passion for knowledge by reading. He began to read everything he could lay his hands on and at all times. He wished neither to play games with other scholars nor to make friends. He became a veritable bookworm, gathering facts and ideas which became imprinted on his mind as on a photographic plate. He lived on books and passed examinations with ease. His father came to the conclusion that his son was a freak. He had wanted his son to be a farmer like himself. He discussed his son's future with his wife and came to the conclusion that he had best become a pastor. Jan passed the entrance examination for Victoria College in the town of Stellenbosch. He was studious, serious, with no sense of humor, frightened of the wicked world, unsociable. He wrote to a professor at the college:

"I trust you will favour me by keeping your eye on me. . . ."
For he considered Stellenbosch "as a place where a large and pu-
erile element exists" and so "affords scope for moral, and, what
is more important, religious temptation, which if yielded to will
eclipse alike the expectation of my parents and the intentions of
myself. . . . For of what use will a mind, enlarged and refined
in all possible ways, be to me if my religion be a deserted pilot,
and morality a wreck?" (From *Grey Steel* by Armstrong, p. 28.)

So Stellebosch was a continuation of Riebeck West and the
somber frightened student continued to bury himself in the
books, studied literature and science, German and High
Dutch, English and Greek and botany. The prim and proper
Jan fell in love with the prim and proper Miss Sibylla Mar-
garetha Krige, a fellow student at Victoria College. He was
seventeen. She was sixteen. He was tall and lanky. She was
small, serious, her hair brushed severely back from her
forehead, and very proper. He wanted hero worship and she
gave him hero worship. They sedately walked side by side
with books tucked underneath their arms discussing the solemn textbooks in which they lived. But the idea of becoming
a pastor vanished. Walt Whitman and Shelley had shaken
his primitive religious ideas. So he decided to study law and
complete his studies in England. He came out of the college
examinations second on the list for the degree of Bachelor
of Arts. He won the Ebden scholarship worth a hundred
pounds a year and a number of small bursaries. In 1891, he
said good-bye to Miss Krige and sailed for England. He went
to Christ's College, Cambridge, and there pursued his isolated, all-absorbing course, as at Stellebosch and Riebeck
West. He was not interested in England and all the life
around him. The pale-faced, long-jowled, thin, weedy-look-
ing man went straight to the books and stayed there working all day and far into the night. He took supreme honors
in the Cambridge finals, was admitted to the Middle Temple
in May 1894, won many prizes, was offered a professorship
at Christ's College, refused it, and sailed for Cape Town,

with a mind like that of a Robespierre in its formal scholastic brilliance and absence of human warmth. All his knowledge was derived from the books and the real battle of life in human association had yet to begin.

Jan Christiaan Smuts was twenty-four years of age when he returned to South Africa to begin his manhood's career. Those years had been eventful in the history of Anglo-Boer relations; the country was on the eve of dramatic developments which were to tear Smuts out of his isolation and fling him into the foreground of world affairs. Up to this time he had had ten years of childhood on a farm on the South African veldt and fourteen years of intellectual swotting in school, college, university, and law chambers. In the midst of those years, the Boers, who had trekked northward and established the Boer republics—the Transvaal and the Orange Free State—had waged a war against the British and come through with their republics intact and the Laing's Nek and Majuba Hill victories to their credit. But in that war, the prelude to a greater one in which the outcome would be different, it was revealed how completely the Dutch of South Africa had become detached from their original stock in Europe and how great was the change that had taken place in the world's imperial relations. The Dutch of South Africa were no longer "homeland" Dutch but Afrikanders, although the Kruger republicans retained the outlook of their forefathers. When they clashed with the British they could no longer count on the support of the Dutch in Holland, just as the French in Canada could not count longer on the support of the French in France, while the British, who in both cases were in the minority in the colonies when the fighting began, could count on and did receive in both cases the full support of the imperial forces from the homeland. The end of the first Boer war could only be a truce which was to end shortly after young Smuts returned to South Africa. But the shaping of the Dutch republics by the northward-trekking Boers was only one phase of the trans-

formation of the Dutch settlers of South Africa into Afrikanders. The other emerged from those who did not trek to
the republics but remained in the British-occupied regions.
These were more numerous than the British settlers, even in
Cape Colony and Natal. They had retained their private
rights of property and their political rights as citizens. They
were friendly to the British in South Africa and thought that
by their majority they could determine the future of South
Africa and build an Afrikander nation. They formed the
Afrikander Bond under the leadership of J. H. Hofmeyer.
The Bond members wanted a United South Africa and disapproved of Kruger's policy of creating Dutch republics cut
off from the Cape. Jacobus Smuts, father of Jan, was an active
member of the Bond. He was also the member for Malmesbury in the Cape Parliament.

In those first twenty-four years of Jan Smuts' life there had
also come the discovery of diamonds and gold and the invasion of the Uitlanders, the new industrialists, speculators,
empire-builders. At the head of the new power was Cecil
Rhodes, the master builder of the British Empire, ruthless,
unscrupulous, a dynamic man who would let nothing stand
in his way. In the days when Jan Smuts was a student at Stellebosch College he had been chosen by the college to reply
to an address by Rhodes to the college students. That reply
arrested the attention of Rhodes because the youngster had
echoed his ideas about the future of Africa. Rhodes had
made friends with the Bond and Hofmeyer. When Smuts returned to Africa he had still not made up his mind as to his
own future. His youthful scholasticism had driven old Jacobus Smuts to abandon the idea of making a farmer of his
son and send him toward the church. But scholastic development had given Jan new ideas about religion and he had become a lawyer. Immediately he returned from England he
set up as a barrister. A barrister needs, however, other qualities besides a profound knowledge of the law. Young Smuts
was constitutionally incapable of exercising those human

qualities which attract colleagues and clients. If his reserved, haughty manner and somber presence kept his colleagues at a distance they succeeded also in keeping clients away. He took on other jobs, examined students in High Dutch for a fee, wrote articles for the Dutch and English papers on such lofty subjects as the "Moral Conception of Existence," "The Place of Thrift in the Affairs of Life," "The Native Problem," "Immigration." Through his work as a journalist rather than his activities as a lawyer he became absorbed in politics. At last he had found his way to common activity with his father. He joined the Bond and his father, member for Malmesbury, brought him to Hofmeyer. The latter brought him to Rhodes, and Rhodes harnessed Smuts to work for his imperial vision of the future of Africa. Smuts became a Rhodes worshiper; Rhodes was his hero and his leader.

He had just broken into his stride as Rhodes' trumpeter when the truce between the Kruger Boers and the British neared its end. There was trouble. There always had been and always would be trouble in the diamond and gold industry centers, until the showdown between Boer and Briton settled the Uitlander question. The Uitlander question could only be settled by the defeat of the Boers and the triumph of the nineteenth century over the seventeenth. There was trouble in Kimberley among the Uitlanders and some of the Dutch members of the Bond, like Olive Schreiner the novelist, suspected treachery on the part of Rhodes. Rhodes came under fire and somebody had to go to a great meeting in Kimberley Town Hall to defend him. Behold! the scholar Smuts, now the banner-bearer of Rhodes, boldly answered for his hero. He enjoyed a triumph, but Olive Schreiner was right and Smuts was wrong. That was but the prelude to the Jameson Raid and the Jameson Raid was the prelude to the great "showdown" between Boer and Briton. The Jameson Raid made nonsense of Smuts' speech at Kimberley and down he fell from his pedestal in imperial politics.

He retired to his father's home in Riebeck West, bitterly disappointed and disillusioned. His hero and leader had turned out to be unprincipled and treacherous! It took a long time for Smuts to live down his Kimberley speech on Rhodes. He was publicly laughed at and ridiculed, and nothing hurt Smuts so much as ridicule. But the Jameson Raid did more than knock Smuts off his pedestal. It turned the Bond against the British. The Bond repudiated Rhodes. The Jameson Raid united all Dutchmen from Kruger down to every Dutch man and woman in all South Africa, and everyone realized that the great explosion was near at hand. Smuts recovered, left his father's home, closed his office in Cape Town, applied to be admitted to the Transvaal Bar, and opened an office in Johannesburg. He toured the towns and villages of South Africa, preaching fierce hatred of the British, and became more Dutch than Kruger. He became Kruger's Attorney General and went to Pretoria, married Miss Krige, and his course was set for a legal and political career. The year was 1898. On October 9, 1899, Kruger's ultimatum to the British expired and the Boers and Britain were at war. At first, Smuts was Kruger's right-hand man at headquarters in Pretoria, but the war was quickly transformed into guerrilla warfare. The Boer army was destroyed and the commandos scattered about the country. Kruger, old and broken, was shipped to Holland. Smuts left Pretoria and office work and joined de la Rey, the cleverest of the Dutch leaders in raiding warfare. Kitchener wanted a quick peace and sought a meeting with General Botha. Botha called Smuts to his side to meet Kitchener and General French, then Chief of Staff of Kitchener's army. The four met at Middleburg. Botha and Smuts demanded the independence of the Transvaal and the Free State. Kitchener refused. The Dutch must recognize the supremacy of the British. Smuts thought the Dutch could still beat the British and refused to budge an inch. The fighting proceeded. Smuts sought to rouse the Dutch of the Cape to rise against the

English. With three hundred and forty men in all he set off, dodged and doubled across the Transvaal and Orange Free State, entered the Cape, plunged into English territory, raided through Cape Colony with adventures innumerable. A new Smuts had emerged. The bookworm had been transformed into a vigorous, daring leader of hazards, fearless and ruthless. One day, in the middle of May 1902, two English officers with white flags came looking for General Smuts and found him. They brought an invitation from Lord Kitchener for him to meet with the other Dutch leaders at Vereeniging, a village on the border of the Transvaal and the Orange Free State, to discuss terms of peace. The end of the war had come. The Boers were beaten. They were faced with the alternatives of making terms or being wiped out as a nation. Thirty delegates from the Transvaal and thirty from the Free State met the British headed by Lord Milner, the High Commissioner of the Cape, Kitchener and French. The Dutch were stubborn, many of them prepared to fight to the death. Smuts was not a delegate but General Botha had called for him as his adviser. The Dutch met separately to discuss the terms. There had been a deadlock with the British. On the night of the deadlock Kitchener took Smuts aside. He said to him:

"Look here, Smuts, there is something on my mind that I want to tell you. I can only give you my opinion, but my opinion is that in two years' time a Liberal Government will come to power and it will grant you a constitution for South Africa."

"That is a very important pronouncement," replied Smuts. "If one could be sure of the likes of that, it would make a great difference."

"As I say," repeated Kitchener, "it is only my opinion, but honestly I do believe that that will happen." (*Grey Steel* by Armstrong, p. 135.)

That conversation was another decisive turning point in Smuts' career. He abandoned the extreme republicanism he had adopted after the betrayal by Rhodes and resumed the

Rhodesian trail, but with the determination to take it out of the hands of the British. What could not be done by military means could be done by political means in the course of time. He glimpsed this possibility the moment Kitchener opened up the perspective of a Liberal victory in Britain and a South African constitution. The Dutch delegation called on him to speak although he was not a delegate. They acknowledged him as a leader and now he spoke as one. Facing the war-weary, yet tough, determined men, he said:

> I am one of those who provoked this war. I accept the responsibility and it gives me the right to speak. As soldiers none of you are afraid. As a military force you are unconquered and you can fight on; but here to-day you represent not the commandos only but the nation as a whole. . . .
> WE fought for independence, but we must not sacrifice the nation on the altar of independence. . . .
> Brethren, we have sworn to stand to the bitter end. Let us be brave, and acknowledge that the bitter end has come. . . .
> It has been a war for freedom . . . Its results we leave in God's hands. Perhaps it is His will to lead our nation through defeat, through abasement, yea, and even through the Valley of the Shadow of Death, to the glory of a nobler future, to the light of a brighter day. (*Grey Steel* by Armstrong, p. 138.)

He had staked his future on the Liberal election victory and a constitution for South Africa. The delegates voted for acceptance one hour before the ultimatum expired, and the peace was made. But the interim period, between the signing of the peace and the coming of the Liberal government in England and the new constitution for South Africa, was a testing time for Smuts. Lord Milner was the High Commissioner and virtual ruler of South Africa. He was no Liberal. Smuts returned to the law, morose and depressed. There was no scope for him. At the Vereeniging Conference the Dutch commissioned Botha, de la Rey, and De Wet to go to Europe and seek relief funds for the Dutch who had suffered in the war. When Botha returned, Smuts swung in behind him as he had done previously behind Rhodes and Kruger, to found a new political party—"The People's Party" —aiming at "complete self-government" for the Transvaal. These two men, Botha and Smuts, became the acknowledged leaders of the continuing struggle of the Dutch for self-government.

At last, in 1906, the Liberal government arrived in England. That was the moment when Smuts stepped into the world's political arena. With Botha's approval Smuts set off post-haste for London for the memorable meeting with the British leaders, Campbell-Bannerman, Lloyd George, Asquith, Churchill, from which emerged "self-government for the Dutch within the British Empire."

Now there was no further questioning as to his course. The Boer War had hammered into him the fact that, however much he and the rest of the Dutch might treasure their national origin and heritage, once the umbilical cord of the emigrating Dutch had been severed and the imperial power of the "mother country" was no longer at the service of its offspring in a distant land, the Dutch "colonials" had not the military means to defeat an imperial power determined to conquer them. What he had see clearly enough as a student and hero-worshiper of Rhodes he now saw from another angle. Then he saw with Rhodes that the future of South Africa lay in the union of British and Dutch into an Afrikander nation of white rulers founding an African empire under the British flag, under the hegemony of the British. He saw that again but differently. It should be under the British flag and have British support for its expansion and support in international relations but it should come under the hegemony of the Dutch. The Afrikander nation that was to be should be basically Dutch and absorb the British settlers and immigrants. The leadership of the Afrikander nation should be in the hands of its Dutch constituents.

The British vision of Rhodes had become the Dutch Afrikander vision of Smuts and he would pursue it with the same relentlessness as the hero of his youth.

The first step toward it had been taken in London when Smuts and Botha secured from the British Government "self-government for the Transvaal and the Orange Free State within the Empire." The next step was to secure the union of all the Dutch and British states within South Africa, reducing them to provinces of the larger Union. That was no easy matter, although on their return from London Botha and Smuts were the virtual dictators of the Transvaal. The Boers of the Transvaal and the Orange Free State had not lost their hatred of the British overnight. Smuts' wife, far better educated than most of the women of these countries, hated the English and would have nothing to do with them. The old Boer Leaders, De Wet, Hertzog, Steyn, Merriman, did not share the vision of Smuts. Indeed, the original division of the Dutch into those who wanted complete independence and those who preferred to dwell with the British in Natal and the Cape remained. But two years later, after a memorable convention of representatives of the colonies in Durban, Botha and Smuts again appeared in London with a draft of a constitution for the "Union of South Africa—a Dominion of the British Empire." The Imperial Parliament debated it, approved it, and King Edward VII signed it in December 1909. The architect of that Constitution was Jan Christiaan Smuts. Botha and Smuts now ruled all South Africa. In the first Government of South Africa, following the elections of 1910, Botha became Prime Minister and Smuts held three ministerial posts, Interior, Mines, and Defense.

Thus, the second stage of the emergence of the Afrikander nation had been reached in quick time. But only the second stage. The old loyalties of the Boers now reshaped themselves and Hertzog founded a rival party to the South African Party led by Botha and Smuts. With Hertzog came Dr.

Malan, a Dutch pastor who edited a Dutch paper, *Die Burger*, who would one day supersede Smuts, and they, with Steyn of the Free State and De Wet and Tielman Roos, formed the Nationalist Party—Dutch, Republican, hostile to the English, and seeking to reverse the course of history. It appeared on the surface of things that the future would work itself out through parliamentary democracy and peaceful political disputations. But South Africa did not exist in a vacuum. It was the most southern region of a vast continent and six thousand miles from Europe.

In this same period of the conquest of South Africa by the British and their conflict with the Dutch, culminating in their formal incorporation within the British Empire, other imperial powers had entered the African continent. One, in particular, had become a close neighbor of the Union. The Germans had formed colonies in South West Africa and in East Africa, and Germany in Europe was on the point of challenging the British Empire for world supremacy. In 1914 the clash of arms began and the new Union of South Africa led by Botha and Smuts was brought face to face with the most fateful choice ever presented to any leaders of men or nation. Should they use this hour of crisis in the affairs of the British Empire to line up with the enemies of Britain, as a means to complete Dutch independence, or should they accept the obligations of Dominion Status within the British Empire as the means to the fulfillment of the Afrikander vision of Smuts? There was no hesitation on the part of either Botha or Smuts in leading the Union of South Africa into the war on the side of Britain. Smuts considered not only that the Afrikanders had already virtual independence and hegemony in South African affairs but that here was the opportunity to enlarge the Union by driving the Germans out of East and West Africa. His vision was of an Afrikander empire, now rapidly taking shape. But the past still held the Dutch National Party, led by Hertzog and Dr. Malan, in its grip. They regarded Britain's difficulties as

Dutch opportunities to strike again for the Dutch republic and severance of all association with Britain. Before ever Botha and Smuts could carry out their plans to conquer German West Africa, civil war was upon them. Without hesitation they smashed the revolt with the same decisiveness and ruthlessness that Smuts had smashed a general strike on the Rand a few months before. The revolt over, General Botha led an army into German West Africa and within a few more months had completely driven the Germans out of their colony. But Hertzog and Malan remained to organize the political opposition of the defeated rebels within the Union. In a General Election, held in 1915, Botha and Smuts were returned to power once more but only with the aid of the English and the South African Labor Party votes. At the end of 1915, the British Government offered Smuts charge of the military campaign in German East Africa with the rank of major-general. He accepted, and for nearly two years he chased the elusive Von Lettow across vast stretches of territory until Botha recalled him to Pretoria. In 1917 he was needed for other work. The British Government had invited the dominions to send representatives to an Imperial War Conference. Botha sent Smuts.

His arrival in London was an event. He was received with applause and hailed as the first successful Allied general of the war who had driven the Germans, wholesale, out of Africa. Now he was in his element, a principal figure in the metropolis of the British Empire. Away from the domestic problems and the bitter conflict of little men fighting to move Africa backward, the full stature of Smuts as a man of vision and purpose among statesmen of his generation was soon manifest. In South Africa he was not popular and never had been but he was intellectually far ahead of any other politician of his homeland. He was, however, arrogant in his intellectuality and impatient in his dealings with the ignorant. He had the mentality of a dictator and resented criticism. His appointment to the Imperial War Cabinet meant he could leave the South African domestic irritations behind and have full scope for his widest interests in the affairs of the world and especially to pursue his vision of the future of the South African Union in the affairs of man.

He arrived in London in the darkest year of the war for the Allies. The U-boat warfare was at its fiercest and Britain and France were exhausting their resources. America showed no signs of joining the Allies. Czarist Russia had collapsed and revolution was spreading far and wide. England and her leaders were conscious as never before of support from her imperial dominions beyond the seas. Hence the invitation to leaders of the dominions to membership in the Imperial War Cabinet. The dominions, in turn, were conscious of the new dependence of Britain upon them and their own development in nationhood. None was more conscious of these things than Smuts on his arrival in London. It was his full consciousness of the realities of power relations within the British Empire which had enabled him to make up his mind as to where he wished to lead the Union of South Africa, and to step surely and decisively in the Imperial Conference of 1917. He had been delighted to accept the invitation to be a member of the Imperial War Cabinet. This act of centralization of imperial authority was a necessity of the war against an external power. But let no one have the idea that such an authority would govern the empire itself. This he made clear at the 1917 Imperial Conference when he affirmed that there should be full recognition of the dominions as autonomous nations of an imperial commonwealth, that they should have an adequate voice in foreign policy, and that there should be effective means of continuous consultation on all imperial matters. It was at this memorable conference that Smuts led the dominions in the demand for independent representation of the dominions at the Peace Conference and won that right. Indeed it went further and ensured that the King should ratify the Peace Treaty only after the Dominion Parliaments had approved it.

Speaking at a banquet organized in his honor by the House of Lords and the House of Commons on May 15, he boldly outlined his views of the changed position of the British Empire:

I think we are inclined to make mistakes in thinking about this group of nations to which we belong, because too often we think about it as one State. We are not a State, I think the very expression "Empire" is misleading, because it makes people think that we are one community, to which the word "Empire" can appropriately be applied. Germany is an Empire. Rome was an Empire. India is an Empire. But we are a system of nations. We are not a State, but a community of States and nations. We are far greater than any Empire which has ever existed, and by using this ancient expression we really disguise the main fact that our whole position is different, and that we are not one State or nation or Empire, but a whole world by ourselves, consisting of many nations, of many States, and all sorts of communities, under one flag. . . .

What I feel in regard to all the empires of the past, and even in regard to the United States, is that the effort has always been towards forming one nation. All the empires we have known in the past and that exist today are founded on the idea of assimilation, of trying to force human material into one mould. Your whole idea and basis is entirely different. You do not want to standardise the nations of the British Empire; you want to develop them towards greater, fuller nationality. These communities, the offspring of the Mother Country, or territories like my own, which have been annexed after the vicissitudes of war, must not be moulded on any one pattern. You want them to develop freely on the principles of self-government, and therefore your whole idea is very different from anything that has ever existed before. That is the fundamental fact we have to bear in mind— that this British Commonwealth of Nations does not stand for standardisation or denationalisation, but for the fuller, richer, and more various life of all the nations comprised in it.

He was distorting history somewhat in giving the impression that the British Empire had been built with these ideas in mind or that they governed its purpose. The fact of the

matter is that the ideas to which Smuts was giving utterance were taking shape in the minds of British leaders and
governments only as the dominions and colonies asserted
themselves as nations and states determined upon self-government. It was the pattern they assumed under pressure. Ireland had staged at least one armed revolt per century during
the last seven centuries and was still governed from London.
The Indian empire was still governed from London, and its
war of independence in 1857 had been decisively crushed by
military means. Canada was the first dominion to be conceded "Home Rule" as a result of its independent fight. It
had taken two Boer wars to produce the Union of South
Africa. But Smuts was the first of the statesmen of his day to
perceive the fundamental difference in the structure of the
British Empire as compared with the American and others.

But he did not limit his actions to the relations of the Union of South Africa to the British Commonwealth. Incidentally it was he who coined the phrase "British Commonwealth of Nations" in his "banquet" speech. It was he, too,
who caught on to the idea of President Wilson that after the
war there should be a "League of Nations" to keep the peace
of the world. He translated the idea into a plan for its constitution. He achieved the reputation in London of being
"a wise counselor" and until the end of the war he was used
by the Imperial War Cabinet for all kinds of special missions and investigations. He lived at the Savoy Hotel, dressed
as a rule in the uniform of a lieutenant-general, quietly
avoiding social functions as much as possible. Lloyd George,
the Prime Minister, used him as a personal adviser and put
him on many committees. He formed a special committee
to advise the Cabinet on war policy, and one to watch events
in the Near East, and he put Smuts on both. He formed a
War Priorities Committee to allot men to where they were
most needed and he made Smuts its chairman. After London
was bombed in July 1917 by twenty-two Gotha airplanes it

was Smuts who worked out a complete plan for the defense of London from aerial attack. It was accepted by the British Government and then he extended the plan to cover all England. On the basis of his guerrilla fighting in South Africa he had built up a reputation, or at least had acquired the reputation, as a "brilliant general." Lloyd George had this view and the War Cabinet were influenced by his support of the Haig plan for the offensive of 1917, an offensive which proved disastrous with the loss of more than four hundred thousand men in the mud and filth and slaughter of Passchendaele. Smuts was a politician and not a military genius. Lloyd George continued to use him as an adviser and as a man to undertake special missions until he became annoyed with Smuts' pessimism concerning the course of the war. At one time after his arrival in England, Smuts held the view that "the Allies would win the war and lose the peace." Now after Passchendaele and the German offensive of March 1916, his reports from France were gloomy. But the Americans came into the war in 1917 and on November 11, 1918, the fighting ended with the Allies victorious.

The war at an end, Smuts was free to prepare for his role in the Peace Conference. Here, he was the voice of the Union of South Africa and he pursued his own line. His part as the representative of South Africa in the War Cabinet had built up for him a great reputation. It had been a great experience for him in which he had learned much, not the least of which was that the war had changed the power relations of the nations. Empires had been shattered by it. A new phenomenon of social revolution, on a great scale, had changed the face of Europe and of Asia. The Russian Revolution, sweeping west and east, appalled him. He had grown up in the old school of imperial thinkers and leaders. Socialism of any kind was anathema to him. Bolshevism was of the devil. He would, if he could, do with it what he had done with the labor revolt in South Africa—smash it ruthlessly and without mercy. A national revolt he understood and was sympathetic to. A social revolt was beyond his comprehension, the American and French Revolutions notwithstanding. He had a philosophy which excluded this phenomenon but encompassed nationalism and imperialism. He gave it the name of Holism, observing that small units unite into big units and big units into bigger units until they include the whole. So the small colonies of South Africa had united into the Union of South Africa. It would absorb German West Africa. Later East Africa, Rhodesia, and more and more along the route of Rhodes' Cape to Cairo vision. Meanwhile South Africa had united with England and the Dominions of the Empire and the empire would now unite into a League of all the Nations not red. He viewed social problems through the eyes of the anthropologist, instead of anthropology through the eyes of social science. Hence he was at one with Clemenceau and the rest in excluding Russia from the Peace Conference, and his project for the League of Nations was conceived as a world bloc against Russia as well as an instrument for maintaining peace among the rest of the nations.

Smuts won a resounding triumph when he took his stand with the dominions of the British Empire to win independent representation at the Peace Conference. General Botha joined him. They were both determined that whatever else might merge from the conference, Germany should not get back her colonies in Africa. They were not only "bad neighbors" but they were convinced that one day all Africa south of the equator would belong to the Union of South Africa. They got out of the Peace Conference a mandate for the "trusteeship" of German South West Africa but not German East Africa. England held on to that. Smuts did not quibble about the "trusteeship" business. He knew in fact that German South West Africa had come within his grip. Later on, he would demonstrate that. For after the Second World War, which buried the League of Nations, the victors created the United Nations which wanted to take over the

mandate system under another name. Smuts refused to allow
"interference" in South African affairs, which, in this case,
meant German South West Africa. But his plan for the
League of Nations at the Peace Conference went through.
President Wilson thought it was "the goods," got on well
with Smuts, and it was Wilson, Cecil, and Smuts who were
responsible for the "Covenant of the League of Nations."

When the conference was over Botha and Smuts returned
to South Africa. Hardly had they arrived when Botha died.
The Governor-General of South Africa, the King's representative, called on Smuts to be Prime Minister of the Union
of South Africa in succession to Botha.

He had now reached the apex of his career. In his young
manhood he had been understudy to Kruger, then understudy to Botha. At last he was understudy to nobody. He had
arrived. Since the beginning of 1917 he had been in England
and Europe handling world affairs with the great men of his
day. Nobody could deny that he had emerged from that experience with added prestige. Now he had to deal with
lesser men and a population more deeply concerned with the
affairs of their homeland than with the tangled affairs of
Europe or other distant continents. And, above all, he had
to face the problems of South Africa which as never before
was feeling the impact of the twentieth century upon its way
of life.

Although the white man's invasion of South Africa had
begun in the sixteenth and seventeenth centuries the vast
majority of the population were still black men. The four
provinces, Cape of Good Hope, Natal, Orange Free State,
and the Transvaal, which constituted the Union of South
Africa had a population of approximately ten millions. Of
these less than two millions were whites. The white population was divided primarily into those of Dutch and British
origin, but there were others besides them—German, Jewish,
Greek, Portuguese, Italian, and French. These comprised,

all told, some two percent of the white population. Nor was the black and other colored population uniform either in its ethnic make-up or in social stratification. The native Africans are divided into Bantus, Hottentots, and Bushmen. But besides these there are some two hundred thousand Indians, and many Malayans and Chinese. The immigration of the Indians began about the year 1860; they were brought for work on estates and in mines by agreement between the Natal and Indian governments, both governed by England. The whites began to fear that Indian immigration would surpass their own and in 1913 strict laws were passed to curtail new immigration. The Malayans were brought to South Africa by the Dutch and used as slaves. The Chinese were imported as laborers like the Indians but their numbers diminished.

Besides the Asiatics there are some 800,000 colored people, located mainly in the Cape Province, who have their origin in the mixture of the early white settlers and the Hottentots and a general mixture of Europeans with the various black and colored peoples.

These ethnic groups also roughly coincide with the social groups. All the non-Europeans represent the lower social-economic strata. At the bottom are the Bantus and the Hottentots, working as unskilled laborers for the whites. The same applies to the colored groups, although there are some among these who are skilled and semi-skilled workers in the urban areas and they have a higher income. The majority of the Indians forms the lower middle-class and is better off than the "poor" white.

Smuts had a definite theory about how to deal with the problems arising from this complex association of differing ethnic stock. It is based, as was generally accepted by the whites, on white supremacy. The theory he expounded fully on a number of occasions after his arrival in England in 1917. At a dinner given in his honor at the Savoy Hotel on May

22, 1917, with Lord Selborne, an ex-High Commissioner of South Africa as his chairman, he held forth as follows:

There are many people in South Africa—and not very foolish people either—who do not feel certain that our white experiment will be a permanent success, or that we shall ever succeed in making a white man's land of South Africa; but, at any rate, we mean to press on with the experiment. It has now been in progress for some two hundred and fifty years, as you know, and perhaps the way we have set about it may be the right way. . . . We have started by creating a new white base in South Africa and today we are in a position to move forward towards the North and the civilisation of the African continent. Our problem is a very difficult one, however; quite unique in its way. In the United States, there is a similar problem of black and white with the negro population. But there you have had an overwhelming white population, with a smaller negro element in the midst of it. In South Africa the situation is reverse. There you have an overwhelming black population with a small white population which has got a footing there and which has been trying to make that footing secure for more than two centuries.

Having set out the premise, he proceeded to lay down certain axioms and rules of conduct. The first of his axioms was there shall be "no intermixture of blood between the two colors," although South Africa already had a population equal to one third the number of whites who are colored, owing to this intermixture. However, the audience would not question that axiom for they accepted it, too. The next axiom he laid down was one which logically followed from it, namely, social and political segregation. He went on to say:

Instead of mixing black and white in the old haphazard way, which instead of lifting up the black degraded the white, we are now trying to lay down a policy of keeping them apart as much as possible in our institutions. In land ownership, settlement and forms of government we are trying to keep them apart and in that way laying down in outline a general policy which it may take a hundred years to work out but which in the end may be the solution of our native problem.

It is perfectly clear therefore that when Smuts became the Prime Minister of South Africa he already had a policy on the racial question. There is no doubt whatever that in this policy he had the support of the white population of South Africa. But the problem was not so simple as his axioms. He had faced it entirely as a conflict of ethnic groups but the problem was made far more complex by the fact that South Africa finally had passed out of the seventeenth century and was dominated by the twentieth, and the ethnic question was now bedeviled by the impact of the economic and industrial civilization of the twentieth century upon the economy of black and colored races. It had not yet dawned on Smuts or his British partners in government that there was a distinct relationship between the economy and the institutions and levels of civilization. Had it been possible to divide the African continent between the blacks and the whites so that each civilization, with its respective economies and institutions, could pursue its own way of life which included their own economies, their respective institutions would have remained intact. That would have been real segregation. But such was not possible and it had not happened. The white man's economy called for the employment of the black man, first as slave labor which was usable so long as the white settlers were agrarians, and then as "free" labor when they introduced modern industry. Modern industry, especially, will not tolerate segregation. By its nature it brings labor together in greater aggregations, and all attempts at segregation, whether in terms of skilled and unskilled, black and white, sooner or later break down. In drawing the black labor into modern industry it also followed that the black man was taken away from his old economic basis, trained to a new technique of production, and severed from his trib-

alism. When Rhodes and then Smuts broke up the old tribal
ownership of land and established private ownership of
land and cultivation of native agriculture, they introduced a
higher form of economy, created new wants in the life of the
black man, set him on the road to education in higher forms
of the technics of civilization, brought him in closer contact
with the white man's civilization. When they drew the black
man into their wars, waged with technically modern equip-
ment, they put the black man to drive modern transport and
use modern machinery. By these means they were blasting
the foundations of tribalism and the whole ancient civilization. This process had already gone far in South Africa during the lifetime of Smuts himself. He had seen the hectic development of the gold mines of South Africa and the growth
of urban centers on the basis of black, unskilled, cheap labor. Would he be able to stop this process with a policy of
segregation? He would not! And he did not. He had the
consolation of knowing that he and the Afrikanders were
not alone in having to face the problems he had to tackle.
They were common to all Africa and to all the white man's
efforts to make of the African continent a white preserve
with the black man underneath. The white man has taken
his civilization to the black continent and try as he may to
hold back the natives from being drawn into it, he can never
succeed. He cannot eat his cake and have it, use and train
primitive labor as labor for his industry, reorganize and modernize the economy of the continent including that of the
natives, and at the same time hold the black man back in his
tribalism and primitive ways of life.

But Smuts would try. If that had been the only problem
he had to face as he became Prime Minister of South Africa
it would have provided him with more headaches than is
justifiable for one lifetime. It was, however, not the only
problem bound up with his imperial dreams and the evolution of Africa. Gold mining was and still is its principal modern industry. This and the diamond industry were the main

sources of revenue for the government and from which the capital resources could be obtained for the urbanization of Africa. The more modern Africa became the more it would be drawn into the orbit of world economy and the fluctuations it experienced. The smallness of the white population and the low standard of life of the native population meant that the principal stimulus for economic expansion was the world economy outside Africa and not the growth of the home market. Smuts soon had these basic facts thrust upon him with terrific force. He became Prime Minister just as the "post-war slump" (World War I) hit his country. He found Hertzog and the old Dutch opposition making great capital out of the situation and laying the blame for the "unrest" and the economic difficulties at his door, his preoccupation with world problems, long absence from Africa, neglect of home affairs, bad administration, and the like. There were labor troubles in the urban centers. Seventy thousand natives struck work for higher pay on the Rand. In German South West Africa, now under South African mandate, a tribe of Hottentots refused to pay their taxes and rose in revolt. A strange religious sect gathered together near Port Elizabeth to wait for the end of the world. There was no lack of decision on the part of Smuts as to what to do. He may have great dreams and high principles but he would have none of this nonsense. Airplanes bombed the tribe in German South West Africa. That finished off the revolt. When the religious sect refused to depart they were driven home under machine-gun fire and hundreds were killed and wounded. He smashed the native strike on the Rand and when those in Port Elizabeth resisted, sixty-eight of them were shot. He knew how to exercise his authority, Christian morality and high ideals notwithstanding. Smuts in Africa hardly seemed to be the same person as Smuts in London. Nevertheless, when the elections came he was returned to power with a substantial majority. But his problems remained. He attended an Imperial Conference in London. It met at a critical time. There was an economic slump in England. Ireland was up in arms and the Black and Tans were busy. Smuts, unofficially, went to see the leaders of the Irish Revolt—Griffith, De Valera, Erskine Childers. It is said that it was Smuts who persuaded Winston Churchill and Birkenhead to favor a truce and a conference with the Irish leaders. He left England, again acclaimed as a great statesman. He returned to South Africa to find the economic crisis at home worse than ever. The trade unions of white workers had become strong with the growth of the urban centers. They were combined into an industrial federation and demanded the control of the mines. On January 1, 1922, the mineowners reduced the wages of the miners by five shillings a day. The miners struck work. Ten days later the gold-mine owners decided to increase the number of black workers employed in place of whites. Twenty thousand gold miners struck work and the engineers joined them. After failing to make negotiations between capital and labor, Smuts called on the owners to reopen the mines and instructed the police to protect all miners who returned to work. The federation called a general strike. The general strike turned to armed revolt and the miners took control of the Reef. Smuts smashed that labor revolt with troops and machine guns and bombing planes.

So he handled "the labor problem" and the "native problem," by means that had become traditional to him. Only once had it really beat him; that was now some time ago when he and Botha were the virtual rulers of the Transvaal and they came up against a man named Gandhi. Indians, British subjects, were flocking into the Transvaal, and surpassed the white men as traders. Smuts determined to stop it and imposed stiff regulations for dealing with Indians who broke the regulations. The Indians, led by Gandhi, protested. Smuts imprisoned some of the Indians, including Gandhi, who had organized passive resistance. When Gandhi asked to see Smuts, Smuts arrogantly refused to meet him. Then he changed his mind and met him. Gandhi said Smuts made promises to him and then never kept them. Gandhi returned to his agitation and passive-resistance methods and the Indians continued to defeat the regulations. It would be difficult to find two men so contrasting in outlook and ways of life. Smuts, well-built, white, steely-blue-eyed, egotistic, reserved, accustomed to rule by power, and Gandhi, small, slim, dark-skinned, quiet, composed, indifferent to threats of violence, a shrewd lawyer and mystic, smiling his way forward. The world was to hear much of him in the years ahead. He was outside the range of Smuts' comprehension.

Smuts smashed the labor movement, ruthlessly. It was a triumph and he went his way. But it tore away from him the parliamentary support which he needed to hold power against Hertzog's opposition. In 1924 he was thrown out of office. The Labor Party of South Africa had lined up with Hertzog. Nor did Smuts quickly recover from the defeat. He was again defeated in the 1929 elections. After his first defeat, he went home to his farmstead which he had named Irene. There, with his wife and family, he lived a simple life. Smuts had never worried about accumulating money. He lived with ideas, and money-making was not one of them. He had been a politician for twenty-five years and from his school days he had been interested in acquiring knowledge. His wife was his old sweetheart of college days who had looked up to him always and given him steady devotion. In all their married life she had lived the life of the wife of a Dutch farmer. In all his travels he went alone. They had a number of children but of them Smuts said, "My children treat me as a distinguished stranger." He had seen them so infrequently. Now he lived again the life of a Dutch farmer in its simplicity, but not as a farmer. His books and papers occupied him. Of course, he had to lead the Opposition in Parliament but he had much free time from that. In these years he wrote *Holism and Evolution*. In the middle of this period of quiescence in leadership, in the autumn of 1927, he expounded his philosophy in a lecture to the Witwatersrand University. He said of it:

Holism is an attempt at synthesis, an attempt at bringing together many currents of thought and development such as we have seen in our day. It is not a system of philosophy. I do not believe very much in systems. . . . Holism—the theory of the whole—tries to emphasise one aspect of thought that has been hitherto a neglected factor.

He worked on the assumption that matter had disappeared into energy and the universe consisted of patterns of energy. What he meant by energy or what it was that was energetic he did not attempt to define; he belonged to the "idealist" school of philosophy. He continued:

If you take patterns as the ultimate structure of the world, if it is arrangements and not stuff that make up the world, the new concept leads you to the concept of wholes. Wholes have no stuff; they are arrangements. Science has come round to the view that the world consists of patterns, and I construe that to be that the world consists of wholes.
. . . Instead of taking matter as the basis of the world, we see there is something deeper than life and mind and personality. Matter is more than it appears. In matter there is a pattern, a whole, which is its very inmost nature. That explains how it is possible for matter to blossom into such forms as mind and life . . .

Having laid down his first principles with regard to matter as having disappeared and become nonexistent, and energy having become a pattern, or whole of nothing, he applied this idea to the universe and to politics, showing a wide range of knowledge of the science of his day. He did not attempt to prove the validity of his idea but simply expounded it and got away with it. He was hailed as a philosopher, scientist, statesman, but he lost out in the elections of 1929, notwithstanding. Defeated a second time and with Hertzog in charge of the South African Parliament for another four years, he decided to flee drab routine and ineffectiveness and tour England and North America.

It was a triumphal tour. He was now in his real element, with intellectual equals, away from the jarring irritation of domestic politics, hailed as an elder statesman of the British Empire as well as scientist and philosopher. He stayed with the King of England at Sandringham. He addressed great audiences of the learned at Cambridge and Oxford, Edinburgh and Glasgow. He delivered the Rhodes Memorial Lecture at Oxford and was made an Honorary D.C.L. of the university. Canada and the United States greeted him in the same honored way. Received by President Hoover at the White House, he had the honor of shaking hands with the Senators as they filed past him on the floor of the Senate House.

In the midst of the grand tour he rushed back to South Africa to oppose a bill restricting the immigration of Jews. He had been one of the first statesmen to support the Balfour Declaration in favor of making Palestine a home for the Jews. He hated the crude nationalism of the Hertzog followers, now inflamed with anti-semitism; but he did not succeed in stopping the passage of the bill. He resumed his tour and on arriving in England once more received the greatest honor and tribute of his career. He was invited to preside at the centenary meeting of the British Association, attended by five thousand scientists of the world. He declared: "This is the crowning honor of my life." Here he gave a remarkable survey of the science of his day, indoctrinated somewhat with his "Holism." He revealed an immense range of knowledge and how well he had kept himself abreast of the scientific and philosophical knowledge of his day. He lectured, too, on the problems of Europe and the world, the League of Nations and World Peace. His effect on public and politicians was amazing. Enough that Smuts had spoken; he was regarded as the fount of wisdom. A possible explanation of this is that he appeared as a guest and as one above the battle of contending social forces in England. For certainly his wisdom was not accepted in such an atmosphere of awe in South Africa. Soon the tide turned for him even in South Africa. It was 1932 when he returned, and South Africa was feeling the impact of the "economic blizzard" which had hit the world. In addition, South Africa had had to contend with severe droughts and a plague of locusts, both of which had ruined great numbers of farmers. Hertzog had kept South Africa on the gold standard after other countries, and Britain in particular, had been forced to abandon it. Consequently, South Africa's exports fell severely and came almost to a standstill. The mines were badly hit. The crisis grew. Smuts promptly denounced Hertzog for keeping South Africa on gold, and soon Hertzog was forced by the crisis conditions to do as Smuts had advocated. Smuts' stock went up and Hertzog's went down. Then Hertzog asked Smuts to join him in coalition. Smuts agreed and in 1933 they, together, swept the country and Smuts was again the virtual leader of the government. On the surface, it appeared that he had now achieved what he had set out to attain when the Union of South Africa was established in 1910—a united Afrikander people. But it was an uneasy coalition and not a fundamental fusing of the conflicting elements into a single body. He was Minister of Justice in the Coalition Government—a post which left him a considerable amount of freedom to exercise his influence on general policy. When it came to the larger questions of imperial policy he was the spokesman of the government. It fell to his lot to bring for ratification the famous Statute of Westminster before the South African Parliament. This statute, passed by the British Parliament, put into legal form the Balfour Declaration of 1926, defining the nature of the relations of nations and states within "The British Commonwealth of Nations." Smuts had always regarded that definition as a sequel to his own stand on the future of South Africa in relation to Britain at the formation of the Union of South Africa. The Statute of Westminster he therefore regarded as the greatest act of statesmanship in the history of the British Empire. He spoke to the South African Parliament on this measure with all the enthusiasm of which he was capable. Heart and mind responded to it. It was so much in accord with his vision for the future of Africa. After explaining its provisions section by section, he said·

This Bill gives us a full sovereign status and is intended to give that; but it also, at the same time, equally emphasises the other aspect of our position, and that is that we belong to a group of friends, a free world-wide association of States. We may leave it in the ripeness of time but that is the group to which we belong. The King is the symbol of this free association, and common allegiance to him, right through this great group, keeps it together. It seems to me that this is the sort of settlement which I would, if I were a dicator, dictate to South Africa. . . . One never knows in this country what the next phase will be. . . . We have had two roots of division in the past: one root was racial and the other was constitutional. The racial root is withering. More and more you see people fraternising and doing away with the dead racial issues of the past . . . Let us now cut the other root. I hope that this Bill will cut the root of the constitutional controversies which, for a generation, have divided South Africa and convulsed it to its foundations. In cutting it we are rendering South Africa the greatest service possible, and laying a sure foundation for the future.

The bill was passed. It was easier to pass the bill than to rub out the heritage of passions and prejudices. How far they had succeeded was soon to be revealed.

New powers had arisen in Europe and the Far East which were challenging the world. 1939 came and the testing time arrived with it. Would South Africa feel itself at one with Britain and other dominions in answering the Nazi challenge or regard itself as a neutral power? How great was the change since 1914 when Botha and Smuts, faced with the issue of supporting Britain in war against Germany, had

to put down a Dutch rebellion before they could get on with
the war. This time there was a debate in the South African
Parliament. Hertzog, who had been party to the earlier rebellion, proposed neutrality. He was Prime Minister. Smuts
moved an amendment rejecting neutrality and proposing
that the Union should cooperate with its friends and asso-
ciates in the British Commonwealth of Nations in waging
war against the common enemy. The Smuts amendment was
carried by 80 votes to 67. Hertzog resigned. General Smuts
once more became Prime Minister of the Union at war.
There was no armed revolt. Hertzog and Dr. Malan went
off to continue their efforts toward separatism and a Dutch
republic, with Malan openly supporting the Nazis. They
had miscalculated their position both in the Parliament and
in the country. Once again, Smuts held the reins of power,
confident that Africa was traveling the way he wished it to
go.

At first it appeared that history was just repeating itself
with minor differences. The war was in Europe. There was
no war to fight this time in what had been German West and
East Africa; but farther north the Italians had to be driven
out of Africa. Once more Smuts flung himself with great
energy into the war which followed during the first eighteen
months somewhat the pattern of 1914, particularly so far as
South Africa was concerned. South Africa was far from the
scene of battle. It had to send its troops some six thousand
miles to contact the enemy. Suddenly, the Japs struck at
Pearl Harbor and the whole aspect of the war took on new
proportions and direction, creating a new world situation.
It brought the war into the Pacific Ocean and put the question of the defense of the dominions situated in it in an entirely new setting. Up to this time New Zealand, Australia,
South Africa, India, and Canada had been sending men and
supplies to the European front. Suddenly, all of them were
brought face to face with the fact that Britain, upon whom

they had depended for defense, could do very little about it because of its preoccupation with the war in Europe, the Atlantic Ocean, and North Africa. Especially did this apply to Australia and New Zealand. South Africa did not feel this to the same extent as they. Africa was still a long way from the range of the Japanese. Nevertheless, Smuts saw clearly enough, as all the world could see, that the war in the Pacific, and the defense of Australia and New Zealand especially, and the Dutch East Indies, fell on the United States of America. In Africa, too, Smuts saw that the war frontier of the Union of South Africa was no longer the northern boundary of the Transvaal and Southern Rhodesia. It reached to the region of fighting in Abyssinia. This changed situation enlarged and changed many of the ideas he had propounded in the course of the First World War when he drafted the scheme for the League of Nations. Then he viewed the world with his feet in Cape Town and his head in London, the metropolis of the British Empire and Commonwealth of Nations, giving only a fraternal glance to the other dominions. This time, when he was not engrossed in the work of mobilizing the full strength of the Union for the prosecution of the war, he stood, as it were, on Table Mountain and glimpsed the horizons of the struggling world as far as he could see. Never did he doubt that the Allies would win or that the U.S.A. would come into the fray. Of Russia he was afraid; of the revolution that had taken place in that vast country he had never been able to comprehend either its scope or its meaning, except through a glass darkly and dimmed with fear.

In May 1941, before either Soviet Russia or the U.S.A. had been thrust into the war by the Fascist powers, he gave a speech on the subject, "A Vision of the New World Order." He glimpsed two possibilities of the outcome of the war, only to dismiss them, namely, a stalemate and a Hitler world. Then he turned his eye on the prospect of an Allied victory.

He asked: "How will the world look, viewed from our perspectives of today?"

He answered his own question thus:

It seems to me that the day of the small independent sovereign State has passed. That is the sign of the times. In the absence of a mighty world organisation the sad fate of the small independent States of Europe in our day is likely to be their fate more and more in the future. . . .

We are unmistakably in for a larger grouping in that Holistic process which fundamentally moulds all life and all history. . . . Already the free Democracies representing the forward movement in our western civilisation, are grouping themselves together under the pressure of the times. That pressure is irresistibly forcing them together in a great world organisation, the outlines and pattern of which we are already beginning to see more or less clearly. . . .

In the inner circle which now forms the heart of the resistance to Hitler, is the British Commonwealth of Nations.

This he regarded as the prototype of the world organization that was growing. Next to the commonwealth he placed the U.S.A. Indeed he criticized America for abandoning the League of Nations and then looked to America to be the leader of a new world organization that would emerge from the war.

In 1944 he went again to England, invited as the Prime Minister of the Union of South Africa to the Conference of Prime Ministers which preceded the setting up of the United Nations Organization. Referring to this project in a speech he made at Birmingham, on May 19, he said:

It would almost inevitably be an improved and reformed version of the old League of Nations. That brave and brilliant improvisation failed in part because it was not clothed with sufficient authority and coercive power to maintain peace. Next time responsibility should be placed on those who have the power, and the great powers who won the war should be made responsible in the first instance for keeping the peace.

He did not mention that he had fought against the League being organized with such coercive powers but went on to plead for regional groupings of the nations. He advocated a federation of the small European democracies with the United Kingdom—an adumbration of "Western Union"— in long-distance perspective. He grouped the British Commonwealth with the United States and within the British Commonwealth he visualized regional groupings such as the war had produced for the defense of the countries in the Pacific. When the Conference of Prime Ministers met once more he took his stand against any centralizing trends which would infringe in the least the autonomous position of the nations forming the commonwealth. Conferences? Yes. Discussion of common problems and common actions? Yes. But the minimum of centralized authority. And, as always, he never lost sight of his imperial ambitions for the Union of South Africa.

The United Nations was formed. He did not play the same major role in its creation as he had done after the First World War in the creation of the League but his course was clear with regard to it. There is, however, irony in the fact that almost at once after its creation he should come into conflict with his imperial policy, for Africa bumped up against the finer conception of internationalism. In place of the mandate system of the League of Nations the United Nations introduced "trusteeship." It asked South Africa to bring German South West Africa, which it had held in mandate from the League, into the "trusteeship" of the new organization. Smuts would have none of it. He took his stand on the fact that under the mandate of the League, the Union was granted full power of administration and legislation over the territory as an integral portion of the Union. It is economically dependent on the Union and the latter has governed it for twenty-five years. There is no prospect of the territory ever existing as a separate state and the native peoples spring from the same ethnological source as the native

peoples of the Union. He advanced other reasons besides
these for South Africa's refusal to bring the territory under
"trusteeship." The fact is that the territory had been vir-
tually annexed by South Africa and the world can rest assured that when Smuts has to choose between loyalty to his
imperial South African dream and loyalty to U.N.O., or any
other international body, he will always choose the former.

After the war was over he suffered the fate of Churchill
and was again rejected by the people of the South African
Union. This time he lost to Dr. Malan, the republican successor to Hertzog. This was not the first time that Dr. Malan
had fought Smuts but it was the first time he had led the nationalist forces to the defeat of Smuts.

Malan is an elderly man, only four years younger than the
older man he had defeated. Born in 1874, in Cape Province,
he was educated at the same college as Smuts, at Victoria
College, Stellenbosch, and at the University of Utrecht. He
was pastor of the Dutch Reform Church at Montagu in
1906 but in later years became primarily a journalist and
editor rather than a minister of the gospel. As member of
Parliament for Piquetberg he has been the leader of extreme
Dutch nationalism since 1919. In the Hertzog government
of 1924-33 he was Minister of the Interior. As a young man
he supported the revolt of De Wett and Hertzog against the
war of 1914-18. In 1939 he opposed South Africa's participation in the war. He held the view that a Nazi victory would
be to the advantage of South Africa and wanted the Union to
break away from the British connection. A rugged, sectarian
Dutch nationalist in the tradition of, and as intense in his
racialism as, Hitler, he had grown up in hatred of the English and it was thought that when he became Prime Minister
of South Africa in 1947 he would lead the way to the formation of a South African republic and a breakaway from the
British Commonwealth. Whether his majority was too small
for him immediately to pursue this policy, he did not make
the break but sent a deputy to the Prime Ministers' Com-

monwealth Conference in October 1948. On October 26, 1948, the *Daily Mail* reports him saying to an audience in Port Elizabeth:

. . . that it was nonsense to accuse his Government of isolationism. The main principle of its policy was that South Africa was a sovereign and independent nation, and that nobody had the right to dominate her or interfere in her internal affairs. The nearest countries to South Africa were members of the Commonwealth to which she belonged, but there she was free and would walk with them only if she regarded it as in her own interests.

Dr. Malan said he intended raising the rank of South African representatives in the Commonwealth countries from High Commissioners to Ambassador as soon as possible.

When he attended the Conference of Commonwealth Prime Ministers in 1949 he regarded the decision to permit a republic to be a member of the commonwealth of the highest significance for South Africa. Besides his republicanism he carries on the fierce racialism of the old Boers. Fierce in his national hatreds and doctrinaire in his fanaticism, he is very close in type and outlook to the Teutonic Nazi. Such is the man who superseded Jan Smuts in the South African elections of 1947.

The triumph of Malan over Smuts was a decisive turning point in the history of the South African Union. It represented an end to the merger principle as applied to the Dutch and the British in South Africa. Since the formation of the Union of South Africa under his leadership, Smuts had worked consistently for their merger in the Afrikander nation, feeling sure that it would remain more Dutch than British. Malan aimed at the conquest of the British by the Dutch. From the outset he made it clear that continuous association with the Commonwealth turned entirely upon whether it served South African interests and not Commonwealth interests. In a statement issued immediately after his election to premiership, he said:

It will be acknowledged that, with the recent admission to the Commonwealth of new members with equal rights, and especially in view of South Africa's experience at Lake Success, the danger . . . of interference is by no means imaginary. The question must inevitably be put, therefore, whether the good co-operation which everyone desires could not be better achieved by independent contacts between the individual members of the Commonwealth than by discussions by general and all-embracing conferences. . . .

We must emphasise that co-operation for common ends will be possible only if there is no prejudice to our status and conduct as a sovereign independent state and if there are no attempts at outside interference in our domestic affairs.

That was a warning to all and sundry to keep their noses out of what Dr. Malan considered exclusively South African affairs. Malan's government proceeded to make stricter immigration laws to ensure more effective "screening" of immigrants from a physical, economic, and political point of view. A British immigrant after proper "screening" could only become a South African citizen, with full rights, after six years' residence. New legislation was introduced directed against the Indian population and a fierce drive was made against the colored natives. India recalled her High Commissioner and terminated the trade agreement with South Africa. A ban was placed on native military training and a similar ban was enacted against native artisanship. Malan repeated the action of Smuts with regard to German South West Africa which the United Nations sought to bring under the Trusteeship Council. Malan refused to make any report on South African administration of this territory and counter-attacked the United Nations, warning that body "if the United Nations continues along that road, it will mean its downfall." Nevertheless, he was wholly in line with the Fulton policy of Mr. Winston Churchill and had a special antipathy to Russia and Communism which led him to endorse the Atlantic Pact and plead for an alliance with other powers having possessions in Africa.

He pursued his race-segregation policy with vigor until it

can be safely declared that he has laid the basis of a racial war throughout the South African Union. Nor has he forgotten the expansionist visions of his predecessor. He shared with Smuts the idea that the Union of South Africa should not be limited to its existing territory. But whereas Smuts was always concerned about antagonizing Britain, Malan has no qualms whatever in this matter. On October 26, 1949, he announced that he would ask the British Government to incorporate into the Union of South Africa the British Protectorates of Bechuanaland, Basutoland, and Swaziland. This would add 300,000 square miles of territory and four hundred thousand natives to the Union. In making this announcement of his intentions, Dr. Malan said:

It is unheard of that in a sovereign independent country like the Union of South Africa there should be territories subordinate to a foreign country. South Africa is getting impatient. The last step, if everything else fails, will be that the Union Parliament will send a petition to the Privy Council.

Nevertheless, notwithstanding the familiar note of "impatience" which was heard so frequently in Europe up to 1939, when the "dollar crisis" hit the countries of the sterling area it hit the Union of South Africa too. When Britain devalued the pound Malan also devalued South Africa's currency. Malan is driving forward with an intensive nationalistic policy in all directions and stormy days lie ahead, threatening a rupture of the commonwealth and all international organization. Were it not that South Africa's economy is so intimately related to the economy of the whole Commonwealth and world economy, it is clear that rupture would be certain. But the economic crisis has acted as a driving force toward common action with the Commonwealth and as a brake on her isolationism.

Meanwhile Smuts continued to lead the Opposition. His defeat was a sad blow to him. He is an old man and a little tired. He is eighty, yet well and strong and holds forth as an elder statesman of the British Empire and Commonwealth and philosopher of Holism. Honors have been showered upon him in the course of his later years. In the First World War he became a major-general. In the second, a field marshal. The universities throughout the world have given him academic honors. Fellow of the Royal Society, he cherished no honor more than that of its presidency on the occasion of its centenary. But he will be remembered most as the leader of the new Afrikander nation which emerged from a blending of the Dutch and English settlers in South Africa and who, as a leader, played a decisive part in the transformation of the centralized British Empire into a commonwealth of autonomous nations. Musing over the course of his years, Smuts says of himself:

I have sampled the world and human nature at many points and I have learnt that it takes all sorts to make a world. But through it all my conviction has only deepened that there is nothing in the nature of things that is alien to what is best in us. There is no malign fatalism which makes fools of us in our dark strivings towards the good. On the contrary, what is highest in us is deepest in the nature of things, and as virtue is its own reward so life carries its own sanctions and the guarantee of its own fulfillments and perfections. That is my ultimate credo; and it is not founded on hearsay, but on my first-hand experience in that cross-section of the world which I have lived through. There is no doubt a slender basis of fact for so large a conclusion. But the final convictions are not inductions from experience, but insights into it. I remain at heart an optimist.

Of the people from whom he has sprung and to whom he has given a lifetime of service, he says:

The temper of South Africa is curious and full of individuality. They are only a handful of whites . . . each private thinks he is a general. . . . Look at the other Dominions, no quarrels, no problems. Everything smooth and easy, how empty, how dull! Now there isn't a single problem under the sun we haven't in this Union of ours. Black, yellow, brown, white, we have them all.

. . . Can it be said we are a peaceful nation? Of course it can't. But it cannot be said we are not an interesting nation. How exciting life is here! (*African Portraits* by Stuart Cloete, p. 452.)

He is the biggest man South Africa has yet produced.

C H A P T E R   V I I I

E   R   N   E   S   T   B   E   V   I   N

No MAN WAS MORE SURPRISED
than Mr. Ernest Bevin when Mr. Clement Attlee called
upon him in 1945 to be Britain's Foreign Secretary. No Foreign Secretary ever appointed had been less prepared by
education and political experience for such a post. Bevin
had expected, in the light of his reputation, career, and
standing in the leadership of the British Labor Movement,
to become Britain's Chancellor of the Exchequer. But Attlee
apparently held the view that Bevin, with his powerful personality and reputation for bludgeoning his way forward
through apparently unsurmountable situations was the man
to speak to the nations of the world in the name of Britain.
Ernest Bevin was already an elderly man when he became
Britain's Foreign Secretary but he was the most powerful and
dominating figure in the British Labor Movement. He was
vigorous and ready to make his impact on world affairs, as he
had undoubtedly made his impress on the economic and social
life of Britain when he was the country's outstanding trade-
union leader and, during the war, the successful Minister of
Labor and National Service.

Bevin was born in 1880 in the village of Winsford in Som-
ersetshire. Of his father little is known beyond the fact that
he was an agricultural laborer. Ernest Bevin never knew his
father, for the latter died before he was born. His mother
was more widely known, for she achieved renown as a sturdy
"Methodist agitator." Her efforts to raise funds for the build-

ing of a Methodist chapel so incensed the vicar of the Established Church in the neighborhood that on her death, when
Ernest Bevin was six years of age, he refused permission, at
first, for her body to be buried in consecrated ground. Only
when the cortege reached the church door and a conference
was held between the vicar and the churchwardens was permission finally granted. The coming Foreign Minister of
Britain received his first lesson in the struggle against "in-
tolerance" in the conflict of the creeds.

The orphan boy went to live with his sister at a place
called Crediton, attended school until he was eleven years
of age, and then followed in his late father's footsteps and
went to work on a farm. Bevin has said, "The farmer paid
me ninepence ($.10½) a week—paid me quarterly, nine shil-
lings and sixpence a quarter ($1.33); and he always asked
for the change out of ten shillings ($1.40)." Here began his
economic struggle. He left this farmer and went to another
who paid him one shilling per week ($.14). He was not tall
but broad and strong and intelligent, tough and aggressive.
Quarreling with the farmer's son, who belabored him
fiercely, he packed up his job, abandoned farm work, and set
off to the industrial town and port of Bristol. There he
worked on all kinds of jobs, washed dishes in a cafe, served in
a grocery store, hawked ginger beer and other mineral wa-
ters, became a drayman and tram driver. All these jobs were
intermingled with spells of unemployment.

Life was hard and fierce and he grew in toughness and not
a little bitterness. But he had not forgotten that his mother
was a Methodist nor lost the religious associations of his
childhood. His education continued along the lines of self-
development, making use of the Adult School Movement
which got him interested more and more in politics and economics. In these studies, as in religion, he was not interested
in theories but in practice. Abstract thinking has never been
his strong point. He had always been in Poverty Street and
he wanted the goods. It was the same with his Socialism.

The days of his youth coincided with the rebirth of the Socialist Movement in Britain. After the death of Chartism, the great resurgent social movement of the new working class which had grown with the industrial revolution and expired at the end of the first half of the nineteenth century, Socialism caused only a ripple on the working class of Britain until the dawn of the twentieth century. Socialism was then reborn. Blatchford wrote *Britain for the British*, Bernard Shaw and Sidney Webb became famous as the leaders of the Fabians. Hardie and MacDonald and Snowden and Jowett thundered on behalf of the Independent Labor Party. H. M. Hyndman pioneered the Social Democratic Federation as the organization of Marxism. Tom Mann and Ben Tillett, the leader of the Dockers Union in which Bevin would rise to power, stormed through the country with the message of syndicalism. The Labor Party was born.

As a young fellow, Bevin led the unemployed in their demand for work and bread. He listened to the Socialists and joined Hyndman's organization. He learned much from its members but what meant most to him was the need for bread and work, and work and bread, and to get them here and now, before the revolution in the economic fabric of society. The grandiose schemes associated with the fundamental demand for the socialization of the means of production seemed rational enough for him but the immediate question of coping with unemployment, finding work, and improving the economic conditions of himself and his fellow men, gripped his mind firmly. His natural egotism and strength of character, a native capacity to speak boldly and powerfully to those in circumstances similar to his own, thrust him into the forefront of the efforts to organize the unemployed of Bristol at a time when unemployment was rife in that city.

There was no "Welfare State," no social insurance against unemployment, and the hunger problem was urgent. This hard apprenticeship in the school of the impoverished equipped him for the job of trade-union organizer in the

dockland of Bristol, and made him a Socialist candidate for
the local council. He was a van driver delivering ginger beer
at fifteen shillings a week plus seven shillings' commission,
when he married, established his own home, and became a
branch secretary of the Dockers Union. From that time onward he gave himself wholeheartedly to trade unionism and
quickly rose from branch secretary to full-time organizer at
twenty-five shillings a week. From organizer he reached upward to leadership of the Dockers Union, from the Dockers
Union to the leadership of the Transport Workers, eclipsing
the old leader, Ben Tillett, in the process. Onward then to
the leadership of the Transport and General Workers Union
which, under his direction, became the greatest trade union
in the country. In all things he was the "practical man." He
scoffed at "highfalutin theory" about "capitalism in decay."
When men were unemployed they wanted bread and work
not an oration about the coming revolution. He organized
the unemployed, collected funds to feed them, and put practical work schemes before the local authorities. When he
got busy as an organizer of the dockers it had long been
drummed into his head by harsh experience that organization meant power and men could get nowhere without
power. "Power is the king of words," Jack London once said.
Bevin would add—it was only the king of words if the reality
of power was behind it. He had learned that from bitter experience and he drove the lesson into the minds of the dockers whom he organized. Trade unionism was a simple matter. It could be boiled down to the simple proposition that
"you could have what you had the power to take." There existed employers and employees. The workers were the employees who had no power whatever unless they were organized. Ergo, organize them and use the power to stop working,
to force a bargain as to the terms of employment. He became a master at the game—the champion bargain-maker.
All his union-building from the first amalgamation of the
Dockers Union with other transport organizations and their

merger with general labor organizations were governed by one principle, and one only—the accumulation of power. Bevin rose to the leadership of the Dockers and the Transport Union with the rise of road transport to a key position in the structure of modern industry, just as J. H. Thomas had before him risen to the forefront of British trade unionism when the railway industry became the supreme means of communication between town and city and village, farm, factory, and industry. But while Thomas and the railwaymen confined themselves to the railway industry, Bevin swept aside all consideration for the structure of industry and the relation of the unions to them and cashed in for more power with a grandiose merger of the Transport Workers organizations and those of general laborers sprawled across any and every industry. Such organization brought with it power and power was the thing that mattered in the making of bargains and squeezing concessions. What Gompers was to the Trade Union Movement in the United States, Bevin became to the British trade unions except that Gompers rested his power upon the skilled workers of industry whereas Bevin represented chiefly the power of general labor.

What he became in terms of leadership in the unions, he was in himself: broad-shouldered, heavily built, heavy-jowled, somber in his gait, dogmatic in utterance, and a powerful demagogue. He has a great memory for things and persons. He is the supreme egotist who expounds all things in the first person singular. The unemployed whom he organized were his unemployed. The dockers whom he organized were his dockers. The Transport and General Workers was his union. The Foreign Office became his office and the staff, his men, and if ever he were to become President of the United Nations Assembly that organization would be his, too, and he would see the world populated by his boys. Nor has there been any half measure in his service to those who came directly under his control. As he achieved more and more power he succeeded in making more and more collective bargains. Grammar notwithstanding, and defective pronunciation overlooked, there was no doubt about his ability to make himself understood in the language of his workmates. Whether it is a part of the technique of the ambitious in their quest for leadership or a law of political development from youth to maturity, it is common to most politicians and trade-union leaders that they begin on the *Left* and finish on the *Right*. Bevin began on the Left and remained there until he had won power; he turned to the Right when he had got power. In his early years he was a member of the Social Democratic Federation, led by H. M. Hyndman, shouting Marxist economics from the platforms. The *SDF* was an organization which was regarded as being on the extreme Left and it talked class war. Bevin, too, was a member of the Bristol Labor Representation Committee which preceded the Bristol Labor Party. He led the dockers and transport workers of Bristol and the western ports in the great Dock Strike of 1911. He was a British patriot in the war of 1914-18. But it was his fight for the dockers in the Shaw Enquiry of 1920 that brought him fame. So great was the effect that when the Councils of Action were formed in that year to stop the War of Intervention against Soviet Russia he was selected to state the case of the delegation of the Councils of Action to Prime Minister Lloyd George and threatened the government with a General Strike.

It was an amazing speech in one of the most critical situations of British political history. The country was nearer to a declaration of civil war than at any time since Cromwell. The speech is worth recalling. He said:

Behind the resolution of the Councils of Action lay the power of 6,000,000 trade unionists of the country, who by their resolutions had passed their opinion on the matter. That opinion and the decision were based upon democracy's inherent sense of fair play. Since the Revolution of 1917 the conduct of the Allies, including Britain, towards Russia had been unparalleled—at war the whole time, yet not declaring war.

We believe that the hidden forces at work in Europe (especially in Paris) have been responsible for the prolongation of this terrible conflict with Russia; that the Polish war is but a climax (or at least we hope it is the climax) of the series of wars promoted by influences outside Russia in the form of war of Kolchak, Denikin, Yudenitch and later, Wrangel. We believe that hidden forces —these reactionary forces—have been endeavouring to manoeuvre the diplomatic situation so as to make Russia appear in the wrong, so as to find excuse to declare war with all the forces of the Allies against her.

. . . Another fundamental principle at stake is that we cannot admit the right, in the event of a revolution in any country, of every other nation sending immediately the whole of their armed forces to crush out or stem the changes that are taking place. Czars have murdered thousands and we have not interfered—but if a people's revolution takes place we appear to be called upon, according to the policy of the last three years, to stamp out a terrible menace. This is a principle that Labor can no longer stand idly by and see develop.

In conclusion, we have no hesitation in putting our cards on the table. We are satisfied of this, that if war with Russia is carried on, either directly or indirectly, in support of Poland and General Wrangel, anyone who is responsible will be setting a match to material so explosive in its nature that the result none of us can foresee. We know our people are with us. It is not merely a political action but action representing the full force of Labor; and we believe, judging by the enormous support we enjoy from other classes of the community, we are representing the desire and will of the great majority of the British people.

That speech represented the high peak of his leftward development. It marked, too, his ascendancy into the ranks of the foremost leaders of the British Labor Movement. From that moment, also, he moved away from the Left toward the Right. It has been debated in various circles whether that great hour, when the whole Labor Movement of Britain was roused as never before and appeared on the verge of a revolutionary upheaval, was not deliberately staged with the cooperation of Lloyd George, to strengthen the latter's hand in his opposition to Winston Churchill who was the driving force in the government for the extension of the war against

Soviet Russia. It was well known that Lloyd George was opposed to such an extension and in favor of recognition and normal relations between governments. Be that as it may, Bevin "put his cards on the table" and was undoubtedly in favor of the policy he described and held the views he outlined.

Less than twelve months later circumstances again brought the Trade Union Movement face to face with another famous crisis. The three greatest organizations within the working-class movement, namely, the Miners' Federation, the Railways Unions, and the Transport Workers Federation, threatened the government with a general strike in defense of the miners against threatened wage reductions. Ernest Bevin was a leader of this Triple Alliance which refused to carry out its pledge to strike with the miners on the day designated forever afterward as Black Friday. Nevertheless, his fame as the "Dockers" K.C. (King's Counsel) lingered and his advance to positions of power continued. In 1925 it appeared for a bright moment as if he had moved to the Left again when Red Friday seemed to obliterate the memory of Black Friday. On a notable day in June of that year he stood at the head of the trade unions, again threatening a general strike in support of the miners once more faced with wage reductions. At the last moment the government, unready to face such a threat, called a truce for nine months, and with the aid of a subsidy of £30,000,000 to the mine owners enabled them to maintain the *status quo* with regard to the miners' wages while they got ready to deal more effectively with the situation. Red Friday proved to be not a revolutionary triumph but a red dawn, the harbinger of a coming storm. The storm broke on May 1, 1926, when the government led by Mr. Baldwin cut out the talking which had been going on for days while the Conference of Trade Union Executives sang hymns and songs and told tales in the Memorial Hall in London. When J. H. Thomas and his colleagues scurried back to the conference hall with the sad news, Ramsay MacDonald and J. H. Thomas turned the conference from singing "Lead, Kindly Light" to a great rendering of the "Red Flag." It was given to Mr. Ernest Bevin to give the signal for the general strike he did not wish to call and for which the unions had not prepared. For nine days the great strike held and in it Ernest Bevin was the man displaying organizational powers far ahead of any of his colleagues. At the end of nine days, to the consternation of the whole working-class movement, although there were no signs of weakening in the ranks of the workers, the leaders collapsed in panic lest the strike should grow and get out of their control. Mr. Bevin led the deputation to Baldwin announcing their capitulation.

That action led the Russian trade-union leaders, headed by Tomsky, to denounce the capitulation as a betrayal of the workers and especially the miners. This denunciation led to the rupture of the Anglo-Russian Trade Union Unity Committee and the end of all tolerance between Right and Left in the British Labor Movement. From that day, too, there was never any dubiety about the position of Mr. Bevin either with regard to Russia and its revolution or toward the Left of the British Labor Movement. Ernest Bevin never could take criticism. Every critic became an enemy seeking to shatter or usurp his power. From that time forward he never missed an opportunity to attack Russia. The Russians "had done him wrong" and he never forgave them. Time and again he would refer to what he had done in 1920 as spokesman of the Councils of Action, only to give himself a moral right for his new course adopted after their criticism of British trade-union leaders in 1926. But Bevin not only swung the trade unions against the Russians. Along with the General Council of the Trades Union Congress he swung Labor's policy decisively from Left to Right in every phase of its policy. The capitulation of the trade unions on that eventful day, when Bevin surrendered to Baldwin and deserted the miners, ended the leftward struggles of the trade unions which had marked their history from the end of 1918. "Never again," moaned their leaders and they meant it. They turned to the employers pleading for collaboration, good will, no more lockouts, no more strikes, and joint action to restore British economy to find work and profits for all. Mr. Bevin was the principal architect of the new collaboration expressed in the schemes of continuous action between the Trades Union Congress, the Federation of British Industries, and the Employers Federation. There would be no more general strikes now he had his grip upon the unions. In fact, there have been no great strikes of long duration. There have been many unofficial strikes but no marshaling of the great battalions which threatened the power of the state. The days lost in industrial disputes per year since Bevin swung the unions into the path of industrial peace were but a fraction of the time lost in these conflicts prior to his rise to power and his virtual domination of the trades unions.

Bevin was on the point of retirement when the war of 1939 swung him off the path of trade-union leadership into the forefront of British politics. Had he retired at that time it is no exaggeration to say that he would have done so with a prestige in British trade unionism as great as that of Gompers in the American Federation of Labor. But that was not to be. When Churchill became Prime Minister in 1940 and the British Labor Party somersaulted from its isolation policy—in the name of Pure Socialism—to Coalition, Bevin was one of Labor's Big Three—the others being Attlee and Morrison—whom he brought into the Coalition Cabinet. The choice of Bevin was unique. He was not a member of Parliament; he had never been elected to Parliament. He had long contented himself with complete devotion to the Trade Union Movement. He is the only man of the British trade unions to have leaped from outside Parliament to Cabinet rank for whom a parliamentary seat had to be found afterward. That was not only a tribute to his personal qualities as an organizer and negotiator but a recognition of his immense prestige and power in the ranks of organized labor. He was given the post of Minister of Labor and National Service and quickly demonstrated his power and capacity in all the affairs of mobilizing labor for the prosecution of the war. His record of achievements in this position was outstanding, however it may be viewed, whether from the number of reforms he initiated in the conditions of labor, the securing of the maximum number of workers in industry by the huge transfer of woman labor, the problem of transferring men and women into the forces, or the organization of demobilization at the end of the war. Had he then decided to put into operation his deferred decision on retirement he would have done so with a prestige second to none in the history of the modern Trade Union and Labor Movement reformers. But Bevin is not the retiring sort. A man of tremendous energy and resource, he now faced a change in the course of his career such as he had never contemplated.

The election of the Labor Government in 1945 and his appointment as Britain's Foreign Secretary was a surprise to the whole world, as well as to Bevin himself. His whole life had been devoted to trade unionism and collective bargaining. Although he had spoken for the trade unions on international affairs he had never been regarded as a politician. Nevertheless, he had a record on these matters. Long ago, as he rose in the ranks of his union, one of his first appointments as a delegate to an international conference was during the First World War when he was sent as a fraternal delegate to the Congress of the American Federation of Labor. There he stated the British trade unions' point of view with regard to the war at a time when America was still neutral. On his return he made his first speech on foreign policy, reporting on his visit to America. In America, Bevin had supported Gompers' proposal for an international labor conference to be held simultaneously with the Peace Conference of the governments involved. He was no pacifist, despite the Methodist associations of his youth. The next occasion on which he held forth Bevin clashed with the pacifists, led by Philip Snowden, at the Workers and Soldiers Conference at Leeds in 1917. Side by side with his old colleague, Ben Tillett, he was in opposition to the conference which proposed to set up Workers and Soldiers' Councils in England. Then, in 1920, came his famous action supporting the refusal of the dockers to load the steamship "Jolly George" with munitions for the fight against Soviet Russia, followed by his still more famous speech to Lloyd George threatening the general strike if the government did not cease its war of intervention. And that was the end of his leftward trend in international affairs.

Whatever else Bevin may be, trade-union leader, politician, organizer, he has always been first and foremost a British patriot. Whatever there has been in his career that may be designated as of class-war politics, whether he has rhetorically talked about the "Phalanx of the workers" or sentimentalized about his yesterdays, the real Bevin expressed himself thus: "I know there are lots of people who believe that the British race—and I am beating no patriotic drum—is finished with, is down and out, and is done for. I do not believe it. . . ." Again, "The British race is very peculiar; it will not go about threatening to 'thug' people, but it will defend itself when it is hit. . . ." Not a theoretician, but a "practical" working man, he was always on the defensive against those who had "done him wrong," always building up, by trial and error, power and more power. Winston Churchill once said of him: "Bevin has a lust for power and doesn't know what to do with it when he has got it." But he fights and he builds. No sooner had Baldwin and his government beaten the unions to a standstill in 1927 than Bevin emerged from the fray, not only with his scheme for collaboration with the Federation of British Industries but a new plan for the organization of the "United States of Europe," a scheme which had a direct bearing on his subsequent practice eighteen years later when he became Foreign Secretary. Hitherto, Socialists had talked about a Socialist United States

of Europe. Bevin led the Trade Union Congress of 1927
away from this idea. It was as significant in his own development as his turn away from support to Soviet Russia to his
anti-Soviet policy which followed the Russian criticism of his
leadership of the general strike. He, on behalf of his union,
proposed the following resolution:

That notwithstanding the political divisions of Europe, this
Congress instructs the General Council to further, through the
international organisations, a policy having for its object the creation of a European public opinion in favor of Europe becoming
an economic entity.

Speaking in favor of this resolution, he said:

. . . I recognise, and my Union recognises, that national aspirations and political divisions are bound to be a great handicap to
us for a long time to come, perhaps longer than we shall be on
this earth. But we also believe that if we are to develop rationally
we have got to show our people unionism in terms of raw material, in terms of harvests, cycles of trade, and exchange.

With this economic lead-in to his argument he proceeded
to use the United States of America as a model for Europe.
He referred to his visit there and said:

I found a frontier 3,000 miles long without a gun, with commerce passing to and fro pretty freely, and I came to the conclusion that if we are to deal with the problems of Europe we have
got to try to teach the people of Europe that their economic interests, their economic development, have to transcend national
boundaries. I am a little bit of a dreamer; I think it is necessary.
We have debated all this week as if Britain had no industrial
problem to solve, but Britain has got a problem, and it is no
use attacking unemployment unless we try at least to make a
contribution towards its solution, and one of the complications
throughout Europe has been the creation of a greater number of
national boundaries as a result of the Versailles Treaty breaking
up the proper organic economic distribution of commodities,
dividing the great Danubian area into several divisions, distribut-

ing and handling the ownership of raw materials from one country to another.

. . . Cast your eye over Europe with its millions of underfed,
with its millions of people with a wretchedly low standard of
living. We can have mass production, we can have intensified
production and we must direct the consuming power in order
to absorb the mass production to the millions of people of Europe,
whose standard of living is not far removed from the animal, and
whose standards are capable of being raised 1,000 per cent by
bringing together their productive capacity in return for the
craftsmanship of Western Europe.

That this had nothing to do with Socialism he proceeded to
make clear, for he added:

We want an indivisible united nation spreading from the
borders of Russia right to the borders of France, but due to political divisions they have been cut up into national sections and
their economic unity absolutely destroyed in dealing with their
own problems. . . . We have to be capable of studying all the
industrial problems associated with our movement, *not with the
idea of making preparations for the nationalisation of production,
distribution and exchange,* but trying to bring an improved
mentality to show how Labor is to face and tackle that problem.

Having laid down a course for Europe, leaving us not quite
sure as to whether Britain was included in the European
scheme or engaging in the useful occupation of putting other
people's countries and affairs in order, he exercised a pre-
eminently influential position in the program-making of the
Mond-Turner combination of the employers' and workers'
organizations. In the course of the next two or three years
this body came forward with schemes for the rationalization
of British industry and improving its competitive position
in the markets of the world. Free trade had to go by the
board and Britain become a tariff country, in fact, with both
free trade and tariffs, abandoning the gold standard, raising
wholesale prices, and stabilizing prices in general. All this
culminated in the presentation to the Trades Union Con-

gress of a memorandum on the British Empire and Commonwealth. It was the 1930 congress. Bevin was in the plenitude of his power with no one in the congress within measurable distance of challenging him for leadership. Gone were the days when he was limited to five-minute speeches before the congress. The congress flung wide the door, suspended the standing orders, granted him unlimited time to hold forth on his grand plan for the tightening up of the British Empire and setting it on the road to become an economic unit. Many a time he had assured the Labor Movement that he was "beating no patriotic drum" when that was just what he was doing. Now he assured the Congress, "I am no imperialist," as he expounded his imperial scheme. He went on:

. . . but an Empire exists in the world. Empires are not limited to the British Empire; the United States of America is as much an empire as the British Empire.

After a polemic about the First World War and the next world war and empires which used every conceivable means to gain control of raw materials, and after showing how certain groups of nations had a monopoly of some materials, he turned to the British Empire, thus:

Within this great Empire there is a tremendous fund of raw materials, and in fact, in certain commodities a monopoly. In rubber there is a majority control. If all the oil in the mandated territories and in our Colonial possessions is developed I think you will find we should have a majority of the world's output. What we appear to do is to use other people's oil and many other essentials of the world's needs. On the other hand, the United States dominates cotton and other commodities. You cannot read of Mr. Hoover in South America without realising the motive that was behind that tour for Pan-American development. . . .

The main object of this report was . . . a proposal for a definite economic organisation within what is called the British Empire . . . we have outlined this economic organisation and we trust that economic organisation will by arrangement with the rest of the country, control ultimately the raw materials within this great Empire. If we are to use Australian wool, Australia needs to understand our problem as much as we need to understand Australia's problem. If we are to use Canadian wheat it is impossible to pay for it with American motor-cars . . . Let me assume that we have organised the whole Empire, because it is not a proposal merely for the Home Government only, but it is a proposal of a fairly representative body elected by these Governments who are to be charged with responsibility. . . .

. . . when we go to a World Economic Conference and we find that one country has oil, another nation cotton, and another nation rubber, it is not a case of armies or navies settling the business; but we shall say to the others, here are the resources at our disposal, resources which will be open to you, there being no restriction of raw material for your needs, but in return there must be no restriction of supplies imposed upon us, so that we, too, may have the raw materials that we need without the fighting and financial struggle that has gone on hitherto. . . .

With a million votes in his pocket, on behalf of the Transport and General Workers Union, his imperial proposals carried the day with 1,878,000 votes to 1,401,000.

All this was in 1930 when the second Labor Government, under the leadership of MacDonald, was in its stride. Bevin was not a member of the government and at that time was the most powerful voice in the trade unions. Within a year of his victory in the congress for his proposal to make an economic unit of the British Empire, Britain was hit by an "economic blizzard." The Labor Government went down before the storm, Britain slipped off the gold standard and became a tariff country and headed toward the Ottawa Conference under Conservative leadership with a view to stepping up the measures required to make the empire function as an economic bloc.

The economic crisis changed the whole world situation. Out of the disorder and ruin of Europe Hitler rose to power in Germany and all attention was diverted from the problems of empire-building and economic rehabilitation to the new menace which challenged the very existence of the British Empire. The Disarmament Conference died and a new armament race began. The League of Nations began to flounder; the preliminaries of the Second World War were set in motion. Japan had struck at Manchuria. Mussolini struck at Abyssinia. Hitler and Mussolini struck at Republican Spain; Hitler swallowed Austria and turned on Czechoslovakia and Poland. Bevin was the first of the British labor leaders to agree with Churchill on the need for rearmament.

In 1936 he forced the Labor Party off its "tight-rope walking" policy in relation to rearmament. In the same conference he was the most powerful supporter of non-intervention on the Spanish issue and without doubt blocked the way to the repudiation of non-intervention.

In 1938, for the first time in his career, he attended the British Commonwealth Relations Conference. Of this conference he said it "was a very peculiar one" because "nobody had to come to a conclusion about anything." When he made these observations he was addressing the Royal Institute of International Affairs at Chatham House, London. "But," he said:

. . . running through the whole discussion and the constant repetition that took place under the various heads, we found ourselves constantly brought back to about five or six main points which can be regarded as the most prominent matters exercising the minds of all the representatives who were there. I put them in this order: the Commonwealth and external affairs, defence, constitutional problems, trade-colonial and empire-migration and social problems. These heads really represent the subjects which were predominent in the minds of those attending the Conference.

After a review of international affairs and their effect on dominions of the empire and commonwealth, he expressed the view that "the present method of handling external affairs between the Dominions and ourselves leaves, in my view, the peoples in the Dominions, as indeed one must confess here at home so far as the masses are concerned, in a state of ignorance." After observing that the League of Nations was ceasing to function, he made the following proposal:

. . . one of the best steps to take at the present moment would be something in the nature of a League Assembly of the British Commonwealth itself, in order that all the parties in the Commonwealth might be represented, and the facts relating to external affairs and other matters might be discussed freely and in a manner to give confidence to those who have ultimately to share the fate of the decisions of governments in these matters. . . . I thought that such an arrangement might even lead to an extension of the Commonwealth idea and provide the basis upon which to begin building up again a League of Sovereign States, something that could be made workable and restore confidence throughout the Commonwealth.

When he came to the discussion on military matters he hit up hard against one of the most important problems which had yet faced the British Empire. Growing up in a centralized empire the new nations had at no time taken any independent means for their own defense. They had been dependent, always, on the mother country. Although, step by step, the dominions had emerged from the settlement colonies, had broken down the authority of the mother country, had achieved self-government in home affairs, and then extended self-government to foreign affairs as well, and finally, had seen these legalized in the Westminster Statute of 1931, they were still dependent on the mother country for defense. Bevin did not like this arrangement and he was quite outspoken on the matter. He said:

We are bound by the Eden declaration of April 1937, in which the British people without question, without being able to say anything, must if that pledge is put into effect, go to war to defend any part of the British Empire and the countries with whom we have treaties. On the other hand, a very striking thing is that the Dominions—and I do think they quite appreciate the point—have no reciprocal obligation if their interpretation of their rights under the Statute of Westminster is correct. And I feel sure that, if the British people were conscious of the fact that they are under obligation to go to war to defend any part of the British Empire, whatever the nature of the quarrel, and, at the same time, that Canada, or any other part of the Commonwealth, can at the last moment through her Parliament declare her neutrality, they would not be a party to such a binding undertaking. I am sure that the fact is not consciously realised by the people of this country.

Continuing in his usual downright fashion, he said:

It is very doubtful whether the citizens of New Zealand and Australia, who have really to face great problems in the Pacific, have any idea of the contribution which has to be made by the British people towards their security, and it has never been examined in a practical, scientific way. The question of liberty of action was particularly emphasised so far as South Africa was concerned, and yet South Africa may represent the very centre of the problems that are looming ahead; and therefore I say that if a part of the British Commonwealth will not accept what are, in my view, obligations, neither, do I think the British people should, willy-nilly, be called upon to give effect to the whole of the Eden declaration.

Mr. Bevin was viewing the relations between the commonwealth nations as if there had been no history of the British Empire and as one totally unconscious of the geographical foundations of the empire. Modern defense rests upon industry and no war industry can be developed unless there exists within the country the foundations of heavy industry—coal, iron, steel, metallurgy, engineering industry. He spoke as one forgetful of the fact that Britain had never encouraged the development of these industries in any of the dominions. On the contrary, it had definitely retarded their independent development of these industries. Nor had Britain ever set about the task of populating the dominions. Canada's population, when Mr. Bevin was speaking, after a century of development, was not more than eleven million people. The

Australian population was not the equivalent of Manchester and Liverpool combined. Even to this day the white population of South Africa, including the Dutch and the British combined, is not equal to more than a third of the population of London. The whole of Ireland had not a population equal to half that of London. Not one of the dominions, in 1938, was physically capable of defending itself. But the strength of their traditional attachment and consciousness of dependence upon the mother country was such that they, with one accord, except in the case of Ireland which had been cut into two by partition, leaped to the defense of Britain, although they themselves were not in danger, only to find Britain totally unable to fulfill the Eden declaration when the dominions of the Pacific were attacked. They had to turn to the United States to take on what the Eden declaration had affirmed as a British obligation. Mr. Bevin could not think in any other terms than of the Collective Bargain and the machinery of power from the standpoint of John Bull.

Passing from this attempt to give a complex power machinery to the structure of the commonwealth he went on to outline a development of his empire-bloc ideas which he had first propounded in the Trades Union Congress of 1930. Referring to the proceedings of the Commonwealth Relations Conference, again, he initiated proposals which revealed that in addition to his plans for making the British Empire and Commonwealth into an economic unit, he was concerned with expansionist ideas. In this connection, he said:

I submit to you that probably the best thing to do would be to broaden the Ottawa system and invite other nations to join in it. In other words, those nations that are prepared to use the Ottawa system to come in on a lower tariff policy, should be permitted to do so.

At the 1939 Labor Party Conference, convened three months before Hitler smashed across Poland's frontiers, and the Danzig crisis was at its height, Mr. Bevin made a remarkable speech in remarkable circumstances. The Labor Party Conference had just expelled from its membership Sir Stafford Cripps, Aneurin Bevan, and George Strauss, all members of Parliament, on account of the waging a campaign for an Anti-Fascist Coalition Government. The Labor Party rejected coalition, on principle, reaffirmed its determination to stand for a pure socialist government and fight all comers in the anticipated election of 1939, which never came. That the party leaders were wholly unconscious of the imminence of war is obvious in every speech at the conference outside the ranks of the advocates of the Popular Front Coalition. Mr. Bevin passed over the war danger to project a grandiose scheme for maintaining the peace of the world. It is important to recall this speech because of the part that Bevin was destined to play in world affairs when the war drums would cease to beat and six years of slaughter would end.

No one reading this speech, in the light of subsequent historic events, need feel surprise that as Foreign Secretary his policy would call for traditional "continuity" of foreign policy in flat contradiction to the policy resolution of the Labor Party embodied in its 1945 election programme, "Let us Face the Future."

He began:

I used a phrase the other day, which I think is worth repeating and expresses what is in my mind. It was that "while we must see Collective Security as the principal weapon to resist aggression, we must always hitch our peace program to a real economic star." . . . One of the most potent causes of world disorder [is our] dominant financial policy. You attack Chamberlain today but what Chamberlain is trying to do is to fit world events into the requirements of that narrow island, the City of London. Behind Chamberlain are the bankers; they are the principal supporters of appeasement for Germany . . . I am anxious to prevent this movement fighting for the preservation of the Paris Bourse, the London Stock Exchange, and Wall Street. . . .
Is not monetary deflation one of the biggest contributors to the

present world problem? It was the cause and the only reason of the Ottawa Agreement—an Agreement which, in my opinion was one of the causes which helped to create the difficulties in Japan, thwarted the efforts of the progressive parties there, and led Japan into a policy which resulted in the attack upon China.

Referring to a visit of Mr. Bennett, ex-Prime Minister of Canada, he said:

I felt bound to call his attention to the fact that when by such an agreement you diverted world economy and attempted to make the British Commonwealth a closed corporation, you created a number of vacuums which you are now trying to fill up with armaments or economic debris.

He would refer to the Ottawa Conference again. Meanwhile he proceeded:

One of the first suggestions I would submit for consideration is the desirability of calling a British Labor Commonwealth Conference; a conference which would be organised on sound lines, with a proper agenda, and which would provide an opportunity for considering not merely how best we can resist aggression, but what contribution can be made from the vast wealth and resources and opportunities of the British Commonwealth, in land, money and raw materials, towards a general solution of the economic problems of the world. . . .

Another reason why I urge this is because we desire to work more closely and in harmony with the United States of America. *The quickest road to the United States is probably through Canada, New Zealand, Australia, Newfoundland, and Africa, and not through Europe.* On the other hand they have vital interests in the Pacific. . . .

I suggest that possibly the quickest approach to understanding with the United States of America is for us to be willing to extend the great Commonwealth idea, in which the United States can be a partner, at least economically, even though it may involve a limitation of our sovereignty.

He went on to repeat his proposals about Ottawa, inviting other countries, willing to cooperate, to "come within our preference system." This, he argued, would bring all the *Haves* together, who would control ninety percent of the essential raw materials of the world. Incidentally, he included the Soviet Union and the United States among the countries which should come into the British Empire preference system. Having got all the *Haves* together, he asked: "What should be our next step?"

He answered his own question, thus:

Our appeal must be to the people of the aggressor countries. That appeal must be genuine, for many of the Germans have said to me "All you have offered us up to now are military pacts— What have the democracies to offer out of their great abundance?" . . . Having pooled our arms, resources and economic power, cannot we then say, and mean it, to the peoples of these countries who, I believe, are as much against war as we are: "Put away your weapons of warfare, discard them as a means of bettering your conditions of life, and you can come in on the ground floor with the rest of us." We can genuinely suggest to the people of these countries that they have another alternative to the shedding of blood—a far better one, and we can pilot the world along towards a World order.

How the British Empire should absorb the rest in her preference scheme he did not explain. How long it would take to pool all the resources of the *Haves* he did not tell the conference. Nor was one word uttered as to how, after such grandiose measures had been adopted, the appeal should or could be made to the people of Germany and Japan who had already been stirred to war fever by Hitler's political and military triumphs and when the Nazis were ready to march again into Danzig and Poland. Was it to be a revolutionary appeal over the head of Hitler, stirring up the German people to revolt by means of promises of economic rewards, or an appeal through Hitler, Mussolini, and the Japanese Emperor to "come in on the ground floor"? He did not trouble to say. The whole thing was rounded off in a tremendous peroration which engulfed all criticism before it could be made.

Japan had already brought Korea and Manchuria within her "preference system," through conquest, the first in 1910, the second in 1931, as the prelude to world war. Hitler had already swallowed Austria and Czechoslovakia, and was ready to smash onward according to his own plan. Three months later, Britain was at war with Germany. The Second World War proceeded to engulf Europe.

When the war came there was no dubiety in the attitude of Bevin. All grandiose schemes of economic reorganization were brushed aside and with all energy he flung himself on to the "job to be done." It was no surprise to anyone when Churchill brought him into his Coalition Cabinet, but it is questionable as to how far the Labor movement of Britain realized the completeness of accord between these two men, one a famous Conservative and the other, ostensibly, a Socialist. The first great shock to the Labor movement, on this matter, came in 1944. Civil war had followed the defeat of the Nazis in Greece. To the consternation of the Labor Movement, the Churchill Coalition Government, which included in the Cabinet Attlee, Morrison, and Bevin, set about the task of disarming the working-class guerrillas, who had fought the Germans, and gave arms to the Fascist Greeks who had been safely ensconced in Egypt. That Bevin shocked the Labor Party Conference of 1944 by boldly supporting and justifying Churchill's policy cannot be gainsaid.

He would not change his attitude when he became Foreign Secretary of the third Labor Government, and he did not. It was obvious from the moment he arrived at Potsdam, with Attlee in place of Churchill, that he thought both Churchill and Roosevelt had gone too far in their concessions to Stalin with regard to the future of Europe. The extension of the revolution throughout the countries of eastern Europe was contrary to his own scheme for the United States of Europe. The latter could only come about through the capitalist expansion of the pre-war economy and not through social revolution. He had been against the revolution in Greece.

He was against revolution anywhere. He would fight it as vigorously as any Churchill. And he did. He was angry with the Communists of eastern Europe for having pushed the revolution so far. He had hated the Russian Communists ever since they had criticized his handling of the general strike in 1926. The struggle in Europe kept him too preoccupied to play a leading role in strictly empire affairs. Attlee and Cripps handled the great change which brought India her independence, although Bevin was present at the 1948 Conference of Prime Ministers when Burma was conceded her independence and India and Pakistan declared for continued association with the commonwealth.

A littler earlier, in 1947, he had indicated to the Trades Union Congress that he was still thinking about the future of the British Empire. Here he expressed the earnest hope that "our Commonwealth and certainly the Empire will agree—as to the possibilities of a customs union for the Commonwealth and Empire." Here had emerged once more the conception of the empire and commonwealth as an economic unit expounded by him at the Trades Union Congress in 1930. He added:

We cannot avoid any longer common defence and acceptance of certain common economic principles if we are to avoid constantly recurring crises. We have within this Commonwealth both primary products and resources which have been badly neglected. The Conservative Party has mouthed 'Empire' for generations and done nothing about it. There are tremendous resources, and the people are waiting for developments and for an upward movement in their civilized life.

In order to keep clear his view with regard to the development of the commonwealth and empire he had reprinted his 1930 speech which he had delivered to the Trades Union Congress outlining his proposals for a British Empire bloc. He sent this around to all members and staff of the Foreign Office. Ever since 1930 he has kept these views well in mind, vacillating from time to time, holding the balance between Russia and America on the one hand and a British Empire merger with America on the other.

As the post-war crisis of the nations assumed increasingly the form of a cold war between Social Revolution in the East, stretching from the western frontiers of Poland to the shores of China, he has been in complete accord with Churchills famous speech at Fulton in 1947.

In 1948, Bevin attended the Commonwealth Conference, in Canberra, and was present also at the 1949 Commonwealth Conference when India, Pakistan, and Ceylon reaffirmed their decision to remain within the commonwealth, while the commonwealth in turn adjusted its constitution to accept the republic of India as a member. But more important, still, was the second 1949 conference which was called to face the financial crisis arising from the "dollar shortage" in those countries whose currencies were geared to sterling. Most profoundly affected of all was Great Britain herself. During the Second World War her increasing dependence on America had become extraordinary. Repeated loans and the Marshall Plan had not succeeded in bridging the gap in the balance of trade between Britain and the United States.

There was a similar gap between the trade balances of the countries of the commonwealth and America but on not so large a scale as that which marked Britain's trade. This gap was draining the gold reserves of the sterling countries which were held by Britain at a rapid rate. The reserves were being drained. Now came the test as to whether the commonwealth would function in unison to cut imports from America as a means of narrowing the gap. The conference, with one accord, agreed to do so. But the crisis continued. The effect of the Cold War, since the end of the Second World War, had been to stop developing trade between East and West. The Marshall Plan had geared the countries accepting its aid to the requirements of the American government, which restricted the kind of trade permitted with the Soviet Union

and the Eastern countries, all of which narrowed the world
market and intensified trade difficulties. It blocked the sterling countries seeking new avenues of trade and which would
relieve their dependence on the United States. The plan itself was the economic phase of the Cold War. Following the
economic pact came the Atlantic Pact, in which Britain and
the Western countries of Europe agreed to a strategic defense
plan.

Thus, instead of a United States of Europe, Bevin has
accepted the division of Europe into two camps. This con-
tractionist policy, in relation to the world market, has had
its sequel in the pouring of American dollars into England
and Western Europe to stimulate production, the proceeds
of which are to be sold within a narrowing range of countries.
Hence, the agreement of the commonwealth countries to
act in unison and contract the market still further did not
solve the problem of the relation of the sterling area to the
dollar. Dollars were still short and the gold reserves continued to be drained to meet dollar commitments.

Again the crisis reached a critical stage and once more the
British Empire and Commonwealth was put to the test of
taking common action. So important was the situation that
this time, August 1949, Mr. Ernest Bevin and Sir Stafford
Cripps traveled to Washington together to confer with the
representatives of the United States and Canada, the latter's
economy and finance being now more closely related to the
United States than to Britain. From that conference came
one more great effort to solve fiscal and economic contradictions within the limits set by the Marshall Plan and the
Atlantic Pact. Britain decided to devalue the pound. The
commonwealth and soft-currency countries followed suit.
Belgium and Switzerland made "Adjustments." Would that
move stop the drain of gold from Britain and stabilize the
currency relations between the countries of the sterling
group and the United States? Mr. Bevin and Sir Stafford
Cripps thought it would. For the Washington Conference of

1949 also agreed to reduce tariff barriers and to invest great capital in the colonies of the British Empire and Britain itself. While Bevin and Cripps optimistically looked forward to the turning of the tide, Mr. Bevin's dream of the U.S.A. and other countries coming within the framework of *Ottawa Preferences* has faded and, in its place, the patron has become the U.S.A. and not the British Government.

Of the Atlantic Pact, Mr. Bevin declared at Washington in April 1949:

The Atlantic Pact is a pact which brings together the largest area of productive ability, skill and enterprise in the whole world. It is not a question of what one nation can give to another. It is a question of what we can put into the common pool. And there will be a common pool of manpower, military assistance, economic assistance and the rest of it. We seek to bring from one great pool of ability and interest an organism which I believe from its very power and wise use can be the greatest contributing factor for world peace that has ever been known.

. . . We shall throw our resources together. But may I make this declaration: it is a fundamental principle of this pact that we will never indulge in aggression—never. But to would-be aggressors, it says: Think twice—think thrice! The Second World war would never have taken place if the aggressors then had had to face a conscious organisation such as we are establishing today.

In January, 1950, Mr. Bevin attended a conference at Columbo, Ceylon, to discuss problems confronting the Pacific regions of the Commonwealth. The meeting was presided over by the Ceylonese Prime Minister, Mr. Senanayake. Called on the initiative of the Pacific region countries, the conference dramatized how completely changed had become the relationship of the nations comprising the Commonwealth. India, rather than Britain, Nehru, rather than Bevin, dominated the proceedings. The new Australian Minister of External Affairs, Mr. J. A. Spender—who had superseded Dr. Evatt after the defeat of the Labor Party at the 1949 Australian general election—entertained the idea of creating a pact of Pacific powers in order to resist social revolution in the East. It would be implemented by an economic program for the Pacific. Mr. Bevin supported the Australian view. But Nehru vetoed the Pacific Pact idea and consequently restricted the scope of the discussions.

The communique issued at the end of the Conference stated that the greater part of the deliberations were spent in "a comprehensive review of the current problems of South East Asia, both political and economic." The main conclusion was that "progress depends mainly on the improvement of economic conditions." Mr. Bevin commented that "a great step forward had been made in accepting the plan proposed by the Australian and Ceylonese delegations for credits and technical assistance to all countries of South and South East Asia willing to join in a mutual self-help scheme." He added, "we must go on striving to bring about sound economic conditions and not merely the right to vote . . . this is the problem which the conference has been trying to understand, if not to solve."

It would appear that the conference, the first to be held in Asia and the first conference to be Asia-dominated, was content to register minor achievements of agreement for self-help because it was frustrated in its larger purpose by the veto of Nehru. The Indian Prime Minister would not be a party to leading his country into one or another bloc of world powers, which had become Mr. Bevin's governing policy. Bevin was not happy with this frustration but he had to bow, like his predecessor, to Nehru and an India which was no longer an appendage of Britain. The Conference ended. Mr. Bevin, who had been ill during most of his visit, prepared to return to London. His program called for a stop-over in Cairo.

When the British Foreign Minister arrived in Cairo he is reported to have requested the Egyptian Government to permit the passage of oil tankers from the Persian Gulf area through the Suez Canal to the Haifa petroleum refineries. This was most important to Britain as these refineries were dollar-earners. The Egyptian Government is reported to have refused his request despite the fact that Egypt has no right to stop international traffic through the Suez Canal. This refusal established a most extraordinary precedent where one party to an agreement stops movement on an international highway. This further blow to British prestige in the Middle East, coming after the fiasco of his almost personal vendetta against Zionism, could not have been relished by Mr. Bevin.

He returned to London in the midst of the February, 1950 British General Election campaign. He did not retire as had been hinted he might. In the course of the election fight he sought to smother Mr. Churchill's manoeuvre in which the latter had suggested "top-level" discussions with the Soviet Union concerning the atom and hydrogen bombs. Bevin's election broadcast address to the people of Britain was a low point of the political campaign. The speech, full of self-justification, was apologetic, defeatist, and, from beginning to end, sounded like a forlorn cry rather than as a rallying call to Labor victory. In his own constituency, however, Mr. Bevin was returned to Parliament by a large majority. When the national results were announced it was apparent that Mr. Attlee would expect Bevin to continue as Foreign Secretary in the Fourth Labor Government.

Mr. Bevin is now an old man. But his somber, heavy figure represents Britain in the councils of the nations. He has grown in power through the years, and believed in the power of the big battalions. He has voiced the views of the central councils of the British Trade Unions in all matters but in none more clearly and definitely than those regarding the British Empire and Commonwealth. Whatever socialism he has preached has been always subordinate to his conservative imperialism. He grew up from the little Bethel Methodist to be a great, patriotic, British statesman whose inspiration in world affairs came not from H. M. Hyndman of the Social Democratic Federation but from Winston Churchill, the imperialist statesman. Try as he might, Mr. Bevin could not retreat to yesterday.

C H A P T E R   I X

H E R B E R T   V E R E   E V A T T

EVERY GREAT CHANGE IN THE structure of the British Empire has been preceded by a storm announcing some significant development in the shifting relations of power between the nations of the world. Out of the storm and crisis conditions there invariably emerged into the foreground of affairs some leading figure who appeared in himself to focus the changes which the crises announced. Mackenzie King typified the emergence of Canada as a nation. Field Marshal Smuts strode across the African veldt and his name proclaimed to the whole world that the Afrikander nation had arrived as an independent entity whose sovereignty over its own affairs must not be challenged. The Boers, at the beginning of the twentieth century, had challenged the might of Britain and out of that crisis was born the Union of South Africa with Smuts at its head. The First World War lifted Smuts from the level of a veldt fighter to world statesmanship, shaping the peace of Europe and putting South Africa on the map as a nation with a new purpose and a new allegiance—The British Commonwealth of Nations. What the First World War did in the case of South Africa and Smuts the Second World War did for Australia, whose principal spokesman in world affairs was Herbert Vere Evatt. The war cracked wide-open the old framework of the relations of the nations in and around the Pacific Ocean and it made Evatt the spokesman of Australia's new needs and new position.

Until the Second World War Australia had been taken for granted as an appendage of the British Empire and in that regard it also took itself for granted. Outside Australia, Evatt was little known. When the Japanese struck at Pearl Harbor they not only committed a dastardly act of aggression against the United States of America but they shattered an illusion which the Australians had cherished for generations—that the British Navy would in all circumstances and at all times be their sure defense. The British Navy and Air Force were fighting for their lives in the Atlantic. The Australians had to look in a new direction for aid and learn quickly of the changes in the power relations of nations that were taking place at a breathless speed. The man who focused this situation was Dr. Herbert V. Evatt. He had become Australia's spokesman as Minister for External Affairs in October 1941.

Evatt was born in New South Wales, in 1894, in the coal-mining district of East Maitland. Son of a storekeeper, he was educated in Sydney at the high school and university and came through with flying colors in a wide range of subjects: law, English literature, philosophy, and mathematics. He became a Master of Arts and a Doctor of Law, his doctorate thesis being a study of the British Constitution. He was not a "bookworm" nor did he isolate himself from his fellow men. He had been a good "mixer" from boyhood onward, interested in all sports, a life member of the University Sports Union, a vice-president of the New South Wales Cricket Association, and the Australian delegate to the Imperial Cricket Conference of 1938. He became a tutor in the College of St. Andrews at Sydney University and, while thus engaged in teaching philosophy and English, began to practice at the Bar. He became an LL.D. in 1924 and soon rose to a leading position in his profession. At the age of thirty-six, he was appointed a High Court judge. Never in Australian history had so young a man been appointed to so high a post.

In 1925 Evatt secured national fame in a keen legal strug-

gle before the High Court judges by his defense of two trade-
union leaders against a deportation order. He won, and the
manner of his victory gave him a national reputation. That
year he became a national politician also by being elected
to the New South Wales Parliament as the member for Bal-
main. He held the seat until 1929. When appointed to the
High Court bench, in 1930, he was known as the "Red
Judge," deepest red to some, palest pink to others. He was
classified as of the fraternity of Sir Stafford Cripps and Professor Harold Laski, the Socialist intellectuals of the British
Labor Party. It is true that Cripps and Evatt are both lawyers
and that with Laski all three are "intellectuals" but there the
comparison really ends. If an English parallel is necessary
then a more accurate comparison would be found among the
English Liberal radicals who came to the conclusion that the
state must take on greater responsibilities in all the departments of life and consequently joined the Labor Party. To
them the "Reds" are anathema, the "rosy pink" are barely
tolerable, and the nearer the party is to "off white" in political color the happier they are. Evatt is an Australian nationalist, a liberal lawyer, a political democrat with socialist
leanings.

The writings of Evatt provide ample proof of the soundness of this classification: *Liberalism in Australia, Convey-
ancing in New South Wales, The King and His Dominions,
Injustice within the Law,* and *The Life of Holman,* the
Australian labor leader who so well typified the liberal radicalism of trade unionism upon which the Australian Labor
Movement grew up. Politics, law, and sport do not set the
limit to Evatt's interests. He has written a story, *Rum Rebellion,* in which he turned his knowledge of the law and
the history of Australia to good account. He is also greatly
interested in modern art and has acquired a collection of
famous modern pictures. Interest in art he shares with his
wife, a lady of American origin, who was the first woman to

hold the post of member of the Sydney National Gallery Art Trust.

The circumstances in which this stocky, yet sturdy figure of a man, busy collecting high honors in law and letters, leaped to the front of Australian affairs and became Australia's spokesman in the councils of the nations of the world, were extraordinary. In 1940 Dr. Evatt was a High Court judge and there was not much higher to climb to the top of the hierarchy of the law. In that year the Australian Labor Party invited him to contest the Barton seat in the federal Parliament. If he accepted the invitation it meant abandoning his legal career, already so well assured, and carving out another one in politics. This he did. In March 1940 he was appointed to the Australian Advisory War Council along with Mr. John Curtin, the leader of the Labor Party. In October 1941, Labor came to power. Mr. Curtin became Prime Minister and, in turn, he appointed Evatt to be Attorney-General and Minister for External Affairs. Less than two months after his appointment Japan struck. Australia's position in world affairs was suddenly changed from that of a country on a far-distant periphery of the conflict into a storm center of paramount strategic significance to the war's outcome in the regions of the Pacific Ocean. What Australians had feared for generations had come to pass. Ever since Japan had emerged as a modern power Australians had felt that a new challenger to their existence had appeared. But fearful as they had been no one had conceived the circumstances in which she would be likely to strike southward, and, beyond bolting the Australian doors to Asiatic immigration, she had pursued her traditional course of reliance on the "Mother Country" to send her fleet to the rescue. But the fleet was not available. The mother country was preoccupied with a fight to the death on her own doorstep, to which Australia had already rallied with the enthusiastic abandon of a country completely unconscious of the imminent danger to herself.

The fact of the matter is that Australia and her nearest neighbor New Zealand had grown up as far-distant provinces of Britain with an outlook as provincial and parochial as that of any other province of the United Kingdom. Territorially, of course, Australia is many times the size of Britain. With an area of nearly three million square miles, a little less than that of the U.S.A., it has a population of just over 7,000,000 people, that is, less population than New York or London. Forty percent of the territory lies within the tropics. The population is scattered along the eastern coast and the southeastern corner while vast stretches of central Australia are desert land and almost uninhabited. Only two cities have populations exceeding a million; Sydney with 1,300,-000 and Melbourne with 1,077,000. The capital of Australia, Canberra, has a population of not more than 12,000. Ninety-five percent of the population is of British descent. The principal industries are rural. Sheep-raising in Australia is a key industry. It produces about one fourth of the world's supply of wool. In 1939-40 Australia produced more than a billion pounds of wool, two hundred thousand tons of butter, six million tons of sugar cane, and two hundred million bushels of wheat. The mining industries are gold, silver, lead, coal, copper, tin, and zinc. Industrialization has been proceeding rapidly and Australia produces increasingly machines and machine tools, textiles and clothing, foodstuffs, chemicals, and wood and paper products. The United Kingdom takes fifty percent of Australia's exports and forty percent of Australia's imports come from Britain. The economic ties are, therefore, strong supplementary bonds to those of racial stock.

The forms of government in Australia have their prototypes in the homeland—the United Kingdom. The legislative power of the commonwealth, established by the Constitution Act of 1900, is vested in the Federal Parliament, consisting of the Sovereign, the Senate, and the House of Representatives. The King is represented throughout the

Commonwealth by the Governor-General who, subject to the constitution, has such powers and functions as the Sovereign assigns to him. In each state there is a state governor and a state parliament. The relations between ministries and the representatives of the people are the same as those prevailing in Britain.

Australia has grown to nationhood as a province of the United Kingdom, twelve thousand miles away from London. The Australians grew up as country cousins of the English, Scotch, Welsh, and Irish. The family relations were good and the economy of each country complementary to the other. One provided foodstuffs and materials for clothing and the other the products of her machine industry, in exchange. Isolated from the great power struggles of Europe, and all threats and challenges to her interests in the Pacific a long way off, there was no great urge to rapid industrialization, immigration, or independence. Self-government in local affairs was a carryover from the country of origin and in no sense a struggle for separation from, and independence of, the mother country. The general homogeneity of the population left the Australians free from the conflict of nationalities, as in the case of Canada and South Africa. The support given by the Australian representative to the War Cabinet of 1914-18, to the proposal of Canada that the dominions should be independently represented at the Peace Conference, was in no sense the result of centrifugal tendencies of Australia. On the contrary, Messrs. Hughes and Bruce, the spokesmen of the Australians on these occasions, regarded their support for the proposal as a strengthening of the bonds of empire, as extra votes for Britain at the Peace Conference. They accepted the Balfour Declaration of 1926 as a clarification of their relationship with Britain and not as an innovation. While South Africa promptly passed the Westminster Statute of 1931 through its own Parliament, and legalized South Africa's independent sovereignty, Australia was unmoved and did nothing about it until October 1942.

Dr. Evatt introduced the Statute of Westminster Adoption Bill in 1942. When every Australian was supremely conscious that Australia had been caught in an entirely unforeseen circumstance, he put the question: "Will the adoption of the statute weaken the imperial tie?" Having put the question, he replied:

My answer is unhesitatingly "No." I go further. I say that the tie between Britain and Australia will be confirmed and strengthened. It would be sorry day if the Australian people were told that their relationship with the people of Britain might be weakened merely because Australians desired that legislation on Australian affairs, passed by their own representatives in their own Parliament should no longer run the risk of invalidation and annihilation by means of a British Act of Parliament which was quite suited to the colonial conditions of 1865 but is quite unsuited to the needs of Australia today—nearly eighty years afterwards. In my submission, the passage of this Bill will give further emphasis to the undoubted fact that the real link between Britain and Australia is not the legal subordination of the Parliament of this great Dominion to the Parliament of the United Kingdom at Westminster but the unity of the Crown throughout the Empire, our common allegiance to the King and indissoluble tie of tradition and kinship which binds the two people. . . .

We are an Australian Government responsible primarily to the people of Australia. We need this legislation in order to remove burdensome restrictions and unsatisfactory delays which still clog the rights of Australians to control their own domestic affairs. Britain does not object to what we are doing. On the contrary, Britain has made our course an eminently suitable one, because in this piece of legislation it has included safeguards to meet the special position of Australia. Why should we not accept this offer in the spirit in which it was made? It will assist us in the exercise of the rights of self-government in Australia.

The belated passing of this legislation testified that Australian independence was thrust upon Australia and not won by their independent struggles against the central government of the empire located in London. In fact, Australian independence was a by-product of the struggles of the Canadians and South Africans. This is true also of her neighbor dominion, New Zealand.

Situated some twelve hundred miles eastward of Australia, New Zealand has an era of 103,934 square miles and a population of 1,634,000. The majority of the population are of Scottish descent. There are also about 93,000 Maoris (aboriginal Polynesians). Again, New Zealand, like Australia, is an agrarian country. Her prosperity is almost entirely dependent on the export of wool, meat, and dairy products. It is essentially a country of small farmers. While New Zealand's record of social legislation is one of the best in the world, in imperial relations it has been the most docile of all the dominions. It reached "Dominion Status" in 1907 and, while giving a nodding approval to the Statute of Westminster, it continued as before. It sells most of its exports to Britain and buys most of its imports from her in return. It has no foreign policy of its own. In its early years it echoed the British Government. In later years, between the two world wars, it echoed the British Labor Party. It looked to the British Navy to defend her and gave herself unreservedly to the service of Britain in her wars. It was a great shock to New Zealanders when they were compelled by the force of circumstances to look elsewhere than to Britain for aid against Japan. For New Zealand was little more than an island village of Britain set far away in the Pacific.

It was this same shock, resulting from the changed relations of the powers of the world and revealed so completely when Japan set forth to conquer the nations of the Far East, that drove Dr. Evatt on to the world's stage in a dual role. He became the champion of the peoples of these two outposts of the British Commonwealth of Nations and the "David" of the small nations against the Goliaths of the great powers. Ten days before the Japanese attack on Pearl Harbor Dr. Evatt made his first speech as Australia's Foreign Minister. Although in that speech he displayed no sense of awareness of impending catastrophic developments in the war, there is a clear indication that Evatt was fully conscious of Australia's geographical position and that she should, with greater vigor, assert her own importance and establish her claims as an independent country. Evatt's speech was an outspoken survey of the international situation. The date was November 1941. He said:

It is a strange feature of the present struggle that, while we are allies of Russia in the fight against Germany, we are still at peace with these three eager satellites (Finland, Hungary and Roumania) and accomplices of Germany.

This was a sharp rap across the knuckles of the leaders of Britain and America. But turning to the Far Eastern situation he said:

Australia has a supreme and special interest in preventing forcible aggression in the Pacific. The Commonwealth Government has recently had valuable discussions with Mr. Duff Cooper, a member of the Churchill Ministry, who was specially appointed to Singapore. In consultation with members of the Advisory War Council, the War Cabinet discussed with Mr. Duff Cooper ways and means for improving the political organisation of the defence effort which is centred at Singapore. Experience shows that the Commonwealth has a great and increasing interest in such organisation, and that *it is entitled to join on a footing of equality* with the United Kingdom in any body which is constituted to deal with political matters of Pacific defence.

That was Round One in the fight by Evatt to establish Australia not merely as an outpost of the British Commonwealth in the Pacific but as the *principal representative of British Commonwealth interests* in that part of the world. From this point onward Evatt begins to shape an independent foreign policy for Australia. The key to his policy is found in his recognition of Australia as the rampart for regional groupings in the Pacific both within the British Commonwealth and within the larger framework of the United

Nations or any other international organization that might replace it.

There is in this same speech an acknowledgment that Britain no longer held the lead in Pacific affairs and that this had passed to the United States. After reporting on the conversations then proceeding between Japan and the U.S.A., he said:

It should be emphasised that the talks are confined to the U.S.A. and Japan, although, of course, they are of very great concern to the British, Australian, Netherlands and Chinese Governments. We are quite content to allow the leadership and initiative in this matter to be retained by the United States, which is very directly affected by any armed aggression in the South-East corner of the Asiatic continent. . . . At the same time, I must express the hope that the talks will result in an agreement. If so a new chapter might commence in the relationships between the leading Pacific Powers.

Hardly had the echoes of that speech died away than the pious hopes of a peaceful settlement with Japan were shot away. On December 16, 1941, Evatt appeared before the House of Representatives to report on what the Australian Government had done in response to the new situation which had caught them all "unawares." Evatt put on a bold front and opened out by asserting that his government's "attitude throughout was clear and unequivocal. We never underestimated Japan's fighting strength. . . ." All that is as it may be. But the whole speech shows the new Foreign Secretary of Australia striding into action as an Australian nationalist, making it quite clear that Australia is no longer ambling along through history at the tail-end of Britain, but as an equal partner with the United Kingdom, and determined to be a *leading* partner in relation to affairs in the Pacific. First, he showed that the declaration of war by Australia was an independent act of Australia in direct association with the King without participation or interference of any kind by the United Kingdom ministers. Secondly, he pointed out that his remarks meant no weakening of the ties that bind Australia to Britain. Then he made his bow to the might of the United States. After that he demonstrated that until the war came into the Pacific, Australia had, at the call of England, sent her forces everywhere, without any special regard for Australia's special interests in the Pacific and in complete lack of anticipation that they would be required for the defense of her own shores. He said:

Before war came into the Pacific, we had entered into commitments all over the world. We are discharging these commitments to the best of our ability. Our airmen are fighting in England. They are training in Canada. Our sailors have fought with indomitable courage on distant shores in Europe, in Africa, in Asia.

But what of the defence of these shores? The Government has been stocktaking. It has inherited a situation in which, for one reason and another, the defence of our country has been treated as a subordinate and subsidiary part of the distant war. From now onwards we shall be thrown back more and more upon our own resources.

Tis well! from this day forward we shall know
That in ourselves our safety must be sought;
That by our own right hands it must be wrought;
That we must stand unpropped, or be laid low.

These were very noble sentiments representing a truly fine spirit. Australia, however, may be a continent in area, but her population numbered a few more than seven millions. Her machine industry was in its infancy. Her Navy, which she could not herself build, amounted to no more than a handful of ships and her Air Force had only just been born. The raw deal which history now handed out to the faraway sons of Britain, maturing in their insularity, was to make them wholly dependent upon the United States of America for their salvation from the depredations of the Japanese.

Here began a struggle to readjust Australia's position to her own requirements, and in accord with her newfound spirit of independence Dr. Evatt was in the forefront of that fight. Here was a man who knew he had a case and knew how to fight for it. Australians may have grown up as the country cousins of the Britons and have been content to be treated as such in the hierarchy of the British Empire and Commonwealth but that was not the estimate by Evatt of the part Australia was called upon to play in the year when he became Australia's Foreign Secretary. Promptly, on behalf of the Australian Government, he requested Mr. Duff Cooper to arrange for the commonwealth representative at Singapore, Mr. Bowden, to take a seat on the War Council which the United Kingdom Government had recently set up.

By the middle of February 1942, Australia's position had become serious. Singapore had fallen to the Japanese. The greater part of the Australian 8th Division—18,000 men— was taken prisoner. Mr. Curtin, Prime Minister of Australia, called this disaster "Australia's Dunkirk." On February 25 Evatt again reviewed Australia's position before the Australian Parliament and launched forth with the demands that Australia's representatives be admitted to the highest councils of Allied strategy and policy-making in relation to the conduct of the war. He said:

I suggest that one outstanding lesson of the campaign is the fundamental need for creating effective machinery to ensure that there shall not be only Allied Unity of command, but a guarantee of a common strategical plan backed by the pooling of Allied resources and the sound allocation of those resources to Allied Forces. . . . In practical terms, the co-ordinating of Allied effort including at least:

(1). Machinery for the higher direction of the war, so that while decisions can be made with speed and firmness due weight is given to all phases of the conflict and to the special situation of the various allies.

(2.) The setting up of a unified command or commands to wage war against the enemy;

(3). Machinery to handle reinforcements and supply in accordance with the decisions of the higher authority.

The capture of Singapore by the Japanese disposed of the Advisory War Council under Duff Cooper. In any case, it was not enough for the purposes Evatt had in mind. He wanted an inter-Allied body, for the higher direction of the war in the Pacific, to be set up in Washington, and Australia to be able to confer with the United States and China on an equal footing. Churchill, who had conversation with Roosevelt in Washington, blocked the way. He would have none of this ex-colonial representation and tried to set up a South West Pacific Command, under General Wavell, without the Australians. The Australian Government would have none of that. Then Mr. Churchill proposed a Far Eastern or Pacific Council, to sit in London. This council was to be composed of representatives of the United Kingdom, Australia, New Zealand, and the Netherlands. The Australians accepted this without ceasing their efforts to get their feet under the same table as the Americans and the British. The council, proposed by Churchill, was a United Kingdom affair only and subordinate to the combined command of the U.S.A. and the United Kingdom sitting in Washington. Evatt put the matter thus:

. . . at no point whatever does any representative of this country [Australia] meet any representative of the United States in any council, committee, or strategic body directly concerned in the controlling of the Allied War against Japan, or for that matter Germany or Italy.

It is quite clear that Mr. Churchill could not free himself of the habit of treating Australia and New Zealand as country cousins of near-colonial status. He showed this again in 1942 when the Australian Government "asked that its representatives should have the right to be heard in the United Kingdom War Cabinet, in the formulation and direction of policy." Churchill took the view that it was not in accordance with constitutional practice, since constitutional practice had consisted of inviting the commonwealth representative to be present at War Cabinet meetings *when anything directly affecting it was under discussion.*

Neither Evatt nor the Australian Government, now thoroughly roused to a full consciousness of Australia's position in Pacific affairs, were prepared to let matters rest there. They felt that they, and the war in the Pacific, were being treated as of secondary importance. The Australian Government, without hesitation, lifted the whole matter out of the realm of diplomatic conversations into the full glare of world publicity. Dr. Evatt was sent on a mission to America and Britain to thrash these matters out while Prime Minister Curtin publicly addressed the people of America over the wireless from Australia. It was a dramatic appeal and a challenge to the British and American Governments. After recounting Australia's part in the war, Curtin said:

We looked to America, among other things, for counsel and advice, and therefore it was our wish that the Pacific War Council should be located at Washington. It is a matter of some regret to us that, even now, 95 days after Japan's staggering advance south, ever south, we have not obtained first-hand contact with America. Therefore, we propose sending to you our Minister for External Affairs [Dr. H. V. Evatt] who is no stranger to your country, so that we may benefit from his discussions with your authorities.

In sending Evatt on this mission, it was soon obvious that here was a man who would not pull his punches and would not hesitate to say what was in his mind. Mr. Curtin had spoken on March 14. On March 28, Evatt was in Washington publicly criticizing the Allies and demanding the establishment of a War Council at Washington for the direction of the war in the Pacific and that the War Council must number representatives of Australia, New Zealand, and the Pacific countries. He said on this occasion:

Australia is specially anxious to improve, in one or two respects, the method of organising our common effort. When several na-

tions join together to achieve victory in war they can only succeed if their accredited representatives consult as to ways and
means. Forces must be combined; physical requirements must be
provided for all the forces. Supreme commanders must be chosen;
joint plans must be made. Effective machinery for consultation is
required. It is not a matter of satisfying national pride, for the
fate of every Allied nation is involved.

Of course, the existence of Allied Councils can never be a
guarantee of success. On the other hand, the absence of regular
consultation may be the cause of failure and frustration. A great
deal depends upon the ability and the moderation of those who
consult. . . .

If existing methods of co-operation are shown to be inadequate,
we change them. . . . In Australia we are not interested in
formulas. We must have action, made quickly, and followed up
energetically right down the line to the point of physical contact
with the enemy. The decisions should be made by the best brains
which the United Nations can call to their aid . . . Each nation,
we believe, should have *some* effective part in the decisions that
are made.

Mr. Curtin believes that, in relation to the Pacific Front a common council established here in Washington would enable Australia to make a more effective contribution to the cause we have
in common.

In early April it was possible for Evatt to record that his
mission had succeeded. Speaking in New York, on April 5,
he announced:

For three months Mr. Curtin has asked for the establishment of
a War Council at Washington to determine how best the war
against Japan can be carried to the offensive. This Council has
now been established. It meets at Washington under the chairmanship of President Roosevelt. On it are represented the United
States, the United Kingdom, Canada, China, Netherlands, together with Australia and New Zealand. I have represented Australia on this body.

This was Evatt's first big political triumph in world politics. Prior to this event he had been an Australian figure,
known only to Australia. With this mission to America and

Britain, and its success, he had made his debut on the international stage. From New York he went to London, broadcast to the people of Britain, addressed a Labor Party conference, traveled to Washington for meetings of the council, and returned to Australia to receive the congratulations of the Australian Government for the mission he had performed.

Evatt thoroughly enjoyed his triumph. He had not only won a case for Australia and truly reflected its now rising nationalism in the most critical stage of its history but he had put himself on the map of the world, too. He had grown up with definite principles, and, like most men who reach the front ranks in any walk of life, his ego was not hidden under a bushel. He was fully conscious that Evatt was making history and he was rather pleased that it was Evatt who was taking the stage. First, he was an Australian, sensitive to the fact that there were only seven million Australians who were belatedly asserting their emancipation from colonial status. Second, he was fundamentally a liberal with Liberalism's emphasis on individualism, self-determination of nations, demanding plenty of room for the little man to become a big one. Theoretically, he was in the tradition of Wilson and Roosevelt but always with the fundamental difference, which developed his precocity and aggressiveness, that while he was the spokesman of a small nation, they were spokesmen of big powers. But time and geography favored him. It may be true that the day of independent small nations is gone, but Herbert Vere Evatt would show that they had an important place in the scheme of things, and that Australians, in particular, were not mere appendages of any great power.

After the Yalta Conference of the Big Three, a conference was held in Cairo in which Churchill and Roosevelt were predominant and to which neither Australia nor New Zealand were invited. Indeed, the Cairo declaration was "news" to them, laying down principles for the peace settlement in East Asia, including new territorial boundaries.

Evatt and his fellow Australians and New Zealanders resented this procedure and were not at all slow in letting the big powers know it. He didn't like being treated as a colonial by Mr. Churchill or as a little fellow from "Down Under" by Mr. Roosevelt. Fearing that this procedure was a forerunner of what would happen in all directions when the hour of victory came nearer, Evatt led the way in a two-nation protest of Australia and New Zealand and demanded their active participation in the peace-planning armistice commissions which would also work out terms of settlement with the enemies.

This served to emphasize the community of interest of Australia and New Zealand and the necessity for united action with regard to all future arrangements in the Pacific zone. On the initiative of Evatt, the Australian Government convened a conference of Australian and New Zealand ministers to work out what became known as the "Australian-New Zealand Agreement." The conference met at Parliament House, Canberra, on January 17, 1944, and completed its work on Friday, January 21, five days later. In addition to the Foreign Ministers themselves, the Prime Ministers of Australia and New Zealand, Mr. John Curtin and Mr. Peter Fraser, attended. This was a happy day for Curtin, who had invited Evatt to become Attorney-General and Minister of External Affairs, although Evatt had not had previous experience in the Federal Parliament when elected in 1941. He and Evatt were good friends, as well as colleagues. John Curtin had been born on January 8, 1885. His birthplace was in Victoria. He grew up as a worker in newspaper offices, the potteries, and factories until he became the Secretary of the Timber Workers' Union in Melbourne. It is said that he was greatly influenced in his political and personal development by Tom Mann, the English syndicalist, one of the greatest orators of the British Labor Movement, and that Curtin's own oratory was much after the style of Tom Mann's. He was an undoubtedly gifted speaker with a rich vocabulary. He was personally very popular throughout the Australian Labor Movement. In 1917 he went to live in West Australia where he edited the *West Australian Worker*, a labor journal, until 1928, when he entered the Federal Parliament as member for Freemantle. Defeated in the elections of 1931, the same constituency returned him in 1934. Shortly afterward he became the leader of the Labor Party in the Federal Parliament and in 1940 the Prime Minister. However much Tom Mann may have influenced him in his youth, Curtin, like most trade-union leaders who turn into politicians, became a moderate.

Mr. Peter Fraser, the Prime Minister of New Zealand, was born in Fearn, Scotland, in 1884. He was of working-class origin and self-educated. As a young man he joined the Independent Labor Party and became well known as an able speaker and exponent of the Keir Hardie brand of Socialism. In 1900 he emigrated to New Zealand and became a dock laborer. In 1910 he was elected to the House of Representatives; twenty-five years later he became Minister of Education, and in 1940 he succeeded to the prime ministership of a Labor government. Fraser had always maintained a close personal contact with the land of his birth. While New Zealand, in its political history, had never had any distinctive foreign policy of its own, its policy, until jolted out of insularity by the Second World War, had been essentially British. "Where Britain goes, we go. Where Britain stands, we stand," was Fraser's motto, although between the two world wars the Labor government of New Zealand supported His Majesty's Labor Opposition in its representation in the League of Nations. New Zealand's representatives and the New Zealand Parliament had been very lukewarm throughout in their attitude to changes within the British Empire. Indeed, Mr. Peter Fraser supported Lord Halifax's empire consolidation speech at Toronto in January 1944. He and his government had been wholly indifferent to the Statute of Westminster. They were well content with the old position of New Zealand in relation to the United Kingdom. Only the isolated position in which both New Zealand and Australia found themselves after Japan opened fire on the Pacific regions brought them to self-awareness and to an understanding of the key positions they held among the Pacific nations.

It did not prove difficult to reach an agreement between New Zealand and Australia, in the newly found sense of urgency. The hand of Dr. Evatt can be seen clearly at work in the terms of the agreement. In it he was laying the basis of his policy of regionalism within the larger framework of international association and staking the claim of Australia and New Zealand as being in pivotal positions for the application of regionalism to the Pacific. This would apply not only to the United Nations Organization, or any organization which might supersede it, but also to the British Commonwealth of Nations. The document itself was very comprehensive, dealing with all existing matters between the two countries and their common policy in relation to the world at large. It defined the means of continuous exchange of information and discussion and declared that "the two Governments agree to act together in matters of common concern in the South-West and South Pacific Areas." They proceeded at once to act by declaring in the agreement itself that the two governments should "be represented at the highest level on all armistice planning and executive bodies." It staked out what should be considered as the regional zone for the South West and South Pacific areas. It "should be based on Australia and New Zealand, stretching through the arc of the islands North and North-east of Australia, to Western Samoa and the Cook Islands." It dealt further with civil aviation and the future of the dependencies and territories in the Pacific, welfare of native peoples under their jurisdiction, migration of peoples, permanent machinery of collaboration, and the like.

Of the relations of this agreement to the British Commonwealth Dr. Evatt declared in his report to the Australian Parliament on February 10, 1944:

The making of the agreement between the two members of the British Commonwealth of Nations is a practical illustration of inter-Commonwealth co-operation. The arrangement is a striking exercise of these powers of full self-government in external affairs which are an indispensable adjunct to Dominion Status. Further, the strengthening of two members of the Commonwealth by their agreement to act together in their external relations would be a valuable contribution to the strength of the Commonwealth as a whole.

That is true, of course, but there was much more significance to the following reference to the agreement which he made in the same speech:

It says, in effect, that Australia and New Zealand have taken to heart the bitter experiences resulting from the failure to achieve collective security and the international order which must be based on security. It says that Australia and New Zealand are resolved to establish in their part of the world a regional system of defence and security. The two countries have undertaken to play their part in these great plans within the framework of a world security system, and by their initiative in making and publishing this Agreement, they have, I think, given a lead on certain vital aspects of international relationships in the post-war world.

The agreement was not entirely original except in its application to Australian and New Zealand affairs and to Pacific questions in particular. But it was clear that Evatt had a policy for Australia and New Zealand based upon a principle which was applicable to a number of regions other than the Pacific and important to any international organization that should emerge from the war. Evatt was supremely conscious that a nation of seven million inhabitants could not travel far on its own. Nor could it go far in collaboration with another nation when the second had a population of less than two millions. In fact, he saw in this plan for regionalism in the Pacific, with Australia and New Zealand as foundation members, the means whereby the small nations could use their combined strength to effect collaboration with the big powers on more equitable terms. In commending the agreement to the Australian Parliament he said:

> The Australian—New Zealand Agreement is not isolationist. . . . The whole agreement contemplates a regional arrangement which, from beginning to end, is made subject to a system of world security. . . . The Agreement invites collaboration with all other countries having interests in this quarter of the globe including France, the Netherlands, Portugal and above all Great Britain and the United States of America.

A much greater assembly would soon know that Evatt was giving to Australia a coherent national policy based upon his conception of Australia's place in the world. From the moment of his appointment he began to build up his department and extend its diplomatic range. For the first time Australia began to act as a grown-up nation. Australian representatives attended the International Wheat, Bretton Woods, and U.N.R.R.A. conferences. Evatt visited America again and later represented Australia in London at the British Commonwealth of Nations Conference to consider the Dumbarton Oaks draft of the U.N. Organization and Charter. In these visits to America and Britain he showed himself preparing to become the spokesman of the small nations, challenging the great powers with the weapon of criticism and mobilizing the "little men." He lectured to the University of California and to the Royal Institute of International Affairs in London. In these lectures he accepted the current thesis emerging from the wartime alliances to the effect that:

> It is fairly apparent that in the immediate post war years the great preponderance of the world's military strength will lie in the hands of the three powers: Britain, the United States and the

Soviet Union. Indeed, the military strength of each one of the three will be so great that any security organisation that does not have the full backing of all three on all matters involving the use of armed forces will have little chance of success. This implies that means must exist or be found for eliminating every possible difference of opinion among these powers. Not only must they act unitedly to deal with aggression in its incipient stages, but they are themselves to be regarded as having undertaken never to use external force as an instrument of national policy. Leadership of the Big Three will be vital because leadership involves specially onerous responsibilities as well as very unusual opportunities and rights.

Having bowed to the mighty, the "representative of the little Davids" proceeded to take account of the giants:

History does not at all support the view that wisdom is confined to the strongest nations, or that knowledge is to be found only at the centre of power.

That was point number one. Then he staked the claim of the small powers. He said:

It is a fact that even the so-called small powers may have an important and even decisive influence in certain regions. Partly for this reason, it is necessary that Powers other than the great powers which are included on the various executive councils of the world organisation should be selected to ensure a fairly balanced outlook on world affairs. Every distinct group of the globe should be considered, and no important group of nations should remain unrepresented upon such executive bodies.

That was the opening of his campaign, anticipating the inaugural conference of the United Nations to be held in San Francisco in April 1945. He followed the speech with another in London in which he raised the issue of the veto powers by the Big Five on the proposed Security Council.

He led the Australian delegation at San Francisco. Whether by accident or design, and almost from the beginning of the conference, Evatt took the center of the stage. He

made his biggest fight on the issue which almost tore the
United Nations apart before the Organization was founded.
Evatt regarded the proposals in the Dumbarton Oaks draft
of the U.N.O. constitution as proposals for Big Power domination and the "nigger in the woodpile" proving that that
was the principle of "Big Five Unanimity." Against this
principle he set the Liberal principle of government by majority vote, as in national parliamentarism. Whether Evatt
saw the full implications of his fight, it is difficult to say. All
the arguments he advanced in the Assembly and in committee were essentially legalistic, Liberal, parliamentarian.
But it would appear that the principle of *Big Five* Unanimity, which in practice at this stage meant *Big Three* unanimity, was evolved to insure a working agreement between
America, Britain, and Russia. This could be established only
by compromise arrangements between the two social systems. Unless the three powers upon whom depended the
peace of the world could agree on common action the international organization would become not an instrument for
maintaining the peace of the world but the means of sharp-
ening their differences and of marshaling votes and power
behind the differences. These appear to have been the considerations in the minds of Roosevelt, Churchill, and Stalin
when they agreed upon the Big Five Unanimity principle,
before Roosevelt's death. As it happened the Big Five came
to the San Francisco Conference already pledged to stand by
this principle. The war was still raging and all the circumstances favored the maintenance of that principle. In the
process, too, they made it difficult to change from that position once the organization had been established for Big Five
Unanimity would be required to alter the constitution.
Should any of the Big Three decide afterward to reject the
principle they would have either to leave the United Nations
or to indulge in some fantastic efforts to build a counter organization while paying lip service to their original pledges.

There is no evidence that Evatt foresaw the developments arising from his battle at San Francisco. He was not only Australia's spokesman but he became the foremost mouthpiece of the small and medium-sized nations, fighting at every step to liberalize the proposed constitution. He achieved a great measure of success, was hailed as the Champion of the Small Nations, and given a great ovation at the end of the proceedings.

He could then claim, as a result of the various amendments he had moved to the original draft of the provisions of the constitution, that the Assembly could discuss and recommend any proposals within the scope of the UNO Charter and that even the scope of the Charter had been enlarged by his amendments to include practically everything affecting the peace and welfare of the world. Through his proposals the *UNO Economic and Social Council* committed all the member nations to a policy of full employment and higher living standards. He also advocated that all non-self-governing countries should be protected from abuses by every trustee power being under the obligation to report regularly to UNO on the economic, social, and educational developments of all subject peoples.

On the major issue of the Great Power veto he did not win. But he let loose into the Assembly a stream of liberal criticism which was to gather momentum outside the UNO and to be given a direction of which he did not then conceive. He scored a further political victory in the San Francisco Assembly, revealed himself in the role of Australian nationalist. He blocked the way to UNO having any control over immigration policies. China and France were sponsoring the counter-proposal. Up rose the Australian, standing firm for a White Australia. Speaking directly to the Chinese delegate he said:

I want to be frank with you. Australia is a good friend of China. But you have insisted on the right to determine the composition of your people. Australia wants that right too. What you are attempting to do now, Japan attempted after the last war, and was prevented by Australia. Had we opened New Guinea and Australia to Japanese immigration after the last war the Pacific War by now might have ended disastrously and we might have had another shambles like that experienced in Malaya.

There spoke the fear of the little Australian occupying a big continent. Nevertheless, he was *the man* of the San Francisco Conference. He fought ably in conference and in committee. He knew what he wanted and went for it. He was not a polished diplomat or an orator of the first order. He was a plain speaker. He had a sense of humor more ironic than good-natured. He was as tenacious as a terrier and prepared to mix it with all comers. He made great headway.

His greatest contribution to the foundation conference of UNO lay, however, in his proposals on territorial trusteeship. The Dumbarton Oaks draft contained no trusteeship provisions—a striking omission. The proposals which Evatt outlined, and which were adopted by the United Nations, sought to pledge all governments responsible for less-developed peoples to regard their responsibility as a trust, to report regularly to the Trusteeship Council of UNO, to provide for the holding of mandates and defining mandate terms with a general system of trusteeship replacing the mandatory system of the League of Nations.

By his work at the United Nations Conference of 1945 Evatt established himself as a world statesman. Instead of the end of the war bringing his retreat to Australia and subsequent absorption in purely Australian affairs he became more active than ever in international affairs. After returning to Australia and reporting to Parliament on the labors of his delegation at San Francisco he went to London for the special conference of representatives of the British Commonwealth Governments concerning problems of the European peace settlement. The time was September 1945. Fighting on all fronts had ceased. The din of warfare as yet unsilenced, the difference of attitude of the Western powers and the Soviet Union toward the social revolutions which had followed in the tracks of the war in Europe and Asia, led to a realignment of the nations and a general deterioration in their relations with each other. Writing in *Foreign Affairs*, after this conference on the failure of the Council of Foreign Ministers to reach agreement on the problems of European peace, Evatt declared:

We are passing through a period of acute pessimism in relation to international affairs. A feeling of disillusionment prevails among our victorious armies, despite the magnificent victories they have gained over our enemies.

Having recorded this mood, he opened fire on the big powers once again. He continued:

A great part of the responsibility for this state of disillusionment must be attributed to those leaders amongst the great Powers who have attempted, and are still attempting, to make the writing and the execution of the peace treaties their own exclusive prerogative.

He reviewed the many occasions during the war when the Big Three had ignored the small powers—the Cairo conference, the early stages of the Pacific war, Dumbarton Oaks, Potsdam, and the Council of Foreign Ministers meeting in London in September 1945. He then told how he succeeded, with the support of the other members of the British Commonwealth, in securing agreement for the peace conference to include representation of all belligerents at a Paris conference.

Again he returned to Australia and on March 13, 1946, reported to Parliament. In this report he drew attention to a striking development in the British Commonwealth of Nations. This arose out of the appointment of three Australians to represent not only Australia but other members of the commonwealth, including the United Kingdom. Evatt said:

It is sufficient to suggest that an entirely new concept in British Commonwealth relations is now emerging. This concept tends to reconcile full Dominion autonomy with full British Commonwealth co-operation. The same principle involves the possibility of a Dominion's acting in certain regions or for certain purposes on behalf of the other members of the British Commonwealth, including the United Kingdom itself. This is evidence that the machinery of co-operation between the nations of the British Commonwealth has now reached a stage where a common policy can be carried out through a chosen Dominion instrumentality in an area, or in relation to a subject matter, which is of primary concern to that Dominion. This principle is capable of extension and suggests the possible integration of British Commonwealth policy at a higher level by a new procedure.

This acceptance of Evatt's regionalism was the first practical example of its operation in the history of the British Commonwealth. He wished to see it extended so that there would be regular conferences convened, first in one dominion and then another, with special conferences for specific purposes in specific regions, the dominions in a region being the sponsors. In 1947 he had the honor of presiding at a conference of the British Commonwealth of Nations in Canberra, Australia. Of this event, he said in a broadcast address in London in 1948:

This Canberra Conference evidenced an entirely new principle that within the Commonwealth the leadership and initiative need not always rest upon Britain herself. On the contrary, in certain areas, and for certain purposes, far greater and perhaps the greatest responsibility, may have to be placed upon one or more selected members of the Commonwealth group.

Evatt's insistence on the principle of regionalism had paid good dividends in the development of the commonwealth, as his fight on behalf of the small nations did for him in the United Nations. For at the 1948 Assembly gathering in Paris Evatt was honored by election to the post of President of the United Nations. If those who voted for him on this occasion did so in the hope that this would turn him into a docile yes-man of the big powers they were due for disappointment. He may not be a far-seeing statesman or grasp clearly the full significance, and long-distance import, of events but he does understand liberal principles, the square deal between men, the position of small nations and their relation to the big ones. There is little of finesse about him and diplomacy is not his strong point. He is an egotist, somewhat vain, but prefers a straight answer rather than a slick reply. When he became President of the United Nations Assembly, post-war crisis conditions were most marked. The peace that should have been established seemed further away than ever. The United Nations assemblies and commissions appeared to have become gatherings for the ventilation of differences between nations rather than meetings to secure the maximum of agreement. Europe was split into two groups of nations. Germany was split in two, the Soviet Union controlling one part and Americans, British, and French controlling the other. At the very moment of his election the world seemed to be once again divided into two camps, the rivals, however, being the one time United Nations. The focus point of the dispute lay, at that moment, in Berlin, over currency control and the establishment of a single currency. Out of the disputation concerning this question between the Allies there had grown up the anomalous situation in which they were waging economic warfare against each other. Arising out of repeated breakdowns in direct negotiations between the Allies, an appeal was made to the United Nations to intervene with a solution to the currency dispute and the termination of the economic war in order that a common basis could be reached to settle the future of Germany as a whole. The Security Council appointed a special committee of neu-

trals to examine the currency problem and make recommendations. In due course the neutrals of the UNO reported how
the currency problem could be resolved and the economic
warfare be ended. To the amazement of all concerned, the
report of the neutral commission was flouted.

This led Evatt, as President of the UNO, and Trygvie
Lie, the General Secretary, to make a most outspoken appeal
to the great powers to come down to earth and remember
their obligations. They were reminded that:

On November 3, 1948, the General Assembly unanimously
adopted an appeal to the Great Powers to renew their efforts to
compose their differences and establish a lasting peace. . . .
We believe the first step is to solve the Berlin question. This
case is still pending before the Security Council. We believe the
history of the Security Council's consideration of this case demon-
strates that it can be solved . . . Fear of another war is crippling
the effort of all nations to repair the damage of the last war and
return once more to the ways of peace. The work of the Assembly
and the United Nations as a whole in every field of its endeavour
is being delayed and undermined. It is within the power of the
leaders of the great nations to which this communication is addressed to end this danger to peace.

This appeal had a profound effect. The day came, not long
afterward, when the blockade of Berlin was lifted and agreement was effected between the four powers primarily concerned. It appeared, at last, as if the cold war of the Western
versus the Eastern nations was about to pass into a new stage
in which the nations would find accommodation in ways of
peace-making. If nothing else had been effected during his
term of office as President of the UNO Assembly than this
easing of the tensions between the great powers by the Berlin
settlement, it would be true to say that Evatt had contributed
greatly in his term of office to strengthening the United Nations as the means to peace.

But his high office in the world organization has not meant
that he ceased to play a part in the development of the Brit-

ish Commonwealth of Nations. In 1949, besides retaining his post as Attorney-General and Minister for External Affairs, he became Deputy Prime Minister of Australia. While he was functioning in the Assembly sessions of the United Nations in America, the famous 1949 Conference of Commonwealth Prime Ministers was held in London. It is very probable that but for the meetings of the United Nations Assembly he would have represented Australia at this decisive Commonwealth Conference. He had attended the 1948 Conference when the representatives of the newly formed Indian states were present and the question was raised as to whether a republic could be a member of the commonwealth. Since then, on the eve of the 1949 Conference, Evatt set forth his views of the new phase of commonwealth development. Writing in *The Times* of March 12, 1949, he took for granted that India, Pakistan, and Ceylon would be permanent members of the British Commonwealth of Nations. He was very emphatic in the use of the title *British Commonwealth of Nations* and denied, outright, that anyone had suggested at the 1948 Conference that the term *British* should be dropped.

He went on to emphasize the importance of retaining the present title and said:

We in Australia would strongly resist the omission of the word "British" not only because of the claims of kinship, but for many practical reasons as well. For the name "British" does not mean that all the people of every member of the Commonwealth come of British stock, still less that the people of Great Britain claim suzerainty or supremacy. But the name does refer to the common bond which united the very diverse members of the group, and no other name could encompass this or indeed accurately describe the unique associations. The bond is composed of many strains— history, nationality, common ideals in political life, the common inheritance of British liberty in government and society, the common objectives of human welfare. This is the light in which the term "British" must be interpreted and should always remain unaltered.

He continued to affirm that ". . . in the case of Australia particularly the bond of the British Commonwealth finds its chief expression in the relationship with the King." Evatt then went on to emphasize the importance of maintaining the "British political tradition of flexibility" and proceeded to assert that much more important than India's adherence to republicanism was "the practical and personal contributions of the three Prime Ministers." Then, once again, Evatt stressed the change in the geographical disposition of the members of the commonwealth with the entry of the three new members and he reaffirmed the importance of "regionalism" in the structure and functioning of the Commonwealth as well as the United Nations. He said:

. . . as partnership in the British Commonwealth is consistent with participation in regional associations, so it is compatible in the fullest sense with the principles of the United Nations. Indeed the objectives of the British Commonwealth and those of the United Nations are in complete harmony so that a stronger British Commonwealth means a stronger United Nations and a surer guarantee of peace.

At the 1949 Conference, however, Mr. Chiffley, the Australian Prime Minister, played the part which Evatt had filled the previous year.

Chiffley had succeeded Mr. Curtin on the latter's death. At that time Chiffley was Federal Treasurer of Australia, is a man of engaging personality, a quiet even-tempered administrator, sixty years of age. In his young manhood he was an engine driver and cleaner in the New South Wales Railways Department. He grew up as an active trade unionist and first became a political leader when he was elected a member of the Federal Parliament in 1928. He is a native of New South Wales. Defeated in the elections of 1931 he was not reelected until September 1940. During his career as a labor leader he was not troubled with unorthodox views but was always outspoken and a man of strong convictions.

A strong supporter of Evatt's policy in Australia's external affairs, and very pro-British, he was most emphatic at the 1949 Conference on the preservation of the title *British Commonwealth of Nations* and on the recognition of the King of England as the symbolic head of the association. But he, like the other Commonwealth Ministers, did not wish to lose India from the association. So they remembered Britain's "flexibility." Hence, implied contradictions notwithstanding, they arrived at a remarkable decision wherein they agreed to permit a republic to become a member of the commonwealth, the King of England to be its symbolic head, and, as Mr. Attlee explained to the House of Commons "we can call the association 'The British Empire,' 'The British Commonwealth of Nations,' 'The Commonwealth,' and we shall be right whichever we use. All are correct."

Dr. Herbert Vere Evatt, looking at the proceedings from the distant pinnacle of the U.N. Assembly Presidency, was content with the result. He felt that his own work as a contributor to the building of the commonwealth had not been in vain. Indeed it had not, even though the December 1949 General Election in Australia resulted in the Labor government's defeat, retiring Dr. Evatt from ministerial office.

C H A P T E R   X

J A W A H A R L A L   N E H R U

Time: 1948.

The scene was the Conference of the Prime Ministers of the British Empire and Commonwealth of Nations. The chairman of the gathering, in St. James' Palace, was the Prime Minister of Britain, Clement Attlee. The conference was unique in every respect: in its personnel, its representation, and the nature of the crisis it had to face. Here were the leaders of the white and colored nations of an empire in transition. Every man present was the spokesman of millions, and each was a leader of men. Here were representatives of Canada, Australia, New Zealand, South Africa, India, Pakistan, Eire, Burma, Ceylon, and the United Kingdom. Never before had the net of empire and commonwealth representation been so widely spread and the principal issue so grave. A new stage had been reached in the evolution of the British Empire. Hitherto, ever since Canada first forced the pace toward self-government for the white colonies of the empire, each critical stage of its transformation had concerned the white colonies of Canada, Australia, New Zealand, Eire, South Africa, until by the Statute of Westminster one and all had achieved virtual independence. The King now accepted the advice of both his British and his Dominion Ministers. The balance of the British Empire remained governed by the British Parliament. Such was the position when the Second World War again shook the British Empire to its foundations. At the end of the war, all that had com-

278

prised the Indian empire (the "brightest jewel in the British Crown") cut loose from the old bondage and stepped into the world's arena, free and independent. The critical issue before the Conference of Prime Ministers was the all-important one of "Where do we go from here?" Would India, Pakistan, Burma, Ceylon, having secured their freedom from imperial control, now join the British Commonwealth of Nations and be partners with the white dominions in a free association or would they turn away? If the colored Prime Ministers from the sub-continent of India, with its population of four hundred million inhabitants, turned away, the British Empire would, instead of being transformed into a new association of free nations, shrink to small dimensions and become a rump of what was once a mighty empire. The issue was sharpened by the fact that Eire, the first of the white colonies to fight for independence and the last to achieve it, made clear that it was out. It would stand as an independent republic. The new representatives from the East had also come from countries which desired to be republics. How could republics swear allegiance to the British Crown? This appeared to be too much of an anomaly and too much akin to the old relationship of Empire.

All eyes in the conference turned to the figures from the East, facing the Prime Minister of the United Kingdom, and fastened especially upon one balding, gray-haired, and refined-looking man named Jawaharlal Nehru, representative of India. Indeed, as the world outside learned of the changes that were being registered by the conference, it also was asking: "What will Nehru do?" It was not easy for him to answer. In himself he bore all the scars of the long and bitter struggle between the brown man and the white, and between India and Britain in particular. Had not the British played cat-and-mouse tactics with his life all through the years of his manhood, putting him into prison, letting him out, putting him in, freeing him, until he had spent not less than nine years in prison? And was not that the common experience of his father—and his great friend and teacher, Gandhi, and many thousands of others who had dared to affirm their nation's right to be a nation of free men? Across the table, watching him, was Prime Minister Attlee—the Labor Prime Minister of Britain. Well, what of it? Had not Attlee been a party to this treatment he and his fellows had received? Had he not been a member of MacDonald's 1929 Labor Government which had filled the jails of India and was responsible for the death of Indians by the thousand? Had he not also been a member of the recent Churchill Coalition Government which had jailed him and his colleagues during the war? Could he write all this off as the "natural process of history" and start afresh? It was not easy to decide. But there were other factors in the situation besides the sufferings of himself and his fellows. There were the extraordinary circumstances in which, at last, India secured her freedom. These must be taken into account, too. It was the same Attlee who had taken part in the oppression, who had struck off the fetters, who had speeded up the withdrawal from India of Britain's armed forces with all their trappings of oppression. Then there was Mountbatten. He had played a remarkable role, cut through the tangled scheme of things, persuaded Attlee to bring forward the date of withdrawal, and organized the withdrawal itself with such speed and good order, and in such a spirit of good will, that he had almost made the Indians feel that they were losing friends instead of ridding themselves of a centuries-old tyranny.

That was sentimentalizing about experience and persons, and Nehru's decision could not be made on sentimental grounds. He was there in circumstances for which his whole life had prepared him as the leader of more than three hundred million people. Field Marshal Smuts might think he had to deal with complex and great problems of mixed races and social backwardness. But Smuts spoke only for ten millions and a small part of Africa. Nehru was the spokesman of thirty times as many people, as varied in their development as any which Smuts could show. The total population of all the countries represented by the white delegates across the table could be put into a corner of the territory now controlled by the Indian people. There was no other Prime Minister representing so many people and faced with so great problems. Truman may lead 150,000,000 Americans but they had grown up with an industrial revolution that had placed in their hands the most wonderful technique of production that the world had known. Stalin may control 200,000,000 people but they also were on the road toward an industrial revolution. Nehru stood at the head of 300,-000,000 people, eighty-seven percent of whom could neither read nor write, whose economic life was as archaic as the ruins of their ancient temples and in whose minds glimmered the darkest superstitions of dead ages. The minority, only, were on the threshold of the industrial revolution so necessary to the fuller life of which he dreamed. If ever a new government and a liberated people needed the friendship and help even of ex-enemies and persecutors it was his government and his people. . . .

Nehru voted in favor of India joining the commonwealth association. Whatever resentment he felt towards Attlee and all those responsible for the grim record of the British military crushing the rebellion of '57, its Rowlatt Acts, the massacre of Amritsar, the Mopla death train, the countless thousands of years that had been taken out of the lives of generations of India's best sons by imprisonment and the immeasurable suffering imposed upon India by the retarding of her industrial development, he repressed, in order that nothing should stand in the way of cooperation and help which would push India through her industrial revolution and lift her out of her tragic backwardness into new ways of life.

The representatives of Pakistan and Ceylon voted with Nehru. The representative of Burma voted against. Thus, Nehru once more demonstrated that in these days of India's transition to independence, he, thirty years an agitator, had emerged as a statesman of reconstruction. For this two men were primarily responsible—his father, Motilal Nehru, and Mahatma Gandhi. Without reference to these men, the emergence and rise of Jawaharlal Nehru to become India's leading statesman is incomprehensible.

Motilal Nehru was a remarkable man in his own right, a man of great courage and extraordinary energy and ability, a lawyer, a man of character, and a builder of the Indian National Congress founded in 1885 to achieve a national revolution for India. The Nehru stock are Kashmiri. The Nehru family lost nearly all it possessed in the Indian Revolt of 1857 and fled from Delhi to Agra. Motilal Nehru was born in Agra in 1861. He grew up to be a lawyer, a good Persian and Arabic scholar, learned English, became thoroughly Westernized and rose to be a High Court lawyer with an extensive practice in Allahabad. Successful and rich, and conscious of the power that wealth gives, he resented that India should be ruled by foreigners, much as he admired the English.

The founding of the Indian National Congress was a very mild act by middle-class Indians and a few white liberal reformers. It was the beginning of a break in the depression which had settled on Indian politics after the British quashed the revolt of 1857. Motilal Nehru grew up in the midst of this lull in Indian politics and succeeded in putting his family on a well-to-do basis. He married a Kashmir woman of culture and refinement. Jawarhalal Nehru was born to them on November 14, 1889, at Allahabad. He was the first child and only son. He was eleven years old when his first sister arrived. Nehru grew up in prosperous surroundings and in cultural and professional ambitions followed in the footsteps of his father. But the period in which he grew to manhood differed from that of his father in one important respect. It was an era of Indian awakening, the passing of the depression and the rise of the National Congress in which his father began to figure actively. He had all the advantages of education that his father had before him. A private tutor at eleven named F. T. Brooks introduced him to literature and science. At fifteen, he sailed for England with the whole Nehru family. They left him to continue his education at Harrow and in 1907 he left Harrow for Trinity College, Cambridge, where for three years he continued to mature and to widen his intellectual horizons. From Cambridge he went to London. He had chosen his father's profession and went to the Inner Temple. For two years he studied there, passed his examinations, was called to the Bar in the summer of 1912, and in the autumn of that year, after seven years in England, he returned to India—a well-to-do Indian intellectual, a lawyer about to begin practice, an Indian nationalist and, he says, "a bit of a prig with little to commend me."

Meanwhile, his father had moved with the times in Indian affairs. Beginning as an orthodox moderate, or liberal nationalist, he joined the Home Rule League organized by Lokamanya Tilak and Mrs. Besant. The latter had had some influence on the younger Nehru when he was about thirteen years of age. She was the most important member of the Theosophist Movement and it appears that Nehru's first tutor, F. T. Brooks, was a theosophist, also. Through him, Nehru became interested in theosophy and amused his father by asking if he might join the Theosophical Society. The elder Nehru had no time to spend on the various religious movements. He thought religion was all right for the women, but to assume that he was a religious man was an insult to his intelligence, although he was good-naturedly tolerant toward the various religious groups. Naturally, he did not interfere with his son's interest in the subject and young Nehru joined the Theosophical Society. The elder man had been through that phase and dropped it as did the younger Nehru, although for the time being he was thrilled by dreaming of astral bodies and flying through the air for vast distances without visible apparatus of locomotion. He left theosophy behind him but always retained an admiration for Mrs. Besant who, besides being a theosophist of renown, played a big part in India's Home Rule Movement, in the years before the First World War. In these years there was a great stir in India and the British Government developed the practice of sending Indian leaders to prison for long terms. This excitement among the Indians drove the National Congress into more active political life and the moderates began to move out of it. The elder Nehru was one who remained, dropping out of the ranks of the moderates, and moving into prominence as Mahatma Gandhi returned to India from South Africa. In fact, the return of Gandhi to India to give leadership to the newly developing nationalist movement led the elder Nehru to cut adrift from his professional life and throw in his lot with Gandhi.

The Indian awakening and the beginning of the new era of struggles drove the young Indians, who were students in England, into extreme nationalism tinged with much romanticism. Although young Nehru had lived the life of an intellectual dilettante in London during his student years he had learned much of English politics. On his return to India, in 1912, he was uncertain of his future course. He turned to law and began to practice, but without any great enthusiasm. The war years of 1914-18 and the clashes of the various nationalist movements in conflict with the British Government finally drove him, enthusiastically, into politics. The Easter Week rising in Dublin, and Roger Casement's great speech in his own defense at his trial in 1916, influenced him particularly. He first met Gandhi at the Lucknow Conference convened by the Indian National Congress Committee. But it was the events following the introduction of the Rowlatt Bills of 1919 that set father and son together on the high road to a dedicated life under the leadership of Gandhi. The Rowlatt Bills met with the resistance of the Indian National Movement. Gandhi gave the lead to disobey the Rowlatt Act and that pointed the way to mass disobedience, all-India hartals, suspension of business, arrests, imprisonment. There came the tragedy of Amritsar, mob violence, firing by the police and military, the massacre of Jallianwala Bagh and martial law in the Punjab. The horror of Jallianwala Bagh shocked the world. Here human beings were made to crawl on their bellies and thousands were mowed down by machine-gun fire in a trap from which there was no escape. Nehru senior presided over the Indian National Congress held at Amritsar in December 1919. This was the Congress where Gandhi became the recognized leader and the great struggle for Indian independence was once more renewed on a national scale. If Gandhi was the foremost leader, as he undoubtedly was, his two principal generals in the struggle were the two Nehrus, father and son.

It should be understood that all three at this time, and indeed the whole Indian Congress Movement, had nothing whatever to do with the Socialism with which the younger Nehru was one day to identify himself. Jawaharlal Nehru himself writes of this period:

My politics had been those of my class, the bourgeoisie. Indeed all vocal politics then (and to a great extent even now) were those of the middle classes, and Moderate and Extremist alike represented them and in different keys, sought their betterment. The Moderate represented especially the handful of the upper middle class who had on the whole prospered under British rule and wanted no sudden changes which might endanger their present position and interests. They had a close connection with the British Government and the big landlord class. The Extremist represented also the lower ranks of the middle class. The industrial workers, their number swollen up by the war, were only locally organized in some places and had little influence. The peasantry were a blind, poverty stricken, suffering mass, resigned to their miserable fate, and sat upon and exploited by all who came in contact with them—the Government, landlords, money lenders, petty officials, police, lawyers, priests.

India, with its hundreds of millions of population, was further down in the historical scale than Russia of Czar Nicholas I. The process of industrialization had only just begun.

India's feudal economy was backward in the extreme. Millions of peasants were without land. Nearly ninety percent of the population was illiterate and sunk in poverty and religious superstition while its social castes were ossified by tradition and religious practices. The social pyramid existed in its most extreme form. Immense wealth was centralized in the hands of a few while poverty and desolation prevailed for the vast majority. There were no political parties such as are familiar to the Western world. India was in the hands of an oligarchy, operating under directions from the British India Office in Whitehall. The Indian National Congress was a middle-class nationalist organization without any social program whatever. The Nehrus were not conscious of the social problems of their country when they launced forth into nationalist agitation. That cannot be said of Gandhi. He was, indeed, the first of the Indian leaders who related the social questions of the time to the national question. But he was far from being a socialist.

From the earliest days of Gandhi's emergence into Indian politics he was recognized as a remarkable man. He came from a lower class than the Nehrus. His full name was Mohandas Karamchand Gandhi. He had been born October 2, 1869, educated at Rajkot and London. In London he became a barrister-at-law and studied at the Inner Temple chambers. He practiced law in Bombay and in South Africa. In championing the cause of the Indians in South Africa he came in conflict with General Smuts and served a term of imprisonment in Natal. He returned to India and in 1919 became the acknowledged leader of the Indian National Congress. But he was no ordinary politician. He combined the qualities of an astute politician and lawyer with those of the mystic. His mysticism found practical expression in the application of non-resistance, in non-cooperation and non-violent civil disobedience. He differed greatly from the Nehrus. Their education had been essentially Western. They were men of literature, rationalists, and lawyers. Gandhi was a man of letters, too, and a lawyer who abandoned the life of his class to live in Tolstoyan simplicity. It helped identify him with the lowest peasant of India and the most poverty-stricken untouchable. He had an extraordinary capacity for reducing problems to their simplest terms and giving them a mystical content. His mysticism ran through his politics and often confused his friends as well as his enemies. For Gandhi a man was rich according to the lack of his material wants and the fullness of his spiritual life. He was neither economist nor statesman and belonged to that category of man whose kingdom is not of this world. It was an accident of history that he was born to face the problems of the twentieth century in which he was never "at home." He disliked its complexities, its speed, and its industrialism wherever he met it. He preferred the simplicity of peasant life, although he would have wished to purify the human relations which grew with it. Gandhi was not a Christian, but if ever there lived a man whose life and thought would stand up to a literal comparison with those of Jesus, it was Gandhi, even to his tragic end, each being killed by political opponents with weapons corresponding to their epoch, one nailed to a cross and the other killed by bullets. The rationalism of both men was geared to the kingdom of heaven and the kingdom of heaven was within them. Both preached and practiced the gospel of non-violence and turned the cheek to the smiter. Gandhi's politics streamed from the impact of his inner vision, of an India set free by love of man for man. The non-cooperation policy which he desired that the National Congress should adopt was not derived from considerations of revolutionary strategy or the paralyzing effect it would have on governments and the opponents of Indian freedom. That would have been a rationalization applied to the social forces struggling for and against Indian independence, possessing definite limits of application. For Gandhi, *non-cooperation* was more than a weapon of conflict. Indeed, he did not regard it as a weapon, but *as a way of life*, an affirmation of the inner kingdom of man. His mind was his kingdom which nothing could enslave, neither power nor prison nor torture. Smuts ran up against it in South Africa and could make nothing of it. The British Government tried time and again to conquer it by imposing on him long stretches of imprisonment. Gandhi accepted their punishments, continuing his way of life without hurry, even though it led to the Golgotha road. It is very awkward for politicians and ordinary folk when a leader combines within himself the qualities of the saint, the stoic, and the lawyer.

Gandhi stepped to the forefront of India's affairs at a crucial stage when the Indian middle classes were awakening to national consciousness at the end of the First World War. Following the events in the Punjab in 1919, the British Government advanced what were known as the Montagu-Chelmsford Reforms, which created legislative councils at the center of British India and also in the provinces, on a very restricted franchise. Central power remained, as always, in the hands of the British Governors. What should the Indians do? Accept these proposals as a step in the right direction, work within the framework of the new institutions or have nothing to do with them? It was here that Gandhi split the leadership of Congress and stepped to the front as the new leader. He proposed *non-cooperation*. It was a hard choice for the middle-class Congress. The new proposals offered so many comfortable jobs for them and their sons. It was the choice which the Nehrus had to make. They made their choice and came down on the side of Gandhi. This was the beginning of the cooperation of these three, Gandhi, Motilal Nehru, and his young son Jawaharlal Nehru, in the leadership of the Congress. Subsequently, the elder Nehru died, an assassin's bullet killed Gandhi, and Nehru, the younger, was left to steer India through revolutionary crises and set India free.

The Nehrus were unlike Gandhi. They were neither mystics nor stoics. Father and son were intellectuals and lawyers who loved the good things of life. They were bourgeois to their fingertips, intensely nationalistic and politically minded. They saw *non-cooperation*, as proposed by Gandhi, not so much as a way of life but as a political weapon to achieve political ends, to be used as an industrial worker used the strike weapon to achieve improvements in his conditions. But it did also mean, in effect, a change in the Nehrus' way of life. For father and son abandoned their professional careers to devote themselves entirely to the leadership of the national struggle for independence. Often, they would be puzzled by Gandhi's application of the policy of non-violent non-cooperation because of their different mode of approach. To Gandhi it was a religion. To the Nehrus it was a rational, political policy. Gandhi on more than one occasion called off a campaign because his followers were not applying his policy in his way. And there was the danger of a mass non-violent movement changing to one of violence. That type of contradiction placed the Nehrus in a dilemma which became for them a question of faith in Gandhi's judgment and leadership. They gave him the allegiance he demanded.

There was no turning back after the die was cast. Within a few months of the first great campaign being launched, father and son were arrested and sent to prison in 1921. Jawaharlal was released first and after six weeks of freedom, in which time he at once went to help Gandhi, he was again arrested and this time sentenced to one year and nine months' imprisonment. Indeed, the story of these three men from the time they ascended to the leadership of the Indian National Congress is a record of campaigns and imprisonment in rapidly changing circumstances as the movement toward Indian independence grew year by year. It is extraordinary, too, that a mystic philosopher, Gandhi, should bring the Nehrus into contact with the real political and social problems of the Indian masses. Indian nationalism was very woolly in its conception, and uncertain of its steps, when Gandhi took on the leadership. The practicality of the non-cooperation method as well as its political soundness in making the issues clear, appealed to the rationalistic minds of the Nehrus and brought them to Gandhi's side. Jawaharlal Nehru had had a fine academic education but he knew next to nothing of the peasant problems of India or of the lives of the oppressed classes and the industrial population. He had made acquaintance with the socialism of the university club but, after graduation, had forgotten his dilettante flirtations with it. Gandhi went to the peasants, led them in struggles for reforms, and made these struggles for improvement in their conditions part of his fight for freedom. It was through this that Jawaharlal Nehru came into contact with the fundamental economic and social problems of India.

Gandhi's remarkable power of reducing questions to their least complex denominator enabled him to speak easily to the most illiterate and backward as well as to the more sophisticated. He had, however, no sense of history but only a grasp of concepts. He gathered from history a conception of the craftsman's and peasant's society in which all could live simply and well, worship, and live the ideal life. His use of the spinning wheel was much more than a hobby and a tactical identification of himself with the life of the humble people of the countless villages of India. It was the symbol of the kind of society he wished to see, a return to a golden age that had perished with the beginning of the British occupation. The vision he conjured up before the eyes of the caste-ridden Indians of the glory of the age of the spinning wheel was a vision which the peasants, steeped in religious traditions and physical bankruptcy, could understand. It rang the bells in their inner heaven and they hailed Gandhi as the savior of men. The contact with the problems of the masses did not lead the Nehrus to share Gandhi's vision of the tomorrows or his economic theories. Father and son had become Westernized and their reaction to the industrialization of the nineteenth and twentieth centuries was entirely different. They had a better sense of history than Gandhi and were confident that, however it was to be done, India must be industrialized and its economy completely changed, not by futile attempts to revert to the age of the spinning wheel but advancing to the age of machines and electricity.

That Gandhi influenced Nehru greatly is undoubted and there grew up between them a great friendship and loyalty. But where the older man's vision was derived from his religious mysticism and was unchanging, the younger man regarded the struggle they were leading as a phase of a vast human and world-wide social conflict from one form of society to another. Nehru says in his autobiography:

History came to have a new meaning for me. The Marxist interpretation threw a flood of light on it and it became an unfolding drama with some order and purpose, howsoever unconscious, behind it. In spite of the appalling waste and misery of the past and the present, the future was bright with hope, though many dangers intervened. It was the essential freedom from dogma and the scientific outlook of Marxism that appealed to me. It was true that there was plenty of dogma in official communism in Russia and elsewhere, and frequently heresy hunts were organized. That seemed to me deplorable, though it was not difficult to understand in view of the tremendous changes taking place rapidly in the Soviet countries, when effective opposition might have resulted in catastrophic failure.

The great world crisis and slump seemed to justify the Marxist analysis. While all other systems and theories were groping about in the dark, Marxism alone explained it more or less satisfactorily and offered a real solution.

As this conviction grew upon me . . . my depression at the non-success of civil disobedience grew much less. Was not the world marching rapidly towards the desired consummation? There were grave dangers of wars and catastrophies, but at any rate we were moving. There was no stagnation. Our national struggle became a stage in a long journey, and it was as well that repression and suffering were tempering our people for future struggles and forcing them to consider new ideas that were stirring the world.

Of Gandhi he said, in these days when he was second in command:

Ideologically he was sometimes amazingly backward, and yet in action he had been the greatest revolutionary of recent times, in India. He was a unique personality, and it is impossible to judge him by the usual standards, or even to apply the ordinary canons of logic to him. But because he was a revolutionary at bottom and was pledged to political independence for India, he was bound to play an uncompromising role till that independence was achieved. And in this very process he would release tremendous mass energies and would himself, I half hoped, advance step by step towards the social goal.

The main influence of Gandhi upon Nehru lay in the field of political practice, in the actual leadership of the movement for Indian independence. So strong was his influence that even when Nehru disagreed with Gandhi most strongly he would bow to Gandhi's will. But Gandhi did not succeed in transforming Nehru into a mystic or winning him over to his religious outlook on life. Of religions, Nehru says he realizes that they offer a

. . . safe anchorage from doubt and mental conflict, an assurance of a future life which will make up for the deficiencies of this life.
I am afraid it is impossible for me to seek harborage in this way. I prefer the open sea, with all its storms and tempests. Nor am I greatly interested in the after life, in what happens after death. I find the problems of this life sufficiently absorbing to fill my mind. The traditional Chinese outlook, fundamentally ethical and yet irreligious or tinged with religious scepticism has an appeal for me, though with its application to life I may not agree. It is the Tao, the path to be followed and the way of life that interests me; how to understand life, not to reject it but to accept it, to conform to it and improve it. But the usual religious outlook does not concern itself with this world. It seems to be the enemy of clear thought, for it is based not only on the acceptance without demur of certain fixed and unalterable theories and dogmas but also on sentiment and emotion and passion. It is far removed from what I consider spirituality and things of the spirit, and it deliberately or unconsciously shuts its eyes to reality lest reality may not fit in with preconceived notions. It is narrow and intolerant of other opinions and ideas; it is self-centred and egotistic and it often allows itself to be exploited by self-seeking and op-

portunities. . . . Usually religion becomes a social quest for God or the Absolute, and the religious man is concerned far more with his own salvation than with the good of society. The mystic tries to rid himself of self, and in the process usually becomes obsessed with it. Moral standards have no relation to social needs, but are based on a highly metaphysical doctrine of sin. And organized religion invariably becomes a vested interest and thus inevitably a reactionary force opposing change and progress.

With such wide divergence between the two men as Jawaharlal reached maturity of thought, the close personal friendship, which had grown between them as they led the Indian Nationalist movement, was possible only because of the nature of the movement which they led and the singleness of the objective at which it aimed. The Indian National Congress was a loosely formed organization. It was founded, in 1885, by an English, retired civil servant named Allan Hume with a program aiming at the formation of one nation out of the numerous groups inhabiting India, toward an equivalent of dominion status within the British Empire. It was, until the coming of Gandhi and the Nehrus, an essentially middle-class institution for the airing of grievances and securing concessions from the British Imperial Government. The new leadership which took charge in 1916-19 gave to the Congress its aim of Swaraj (freedom), widened its social basis in securing the support of a large number of the peasants, and passed to direct action to secure its objectives. Two trends of opinion developed under the joint leadership of Gandhi and Nehru, one radical and reformist, and the other Socialist. Not until most recent years have these trends begun to take shape in the form of political parties corresponding to the parties of Western countries. And only from the time that India's industrial revolution got under way did the various social groups within the Congress begin to organize. There appeared on the scene a trades union congress, All-India Peasant League, Congress Socialist Party, and Communist Party of India. The differences of class interests in the Congress showed themselves ever more clearly as the varying social elements became organized and pressed forward upon the Congress their demands for reforms. But the dominant issue of India's independence, and the consistent struggle maintained by the Congress against the Imperial Government, held all its forces together with the exception of one which pursued its independent way. The Moslem League, formed in the years when the Indian National Congress was first taking shape, stood for Indian independence and a working agreement with Congress, until there were radical changes of policy introduced by Gandhi. Thereafter, under the leadership of the late Mr. Jinnah, it would have nothing to do with Gandhi's non-cooperation policy; instead, it demanded Pakistan, that is, a separate state for the Moslems. It denied the claim of Congress to speak for the Indian people as a whole and refused to accept the minority status which the Moslems would have in a single Indian State. This division was to be maintained throughout the struggle for Indian independence and ultimately lead to the setting up of two states, one essentially Hindu and the other Moslem. This applied to what was then known as British India, with a population of over 310,000,-000 persons. Besides British India, however, there were the Indian states, some of them large, some small, with, all told, 65,000,000 inhabitants. These were feudal states with their own laws and administration under British protection.

In 1929, Nehru became the General Secretary of the All-India National Congress Committee. President of Congress in 1929 and 1930, and again in 1936, he had not always been in agreement with Gandhi, even on questions of policy in the fight for independence. Two occasions stand out in their careers most prominently. The first was on the occasion of the Round Table Conference in London in 1930. Gandhi and the Indian princes attended what proved to be futile conversations. Nehru led the radical elements of the Congress to boycott the talks. The second was much more serious and illustrates how fundamentally different was the approach of the two comrades in leadership to the problems they had to face. When the Second World War crashed upon mankind, both men, with all the Congress, protested against the act by which England declared war for India without consultation with her people or her representatives. But Gandhi as an absolutist pacifist went further and denounced the war outright. He asked to be relieved of all responsibilities of leadership for the National Congress. But Nehru was not a pacifist. He was a socialist and anti-fascist. He did not come down on the side of active support for the Allies but took his stand as an anti-imperialist, proclaiming that Britain should grant to India the freedom for which she declared she was fighting the war, and then India would ally herself with the Allies as an independent state and join actively in the war against the fascist powers. Nevertheless, the personal relationship remained always that of friends who had the deepest respect for each other. Gandhi had a personal policy which Nehru was never able to share although it called forth Nehru's admiration. Besides the collective policy of non-cooperation in which Nehru and their followers participated, Gandhi used individual acts and his personal prestige, derived from his doctrine of non-violent non-cooperation against evil. Time and again he would refuse food and drink and threaten to starve himself to death. This personal conduct was repeatedly used as a weapon against the British Government, making the government responsible for his fast. Time and again the government, which had the blood of thousands of Indians on their hands, feared to be held responsible by the millions of India for the death of their leader. Only a man of iron will and tremendous faith in himself and his doctrine could have applied it with such telling effect. Nehru never attempted to emulate Gandhi in such ways. Although Nehru shared with Gandhi in power over masses of people, and is by no means an aggressive person, this form of self-immolation has never appealed to him.

In two of the interludes between the serving of prison sentences, Nehru visited Europe and England. The first occasion was in the spring of 1926. His wife (whom he had married in 1916) became seriously ill. After many months in a Lucknow hospital, it was deemed advisable to take her to Switzerland for further treatment. Until nearly the end of 1927 Switzerland was his center but he took the opportunity to visit Berlin, England, Moscow, Paris, and to become more deeply drawn into the Socialist movement. He attended the famous Brussels Conference of the League against Imperialism, and visited the English coalfields during the miners lockout following the collapse of the General Strike. His father joined him in Switzerland in 1927 and later in the year the whole family, father, wife, young sister, and Jawaharlal visited Moscow, during the tenth-anniversary celebrations of the Soviet. They were not long there but what they saw impressed them. Then to India the Nehru family returned, leaving the elder Nehru to conduct a case before the British Privy Council. Then another spell of agitation, prison, agitation, prison, and the years sped by with the world hastening toward the second round of the world's Armageddon. Already the peace system following the first war was crumbling to pieces and the lineaments of the coming world wide clash of arms were clearly discernible. In 1935 the younger Nehru came to Europe and England again. He participated in the great Peace Congress held in Paris, visited London, and made contact with the socialists in the intervals between meetings on the question of Indian independence. On this occasion he and Sir Stafford Cripps became friends, at the time when Cripps was leading the Socialist League for constitutional "revolutionary" socialism. This was a friendship that was to last through the years. It drew Sir Stafford into the Indian struggle and called on him to play an extremely important role in its future stages.

Nehru returned to India and again became the President of Congress and recognized as the man standing next to

Gandhi in the hierarchy of leadership. The outbreak of war finally placed him in the post of actual leadership when the Indian National Congress Committee could not endorse Gandhi's pacifism as Indian Congress policy. Gandhi asked to be relieved of all responsibility for Congress policy during the war, and Nehru stepped into the foreground with the revolutionary socialist policy of demanding Indian independence as the price for cooperation with the British Government in the prosecution of the war. History was stepping on the accelerator and events were moving to a climax. Cripps came to India in the winter of 1939 on a personal mission, hoping to secure Indian cooperation with the British during the war if the British Government would promise dominion status to India immediately after the end of the war. He felt that if he could get the Indians to agree to his project that he stood a good chance of persuading the British Government to make such a declaration on his return to England. He saw Nehru and Gandhi and all the leaders of the various Indian political movements. Nothing came of it, immediately. The opposition of Nehru and Gandhi and the Congress to the war led them once again, to prison. The war continued. Japan struck and her forces reached the frontiers of India. Unrest grew. In 1942 the Indian leaders were let out of prison again, as the prelude to the coming of the famous Cripps Mission. This time Cripps came as an Ambassador, representing the British Coalition Government, led by Churchill. Friend met friend and the representative of Britain's might faced the representative of the Indian people demanding to be free. The mission failed. Repression returned and prison gates once more opened to Nehru. Not until the war ended did freedom come again, and with it came the climax of the Indian struggle as the leftward tide of opinion in Britain swept the Conservatives out of power and installed the Labor Government headed by Attlee. In India, too, the tide was flowing fast. The British Government was no longer sure of the Indian troops. The nationalist temper throughout the vast country was rising and the British Government felt that pacifistic non-cooperation was being transformed into revolutionary mass action. Fearful that if they did not give independence the Indians would take it, the British Labor Government, programmatically pledged to give India "Dominion Status," sent another mission, again headed by Cripps and two other Cabinet Ministers, to negotiate a peaceful transition to a free India. As on the occasion of the 1942 Cripps Mission the British Government laid down the terms upon which they were prepared to concede "Dominion Status" or independence. The terms of 1942 insisted that all India, divided into communal groups and states, must come together in a representative Constituent Assembly based upon the existing franchise of the provincial electorates in British India along with representatives of the heads of the feudal states. This Constituent Assembly must, in turn, produce an agreed constitution for all India and a government which could receive power from the British. The communal and state minorities, although having participated in the shaping of the new constitution, would have the right to contract out from the new Indian regime established by the Constituent Assembly and maintain their existing relation with the British Government. Until this procedure had been carried through there would be no withdrawal of British authority. Meanwhile, a Provisional Government, representative of the communal groups and states, should function under the Viceroy as an interim government of India.

The Indians, under the leadership of Gandhi and Nehru, rejected communalism and aimed at an all-India National Government and constitution which would give full scope for communal minorities to have proper representation and freedoms. The largest communal group, the Moslems, led by the Moslem League under Jinnah, rejected the plan of the Indian National Congress on the grounds that it placed the Moslems permanently under the Hindus. They demanded Pakistan, that is, the setting up of a Moslem state, separate from the Hindus. The Indian National Congress were opposed to this "splitting of the nation" as a backward step for India politically and economically. Had the British conceded Indian independence ten years earlier by recognizing the Indian National Congress as the voice of the Indian people, it is probable that there would be no Pakistan State today. But by this time the Moslem League had become a power in the land and the British, as always, played one off against the other. They held that the lack of agreement among the communal elements was a good cause for withholding independence. Gandhi and Nehru always answered: "Let the British get out of India and the Indian people will settle their differences quickly by agreement." They could not agree to Pakistan for the Moslems before British withdrawal, and the Moslems held fast to their demands. Negotiations broke down, however, on the question of the immediate transfer of power to an interim Indian government.

When the Cripps Mission of 1942 came to India, Cripps was a delegate presenting an offer which no discussion could modify. This time he arrived with substantially the same proposals and the Indians held fast to their claims. Again, the negotiations broke down after three months of effort on the part of the Labor Government's Cabinet Mission. The National Congress, led by Gandhi and Nehru, stood firmly to their program. So, too, did the Moslems. But the circumstances in which they negotiated had changed completely. Indian people, of all sections of the population, were awake. Threats of revolution filled the air. Suddenly the British Government changed its course. Up to this time every British Government that had entered into negotiations with the Indians had done so with the determination to postpone the day of departure from India as long as possible. Now it went into reverse, fixed a date for departure, and began to hold their departure over the heads of the Indians as a threat! They said they would give the Indians a time limit in which to settle their differences and apply the scheme they had recommended to the Indians or they would leave them to stew in their own juice. Mr. Attlee and his government had decided to do what Gandhi had long been asking the British to do. First, they fixed the year of departure as 1948. They changed viceroys and appointed Viscount Mountbatten in place of Lord Wavell. At first he repeated the efforts and offers of his predecessor but quickly saw they were of no avail. He then changed the line. Having abandoned the old intention not to get out of India, there was no point in continuing to use the communal differences of the Indians as a means to justify delay. Instead, Mountbatten took the measure of the strength of the Moslems and the Indian Congress and with Solomon-like judgment brought forward the date of departure, severed India into two states, one in the hands of the Indian National Congress with Nehru as Premier, and created Pakistan for the Moslems, under the leadership of the Moslem League and Mr. Jinnah. Each had to have its own Constituent Assembly and constitution, and the fate of the Indian feudal states had to be settled between them.

There had been nothing like it in history. Never had an imperial government ceased its imperial sway over a colonial people so completely, and with such precision, or bid a people to go its independent way after so long and powerful a grip upon them. It was at one and the same time a triumph and a disappointment for Gandhi and Nehru and the Indian Congress. They had aimed at all-Indian unity in freedom, the fusion of all communal groups into a single nation under one flag. The splitting of India and Pakistan was a disappointment. Nevertheless, at last, the Indian people could stand free and independent of British control! That was a triumph which made the long travail of prison and suffering worth while.

No nation can flourish in bondage. Until India was free, full life for the Indian people was an impossibility. The very idea of it all filled the mind and thrilled the heart. But the reality of the birth of a nation into freedom, however splendid it be, is a testing time for every man. In this case it was a testing time for Jawaharlal Nehru. Indeed it provided him with the supreme test of his life. The life of an agitator is one thing. That of a statesman is another. It is one thing to fight for power, another to hold it and use it to rebuild society. That was Nehru's test. He had to pass overnight, as it were, from the life of an agitator and iconoclast of national independence to be the leading minister of state.

There was no time to sit back and bask in the glory of the new freedom. The change-over unleashed passions that had been long controlled in the bosoms of Hindu and Moslem alike. When the two countries, India and Pakistan, became defined and established on August 15, 1947, the long-pent-up feelings began to express themselves in savage massacres on a scale without precedent. Hindus and Moslems were not evenly distributed in the newly defined territories of the respective states. Six million Moslems had to be transferred from India into Pakistan and four million Hindus and Sikhs transferred from Pakistan to India. The transfer became a spontaneous movement of people instead of an organized transfer, and Moslems pillaged and murdered Hindus as Hindus pillaged and murdered Moslems. Panic and savagery held sway over great stretches of territory. Roads, railways, property suffered greatly from the impact of this primitive movement of masses. The conflict and migrations continued all through the autumn and winter and ten million people became refugees in the respective states.

Such was the storm let loose on the day of freedom, and the burden of it fell on the newly formed governments of India and Pakistan. Had the governments been experienced in administration and their institutions been untouched by the problems raised by this clash of communal forces, the problems would still be enormous. But the governments were new in every respect and the issue of communalism ran through every department of administration. The age-old caste system cluttered the apparatus of government at every step. A large number of the railway workers of India were Moslems and they, feeling they would be safer in Pakistan, fled there. The clerical service of banks and institutions was mainly Hindu. These fled from Pakistan to India. India was overstocked with clerical workers; Pakistan understocked. And so it ran through every department of economy and industry and through every institution. Nehru and Gandhi now learned from experience what a revolution was like in practice, when the masses take things into their own hands without direction and control. Their task was immediately to take control of it, direct it, subdue it, consolidate it, bring order out of chaos and stop the massacres. Gandhi did not become a member of the new Indian Government of which Nehru was the Prime Minister. He was advanced in years and played the part of adviser, consultant, and elder statesman. But when these events began to unfold, he stepped to the front of the struggle and pitted all his personal powers of mystical appeal to stop the slaughter and end the violence. Indeed, all the forces of the government in both the new countries strove with all their might to control and subdue the storm.

But there were external dangers, too, with which the new Prime Minister had to deal. There was danger of war with Pakistan. Had there not been military weakness on both sides it is possible that nothing would have prevented it, not even the influence of Gandhi and Nehru. It had been agreed that the ruler of any Indian state was to decide to which dominion he would accede or remain independent. Kashmir was governed by a Hindu ruler but the population was predominantly Moslem. He hesitated to decide and in September a Moslem exodus began. Moslem tribesmen from the North West invaded Kashmir to avenge their kinsmen. In another part of Kashmir a rebellion began. By the end of October the Maharaja had decided to accede to India and both governments began to move troops into the area. Pakistan gave help to the tribal raiders. Nehru appealed to the United Nations to prevent war.

In the midst of these hectic months of upheaval and proximity to war between the newly formed states, Gandhi was assassinated. He was on his way to prayer when a young fanatic, believing that Gandhi had betrayed India, riddled him with bullets and the great, little man, who had awakened the soul of a continent and set four hundred million people on the march to the new day, was dead. The blow stunned the people of India and shocked the world. It may be that in the hour of his death and by it he did more to bring the communal war to an end than in all the wonderful efforts of the closing months of his life. Friend and foe bowed their heads and paid tribute to the saintly stoic who had walked by faith, believed in human brotherhood and peace, and practiced what he preached in serenity and with great courage. Nehru's great consultant was gone. The trinity of leadership which had guided the Indian movement for independence existed no longer. The elder Nehru and Gandhi were no more. Henceforth, the younger Nehru had to be his own adviser and shoulder the fullest responsibility.

The storm abated but enumerable problems crowded in upon him. It should not be overlooked that around Gandhi and the Nehrus, in their leadership of the Congress in the course of the years, there had gathered a team of able men. The passing of the older men drew men closer to Jawaharlal Nehru, especially as he quickly proved that his transformation from agitator to statesman was accomplished and complete. Foremost among the team of Congress leaders who have become members of his government is Sardar Patel who, like the Nehrus, gave up a flourishing law practice to follow Gandhi. He is now an old man but full of vigor and of great ability. His first job, carried through with distinction in the new regime, was the amalgamation of the many princely feudal states into larger and more orderly units with democratic constitutions. There were hundreds of these, both in the east and west of India. The big states, like Mysore, have retained their princely rulers but have agreed to form constitutional governments.

Patel has often been regarded as an enemy of Nehru. It is true that their outlooks differ fundamentally on some things. Patel is essentially a capitalist lawyer and political statesman. Nehru is a socialist. Nevertheless, they have worked together, through the years, with Gandhi who was no socialist and there is no reason to suppose that Patel and Nehru will not continue to cooperate. Patel is Home Secretary with immense responsibility. Nehru is not attempting to run all the ministries himself. None knows better than Nehru that India must travel far before she can become Socialist. The ground for common action between him and Patel is obviously wide and there is scope for long collaboration. Then there is the man whom Gandhi called Maulana Sahib. His full name is Maulana Abul Kalam Azad, President of the Congress and fellow-negotiator with Nehru during the Cripps Mission in 1942. He is a great Muslim scholar. All his life he has been a devoted friend of Gandhi and the Congress. He is now Minister of Education. He is a magnificent-looking man and of fine speech. His great preoccupation to-day is to get a million school teachers as quickly as possible to spread the light of learning amongst the young. No one is more conscious than he of the extent of illiteracy in India's people. He has proposed to conscript university students for one year's elementary teaching as a qualification for matriculation and two years of elementary teaching as one of the qualifications to get a degree. There is also Rajaji, that is, Mr. Rajagopalachari, former governor of West Bengal, who was with Nehru in all the negotiations with the various British missions. He is now Governor-General of India, in succession to Earl Mountbatten. Two women, who were devoted disciples of Gandhi, were given prominent positions in his ministry. One was a Sikh princess, Rajkumari Amrit Kaur. She is Minister of Health. The other, Mrs. Sarojini Naidu, a poet and a woman of great talent and wit, recently deceased. Both these women gave up their own way of life to follow Gandhi. With these companions Nehru worked excellently.

His government was of course a temporary government pending the nation-wide elections for the new Parliament shaped by the Constituent Assembly upon which the present government rests for its authority. Temporary as it may be, it is unquestionably supported by popular consent. Is this perhaps but a carryover from the days of the anti-British struggle, a riding forward on the tide and destined to ebb? For what of the country and the people at whose head stands this government under Nehru's leadership? They have struggled for their freedom in order to change the lives of the millions who have had brought to them the beckoning light of a higher civilization. The Indian Congress had long since set its face against communal conflict and had put forward the higher conception of an Indian nation. It was not the fault of Nehru or Gandhi, or of any within that Congress movement, that their freedom from the grip of Britain had been accompanied by tragic conflict with the Moslems and the establishment of Pakistan. That splitting of the continent has brought its own problems of state relations but on the other hand it has simplified considerably the liquidation of the communal problems within these new states. Considering the vastness of the upheaval accompanying the change-over, involving the switching across great stretches of territory of ten million panicky Hindus and Moslems, the storm subsided quickly and the leaders of India and Pakistan lost neither prestige nor power for the manner in which they countered the violence and secured its subsidence.

There is an extraordinary similarity in the position of Nehru today and that of Kerensky in the Russian Revolution of 1917. There are of course great differences, too. But the similarities are there and worth noting. The great social tide, a mixture of all social classes, swept the Czar from power and established a Provisional Government with Kerensky at its head. Kerensky was a lawyer and a socialist. The Provisional Government was composed of lawyers, capitalists, intellectuals. The masses of Russia who supported them were as illiterate as the masses of India, and as steeped in religious superstition. They were not of one ethnic stock but of hundreds, each with its own language composed of numerous dialects. The country was vaster than India and as little industrialized.

The great Indian awakening of all classes set in motion a tide before which the British withdrew from India. A Provisional Government was formed with Nehru at its head. Nehru was and is a socialist and a lawyer. His Provisional Government is composed of capitalists, lawyers, intellectuals. The masses of India, upon whose support they rest, are illiterate and steeped in religious superstitions. They are not of one ethnic stock but of hundreds, each with its own language composed of numerous dialects. The country is not industrialized and stands only on the threshold of its industrial revolution.

The Russian Revolution came at the end of a war and Kerensky and his government had decided their attitude to the war. The Indian revolution came at the end of a war and Nehru and his Provisional Government had to define their attitude to the other states and particularly to Britain. Here were differences truly, as well as similarities. But the greatest similarity of all lay in the character of the problems that faced them. The old economy, challenged by the new rising capitalism, created vast social problems which demanded quick answers which could be given only on the basis of the rapid industrialization of the country. Such was the character of the challenge facing Kerensky and his government, who proved incapable of dealing with it. They were flung overboard because they had no answer to the social question which had been reduced to its most elemental form in the demand for bread and peace.

Nehru and his government are not entangled with a war problem. But the immensity of the social problems, all of which have been related to the question of national freedom, is as great as anything which Kerensky, the Socialist lawyer, had to face. The backwardness of the economy of the country, the belatedness of industrialization have all been laid at the door of the foreigner who had dominated their lives. The foreigner is no longer in control. Fair and square on the shoulders of Nehru and his colleagues in government lies now the responsibility for the continuation of the social grievances of the masses in their freedom. The composition of the Indian National Government is similar in kind to that of Kerensky's—a Socialist Prime Minister, Liberals, Conservatives, but without party organizations behind them, and intellectuals who were devotees of Gandhi. Maybe man for man the Provisional Government of Kerensky is not comparable in personal qualities to Nehru's, nor so suffused with idealism. But the political content and the social characteristics are the same. The basic problems they have to face are the same—the land question, modernization of agriculture, industrialization, development of political and economic democracy, cultural development of the nationalities, and so forth. Will Nehru succeed as a statesman where Kerensky failed?

With a mind trained to Western modes of thought he knows the problems of the situation. He knows with what he must deal. The test which he has to face lies not in knowledgeability of the economic and political problems to be dealt with, but in his capacity as leader to carry with him his colleagues in leadership and the social forces upon which he depends for power. Will the devoted disciples of Gandhi, with his backward-looking idealism, give the same devoted loyalty to Nehru in the carrying through of the social transformation of India that they and he gave to Gandhi in the fight for Indian freedom? Can he harness them to the new cause, as Gandhi harnessed them to the old? With the mixed social composition of the National Congress and the party formations within it yet in their infancy, can he carry the Congress unitedly forward with a program sufficiently rapid in its operation to cope with the social needs of the people and prevent the rapid development of a rival power, sufficiently conservative to prevent its repudiation and the splitting of his forces from the Right? India is in one of those remarkable stages in the history of human society when a people is compelled to change its methods of production in order to survive and, in changing them, come into mortal conflict not only with the old ways of life but with all the cherished fantasies and traditions and ideologies to which the old mode of life has given rise. Just as in the Middle Ages of Europe the people of a whole continent, under the domination of the Christian Church, lived in a world of gods and devils, saints of heaven and devils of hell, holy grails, angels and archangels, holy men and witches, and countless taboos, and changed the manner whereby the people secured a livelihood, developed a way of life which shattered the power of the church, dissolved the fantasies and abolished the taboos, compelled the ghosts to depart, so in India a similar great change begins. Nehru is conscious of this. His latest book, *The Discovery of India,* tells of his own delving into the historic treasures of his native land, of what he discovered of its art, its literature, architecture, philosophy, and religions through past centuries.

South of the vast mountain range known as the Himalayas there juts out into the Indian Ocean the peninsula named India, more geographically isolated from the rest of the world than any other great country. In the old historical times there was only one road of invasion along which the three great invasions of the earlier centuries came: Over Hindu Kush and the Khyber Pass. Along it came Alexander the Great, the Moslems who stayed, and the Persians who returned. Out of the 330,000,000 people in what is known as India today there are 38,000,000 of Moslem stock who did not move out when Pakistan was formed. From prehistoric times onward, there grew up the culture of Hindu polytheism with its multitudes of gods and its primitive division into castes according to the functions performed in society—the Brahmins, the teachers; the Kshatriyas, the warrior guards; the Vaishyas, the holders of the purse; the Shudras, who plowed the land. These main divisions were supplemented by thousands more and no man could do work other than that of the caste into which he was born. Every sect within the Hindu religion has its varying practices, rules, and taboos, while there are innumerable languages and dialects peculiar to the village life of the millions scattered across the continent. The invasions of Mohammedanism, Confucianism, Christianity, with their numerable sects, extended the fantastic imagery of the symbolic world of Indian civilization as it slowly spread throughout the continent without plan or purpose. But always it was an agrarian civilization with its handicraftsmen in stone, wood, metals, and clay. The three great invasions, before the British came, brought no new economy with them. They were rivals within a single civilization and not a new type crashing in with new ways of life. The Greeks and the Persians came and departed. The Muslims came, remained, were absorbed, and became one with the civilization of India. The British invasion was different from its predecessors. It was more than the conquest of one nation by another. It was the invasion of a new type of civilization, the impact of modern capitalism and its industrialism upon a primitive economy. It was not an ideological conquest whereby the white Christians imposed their religion upon the brown Hindu. The British were not worried about what went on in the heads of the Indians or concerned about their eternal destiny so long as they remained quiet. They were concerned about their own trade and capital and industry. They conquered not by numbers but by the technique of superior weapons, representative of the level of the productive technique of England. The British were not of a race that could be absorbed by the Indians. Nor could the Indian civilization absorb the civilization of the British or the British absorb the Indian. The conquest of India by Britain was a political and military conquest which history has now rectified. But the invasion of Western civilization, with its higher technique of production, opened up a war to the death against the ancient civilization, which the latter must inevitably lose. The irony of the situation lies in the fact that the British neither understood this aspect of the situation nor wished to disturb what was euphemistically described as the indigenous civilization with its religions and institutions. They wished to eat their cake and have it, to have the best of both civilizations. So they conducted themselves to secure the maximum of exploitation with the minimum of social change in the life of the Indian people. Hence, instead of consciously aiming to transform the civilization of India, to introduce techniques of modern industry and economy, it served only to disintegrate the old without carrying India forward to the new. They treated India as a source of raw materials and a market for their manufactured goods. They brought Indian economy into the orbit, and under the control, of modern finance capital, deliberately retarding the development of the heavy industries without which no country can develop its own power to revolutionize its economic life to the levels of Western civilization.

Thus, out of a population of 330,000,000 India today has only 1,600,000 industrial workers. The vast majority of the population consists of poverty-stricken peasants. Most of them are tenants of landlords and their farms are very small, with methods of cultivation that are exceedingly primitive. In one province alone 20,000,000 peasants have become entirely landless and wander through the countryside in unheard-of poverty and misery.

Nevertheless, it is not the consciousness of these facts that has sunk into their minds. These facts belong to the enlightenment of the present. The vast majority of the multitudes who are now looking to Nehru still think the thoughts of their forefathers, dwell with the polytheistic gods, practice their codes of conduct, exercise the taboos, live in the fantastic traditional worships of a civilization which is, historically, nothing more than a living corpse which Indian freedom must leave behind lest India's people die faster than they die today. Already their life-span is shorter than that of any other nation.

Nehru is a socialist statesman who knows full well that these facts mean that history has thrust upon him the task of leading what the specialists call a bourgeois democratic revolution.

He knows, too, that what has taken place in India is part of a vaster movement spread over all the lands of Asia and that, therefore, his role in India has a much more far-reaching significance than the ordinary "nationalist" can recognize. He saw this long before India was set free and, speaking to the Constituent Assembly of India in December 1946, he said:

. . . the new constitution for India will lead India to real freedom. It will lead also to the freedom of other countries of Asia because, however unworthy, we have become—let us recognize it—leaders of the freedom movement of Asia, and whatever we do we should think of ourselves in these larger terms.

In the following spring, Pandit Nehru opened an Asian Conference in Delhi which representatives from all the countries of Asia attended. In his opening speech he showed how clearly he saw this mightier process. He said:

Standing on this watershed which divides two epochs of human history we can look back on our long past and look forward to the future. Asia after a long period of quiescence has suddenly become important again in world affairs.

Nehru was indeed conscious of his place in the history of Asia. Two years later at the end of the famous Conference of Prime

Ministers of the Commonwealth in May 1949, he said to
an English journalist representing the *News Chronicle* of
London:

For hundreds of years Asia was more or less dominated by
Europe. That period has obviously ended, and what remains of
that domination is rapidly ending, and bound to end although
some countries in Europe seem peculiarly blind to that fact.

Now something really big is happening in Asia which cannot
be classified by any name that can be put on it. It is an upheaval,
with possibly good and possibly evil in it if it is not properly
handled.

This statement, part of a larger interview on the results
of the Prime Ministers' Conference of 1949, reaffirms this
Indian liberation movement as part of the greater Asiatic
liberation now under way. Dramatic developments have
taken place since Nehru became the Prime Minister of India.
These have been years of great excitement in which his capacities as a statesman and his grip of the support of his fellow countrymen have been put to a continuous test. By his
side, at this fateful conference of Prime Ministers, were the
representatives of Pakistan and Ceylon. No one had fought
more tenaciously against the splitting of India into two parts
—India and Pakistan. Nevertheless, when he was faced with
the accomplished fact of this division he promptly adjusted
himself to recognize that his goal of a united India, free from
communal differences, would have to be a more "distant
point" than he had hoped, and he set himself to win the
friendship of Pakistan. His neighbors at the conference, who
were sharing the unique position of Asiatics at a commonwealth conference on equal terms with the white men of
other commonwealth countries, where Liaquat Ali Khan
from Pakistan and Mr. Senanayake from Ceylon. Middle-
aged Liaquat Ali Khan had been a devoted lieutenant of
Jinnah, the leader of the Moslem League. He had been Finance Minister in the interim government and was an able

administrator. Although he is not formally the successor of Jinnah in the leadership of Pakistan, he is actually leading. He was anxious to consolidate his position and to stabilize the new regime.

Pakistan presents strange problems. With one half of the country in the west and the other in the east of India, and more than a thousand miles of India between the two halves, its future is wholly tied up with that of India. There are still large minorities of Indians (30,000,000) in both parts of Pakistan as there are millions of Moslems in India (40,000,-000). From a geographical and economic point of view the partition decision was unjustifiable. The division was a political decision based upon reactionary communalism which sooner or later will have to be amended. Pakistan, of necessity, must cooperate with India. Ali Khan is not of the same type of man as Nehru. He is not a revolutionary in the same sense as is Nehru. He is conservative and rather fearful of being drawn into the great changes confronting Asia. He is the representative of a small nation anxious not to be drawn or driven by great powers or great revolutions.

The other representative, by the side of Nehru, was the elderly Mr. Senanayake, the Prime Minister of Ceylon who had steered the Ceylonese from the status of colonials to Dominion Status as defined in the Westminster Statute. In February 1948 Ceylon became independent and, under Senanayake's leadership, applied for membership of the British Commonwealth. Ceylon is a small island country situated at the south of India, producer of tea and rubber, and an important place of call for transport lines to Australia and the Far East. Senayake is a liberal statesman and politician. He rode along on the tide of India's movement for independence.

All these were met together to consider one question only. It had arisen out of the conference of the previous year, when they had discussed the future of the British Commonwealth of Nations and Nehru had made it clear that India would become a republic. He had then indicated the desirability of

India becoming an independent republican member of the commonwealth. Now they were meeting to consider the constitutional issues raised by India's decision. Could a republic be a member of the commonwealth? When, the previous year, Burma and Eire assumed that a republic could not, nothing was done to correct their assumption and both countries pursued their republican course. After six days' discussion at the London Conference of Prime Ministers there was issued the remarkable declaration which agreed that a republic could be a member of the Commonwealth of Nations. It was agreed by all that the one man who made this possible was Jawaharlal Nehru.

On his return to India he had to meet the criticisms of Indians who accused him of having entered into commitments concerning the Western Union of Europe and the Atlantic Pact. These criticisms he repudiated and took his stand on his outline of India's foreign policy which he had made before he attended the Commonwealth Conference. Then he had stated:

India has a vital role to play in world affairs. There is absolutely no reason why we should be asked to choose between this ideology and that. In the past India spread her cultural doctrine to other countries, not by force of arms but by the strength and vitality of her culture. There is no reason why she should give up her own way of doing things simply because of some particular ideology emanating from Europe. By aligning with any particular group we lose the tremendous vantage ground we have of using the influence we possess—and that influence is growing— for the sake of world peace. We do not seek domination over any other country, and do not wish to interfere in any other country's affairs, domestic or other . . . The supreme question today is how can we avoid a world war. . . . Therefore it becomes all the more necessary that *India should not be lined up with one group of powers or another* which for various reasons today are full of the fear of war and are preparing for it.

When Britain devalued the pound in 1949 it was a matter of the relation of Indian economy to the sterling area which led India to devalue the rupee and there was no political pressure of any kind exercised by Britain in the matter. It simply revealed the economic ties of the commonwealth countries.

Shortly afterward, Nehru visited the Untied States and once again it was suggested that he was about to draw India into the Western bloc of nations and make possible an Asiatic Pact similar in kind to the Atlantic Pact. To the disappointment of the prophets he broadcast speeches far and wide based upon the statement of India's foreign policy which he had already made in India.

Thus, India's first independent Prime Minister and first representative to the commonwealth, the successor of Gandhi in the hearts and minds of India's millions, holds his course, claiming that there is a way forward through rational agreement between nations and peoples as an alternative to the ways of power politics and war.

India was once the brightest jewel in the Imperial Crown. Today, under Nehru, it is the most significant power in the Commonwealth. Without India, the Commonwealth would disintegrate into insignificance; with it, India may yet lead the way to a reconciliation between East and West. That is the ambition of Jawaharlal Nehru, first Prime Minister in the first epoch of India's independence.

C H A P T E R X I

T O W A R D A G R E A T E R S Y N T H E S I S

WHEN THE 1949 CONFERENCE
of Prime Ministers announced that henceforth a republic
could be a member of *The Commonwealth* or, as it had
been termed previously, *The British Commonwealth,* it was
hailed as a great triumph, particularly for Mr. Attlee and
Pandit Nehru, one the Prime Minister of the oldest of the
extant empires and the other the Prime Minister of the
youngest of the Republics. It was a triumph of reason over
symbolism, tradition, and prejudices, and of accommodation
through freedom. The decision amounted to an affirmation
that whatever, and whoever, may be the titular heads of the
states of the changing empire they could hold together in
common association in freedom so long as they had mutual
interests and common purposes. It meant also that the British
Empire, through a process of devolution of authority, set in
motion when the first thirteen settler states of the British
Empire in America cut loose and proceeded to found a new
nation, had almost completely changed its character and its
structure. It was no longer a centralized block of nations
subordinate to a central authority in Britain or anywhere
else. It is true that a large number of colonies, including 60,-
000,000 colored people, are still so subject to the British Government. It is, however, not difficult to see in the revolt in
Nigeria, the racial conflict in South Africa, the stirrings in
the West Indies, the same process at work which has culminated in the formation of the commonwealth. The character

of this commonwealth is the opposite of its ancient imperial association. Indeed the association has become so free that it is little more than a system of conferences between representatives of nations, equal in status, in which their mutual interests between each other, the American, and the Soviet nations and the *larger synthesis*—the United Nations—are discussed.

In the First World War the white dominions of the British Empire first fully asserted their right to function as independent nations in the making of the peace, won the right to be represented at the Versailles Conference, and, in so doing, made necessary the famous Balfour Declaration of 1926 which redefined the position of the dominions as they paved the way to the commonwealth of 1949. From that time the dominions were not only a part of the British Empire but of the larger international association, the League of Nations. They remained in it as independent nations up to its dissolution at the beginning of World War II. Today, every one of the now more numerous constituent nations of the commonwealth is also a constituent member of the United Nations, which is the direct product of the collaboration of the three great empires who won the war. It is a striking fact that the project for the United Nations, in the form of the Dumbarton Oaks proposals, came from the U.S.A., the U.S.S.R., and Great Britain, while it is equally a matter of fact that the representatives of the commonwealth states made great modifications which largely determined the final shape of the United Nations Organization. The main criticisms leveled at the original project for this international organization consisted of challenges to the centralization of power in the hands of the Security Council—precisely the criticism and the challenge they had made against the powers of the British Government within the British Empire. The principal changes which were adopted and embodied in the constitution of the United Nations at San Francisco were essentially the same as those which the dominions had won in the shaping of the commonwealth. At San Francisco they checked the power of the Security Council in favor of more power for the Assembly. At the same time they won recognition for the principle of regionalism in the administration of the larger body, precisely what they had succeeded in doing with the development of the commonwealth.

The United Nations Organization started its career as the nearest approach yet seen in history to the synthesis of the political representation of the nations of the world in a common parliament. But from the moment of its first assembling, there began a reversion to power groupings based not upon the acceptance of the common political purposes and aims which had marked its inauguration but upon the ideologies associated with their different economic and social systems. At the end of the war the varying economic interests of the nation states began to operate in rivalry. While the political reorientation and grouping followed the ideological split of the nations into two rival camps, the economic rivalry and dependence of one nation upon another added confusion to the relationship of the nations.

This re-grouping of the nations, grappling with each other in what is called "cold war," now forms one phase of the new world crisis. The "dollar gap" crisis of the Western nations constitutes another principal phase. Over all hangs the threat of the transformation of the crisis into the atomic blast of a third world war. These features of international affairs overshadow all other matters and obscure the significance of the remarkable transformation of the British Empire and the significance of the creation of the United Nations Organization itself.

The United Nations Organization was created as a permanent assembly of independent nations united in the common purpose of insuring the peace of the world without any one power or group of powers dominating the rest, irrespective of the ideology of its constituent elements. This was the significance and meaning of the adoption of the unanimity principle in the functioning of the Security Council. The attempt to make the United Nations Organization function according to the ideologies of its members is not only contrary to the principles upon which the United Nations was founded but it has be-deviled the economic problems which beset the nations and threatens to precipitate economic and social chaos. The principles enunciated by the U.N.O. were clear enough. They were based upon the full recognition of the sovereignty of all nations within the United Nations Organization, irrespective of their ideology or their economic and social systems. Had they laid down that there must be one ideology or a single economic and social system, as a condition of common action and membership of the United Nations Organization, there would have been no San Francisco Conference and indeed no victory in the war. The practicability of nations with differing ideologies and social systems cooperating together for common ends was demonstrated in the war from which we have only recently emerged. The unanimity principle was adopted by the great powers who initiated the formation of the United Nations Organization to insure the continuation of that same cooperation of diverse elements which proved so strikingly successful in the war against the Fascist powers. There was in that time no diversion from the common tasks by violent discussions of rival ideologies. Churchill ceased to denounce Stalin and hailed him as "Stalin the Great." Roosevelt did not denounce Churchill as the custodian of British imperialism. Whatever the respective statesmen thought concerning the others they kept it to themselves and concentrated on those things upon which all were agreed. It is the reemergence of ideological conflict into the United Nations that is bedeviling the *greater synthesis* of its organization and blocking the road to the realistic and practical way to the solving of the major economic problems which beset the world. It has transformed the unanimity principle into a weapon negating agreement instead of affirming cooperation.

The effect of the political cold war has been to shut off almost half the human race from the world market while at the same time the Western half of the world is engulfed in what is known as the dollar crisis. Expressed in financial terms, this means that all the countries of the commonwealth, plus the countries of Western Europe, are suffering from a shortage of American dollars. This shortage has led to a fantastic scramble for dollars in the countries whose currencies are geared to sterling. The most spectacular phase of this crisis was reached with the British devaluation of the pound in 1949. This was followed by the devaluation of the currencies in all sterling countries. The financial crisis itself was caused by the withdrawal of gold in lieu of dollars from the banks of the sterling countries to pay the U.S.A. for the goods she had sold to them and for which she could not take payment in goods. The center of the financial storm which blew up was in London where the gold reserves of the sterling countries were held by Britain.

The roots of this financial dilemma, however, lay deep in the economic situation, primarily in the fundamental economic relations of the U.S.A. to the rest of the world. This was obscured during World War II by Lend-Lease although in reality it was demonstrating to all the world that stupendous changes in power relations between the nations were taking place at a terrific rate. It was shown in its completeness when the war ended and the United States cut off Lend-Lease with extreme suddenness. It revealed that the United Kingdom had a debit balance of £4,200,000,000 on her Lend-Lease account with America. That was only one account: but the largest. This colossal sum, which could not be repaid, and certainly could not be received in goods by the U.S.A., even should Britain become able to produce them, was promptly canceled. On the heels of this action, the U.S.A. loaned Britain another £1,000,000,000. This was speedily absorbed and followed later by what is known as Marshall Aid. Although with a rapid recovery in productive power the

lus than World War I, while simultaneously it cracked the foundations of British power. The wars did not touch American shores, nor did aircraft bomb her factories or her towns and cities or destroy any of her industries. Her productive power was multiplied and her production equaled more than half the world's total production. Britishers may moralize and justify on these grounds that at the end of World War II, Britain was nearly four and a quarter million pounds on the debit side of the Lend-Lease Account and a further billion pounds in debt to America by 1946. But there the facts rest. To these great sums must be added all the Marshall Aid Britain has received since this plan came into operation. Nothing of these sums has been repaid or is likely to be repaid. However these facts be reviewed, approved or disapproved, they reveal and emphasize the completeness of the eclipse of Great Britain and the whole British Empire by the U.S.A. If we measured their respective strengths in terms of military power the eclipse is still more complete. Britain could no more contemplate war against the United States than a domestic cat could contemplate war with a tiger. Indeed, from a purely military point of view, the United Kingdom is looked upon as an airdrome outpost off the shores of Europe and her colonies and the dominions of the commonwealth as strategic calling stations of her global strategy.

At the same time, it must be emphasized that the British Empire and Commonwealth has long since ceased to be a vast entity spread across the globe and upon which the sun never sets. That is a very romantic picture useful for the teaching of geography to schoolchildren, but bears no relation to the realities of today. It is a collection of nations, each with its own national state, its own economy, its own level of civilization. For example, the United Kingdom has approximately 50,000,000 people, with 23,000,000 gainfully occupied in industries of one kind or another. The Union of South Africa is 6,000 miles away from the United Kingdom and has a total population of 10,700,000 people of whom only 2,500,000 are white. The rest are black people on a low level of civilization. The economy of the country is predominantly agrarian plus the mining of gold and diamonds. New Zealand is 11,373 miles away from the United Kingdom. Its area is one sixth larger than that of the United Kingdom. Its population not more than 2,000,000, all told. This population is engaged largely in farm production, light industries, and commerce. The whole population is less than what is contained in the city of Glasgow or the borough of Brooklyn, New York. To New Zealand, we must add Australia with its area of nearly 3,000,000 square miles. Its population is less than is contained in the city of London and totals 7,500,000. It is a great stock-rearing country, raising more sheep and producing more wool than any other country. It has only just started on the path of industrialization.

To these must be added India, Pakistan, and Ceylon. In these lands the populations and the territory are great. Together they constitute a sub-continent. But the level of the civilizations, with their 450,000,000 people, resting on a primitive agrarian economy, has reduced their existing market capacity in relation to the U.K. to less than that of Australia and New Zealand combined. To these, of course, must be added Canada with its vast territory but a population of not more than 12,000,000. Add all these together, and for the moment be forgetful of the fact that Canada has become an economic enclave of the United States. Add to them the low-leveled civilizations of the 60,000,000 natives scattered among the many colonies of the British Empire. These, all told, before the war, did not account for more than fifty percent of the external trade of the United Kingdom, and today they do not account for more than thirty percent of the world's external trade. Each country has grown up and is growing as a national entity. None has been able to create an autarchy of its own. It exists in competitive relations with all countries, including Britain. While there is a degree of interdependence, each is forced to look elsewhere than to the U.K. for the disposal of its products and the purchase of goods. Each state has its own tariff policy, its own economic structure, its own currency, its own variable economic resources and variable rate of economic development. These facts rule out completely the theory that the commonwealth and the Western Union of Europe constitute a new empire in the making. In fact, a similar analysis of the countries of Western Europe would show it as a collection of national states, each one of which is a competitive unit in relation to the others, the commonwealth, and the U.S.A. The fact that the United Kingdom, the commonwealth countries, and the countries of Western Europe acted with a few exceptions, in accord with each other in the currency crisis, and proceeded to devalue their currencies after the United Kingdom devalued the pound, was not because a new centralized empire was in the making but because every national economy within the commonwealth and the Western countries of Europe stood in the same relation to the economy of the U.S.A. Again it must be emphasized that the fundamental feature of the situation is that the productive power of the U.S.A. has become so enormous that it can completely meet its own requirements and export in such volume that it cannot take payment in goods for the goods it exports or the capital it lends. The internal market of the U.S.A. is literally saturated by American goods. So much is this the case that already an overproduction crisis is developing. Any American or foreigner who talks of Britain and other countries pushing seriously into the American domestic market by better window-dressing and smarter tricks of salesmanship is talking through his hat. In 1938, Britain imported from the U.S.A. £118,000,000 of goods. In that year she exported to the U.S.A. £20,500,000 of goods. Such was the position before the war, before Lend-Lease, before Marshall Aid. The war has not narrowed the trade gap but widened it. Not only is this the case between Britain and America but also between Britain and Canada, one of the largest of the commonwealth countries and outside the sterling group of nations. Canada stands parallel with the U.S.A. in her economic relations with Britain and is another of the great creditors to Britain unable to take full payment in goods from that country.

The anomalous character of the situation stands out clearly. In 1947, Britain received forty-two percent of her imports from the Western Hemisphere and sold in return to it only fourteen percent of her exports. The fact that Marshall Aid, i.e., the dollar means of payment, is far from sufficient to fill the gap is seen in the failure, after three years of strenuous effort, to close it by means of penetrating the dollar market, and the existence of the financial crisis due to the drainage of the gold reserves of the sterling countries. The sequel was logical enough. The shrinkage of the gold reserves of the sterling area compelled all the commonwealth countries to agree to severe cuts of imports from America. That meant a shrinkage of American exports. This did not stop the drainage of gold from the sterling area. In October 1949, Sir Stafford Cripps, Britain's Chancellor of the Exchequer, and Mr. Ernest Bevin, Britain's Foreign Secretary, went to Washington to confer with similar representatives of the United States and Canada. The conference arrived at extraordinary decisions. *All agreed that the solution lay in the direction of aggravating the competitive relations between the commonwealth countries and the sterling countries and the U.S.A.!* The U.S.A. agreed to consider the reduction of tariffs to aid her competitors in the penetration of the American market by goods from the sterling area. Britain led the way in the devaluation of the sterling currencies by reducing the exchange value of the pound by thirty percent, in other words, to cut her export prices by thirty percent and raise her import prices from the dollar countries by more than forty-two percent. All the commonwealth countries with the exception of Pakistan and Canada (who devalued by ten percent) followed suit. Then followed further drastic cuts of imports by the sterling countries from the dollar countries. Here was a two-way attack upon the American economy, contracting her exports and undercutting her prices in her own and the world's markets. At the same time the commonwealth countries appealed to the U.S.A. to invest its capital in the colonies of the empire and commonwealth countries. The logical, long-term, outcome of these developments can be only an intensification of the trade war between the commonwealth countries and the U.S.A., between the countries of Western Europe and between the countries of the commonwealth. To this should be added the restoration of Germany as a principal competitor. Already price-cutting retaliation has begun alongside all kinds of rationalization measures to intensify and increase production at cheaper rates in every country concerned. Had the nations of the Western Hemisphere deliberately aimed at developing an overproduction crisis, they could not have decided on more effective measures for the purpose.

It is only necessary to look the facts of the situation fairly and squarely in the face for this conclusion to be demonstrated. After World War II, the U.S.A. was producing fifty percent of the world's goods. Although her export trade formed not more than ten percent of her production it has been increasing in importance to the American economy with every increase in her productive capacity. In 1938 she had become the world's greatest exporter, with fourteen percent of the world's export trade to her credit. In 1947, she had thirty-one percent. All the countries of the Commonwealth together had between them 25.6 percent of the world's export trade in 1938 and 24.9 percent in 1947. Observe, then, that in 1948 the American share of exports fell to 22.8 percent and the Commonwealth share rose to 28.4 percent. At the same time the European share of exports rose from 21.1 percent in 1947 to 24.2 percent in 1948. Thus, the year of recovery, at the expense of the U.S.A. taxpayer, had its sequel in the contraction of her export market. The huge program of cuts in imports from America, agreed upon by the commonwealth and European countries for 1949-50, means a further contraction in American exports. Had the U.S.A. not embarked upon a huge rearmament program for herself and the countries signatory to the Atlantic Pact, the U.S.A. might already be languishing in the depths of a slump. But examine the import side of the picture. In 1938, the U.S.A. took nine percent of world imports, a disparity of five percent as compared with her exports. When, however, her exports rose to thirty-one percent her imports increased only to the extent of twelve percent.

It has become a habit of the British, even in their statistical data, to present the problem as if the commonwealth was functioning as an economic bloc, with Western Europe as another bloc. The fact is that they are political groupings of nations with common economic problems in relation to the U.S.A. and the Eastern World but dissimilar economic problems in relation to each other. This is best illustrated by Canada. Canada's exports to the U.S.A. in 1938 amounted to £53,000,000. During World War II Canada's production output rose from 5½ billion dollars to 15½ billion dollars. Her exports to the U.S.A. rose to £372,000,000 in 1948. But her imports rose in the same period from £95,000,000 in 1938 to £493,000,000 in 1948. Canada thus has her dollar gap in relation to the U.S.A., in common with the United Kingdom. That, however, is not the only gap. In 1938 the United Kingdom imported from Canada £79,000,000 worth of products and Canada received from the United Kingdom in that year just £23,000,000 of goods, i.e., less than one third of what she had exported. In 1948, the contrast was greater still. Canada exported to the United Kingdom £217,000,000 of goods and imported from the United Kingdom only £70,000,000 worth. As exporters, then, Canada and the U.S.A. stand in the same relation to the United Kingdom but in relation to the shortage of American dollars Canada is in the same dilemma as the United Kingdom. Examine the position of Australia. This country imported from the U.S.A. not more than £18,-000,000 of goods in 1938, rising to £59,000,000 in 1948. Her exports to the U.S.A., while showing only £1,000,000 in 1938 rose to £28,000,000 in 1948, and still there remained an adverse balance of £38,000,000. But it would appear that the British colonies, as distinct from the commonwealth countries, have established a different relationship with the U.S.A. Here is sheer irony. The British colonies have exported to the U.S.A. as follows: in 1938, £29,000,000 of goods; in 1947, £92,000,000; and in 1948, £106,000,000. The British colonies received in return from the U.S.A. £16,000,-000 in 1938, £82,000,000 in 1947, and £86,000,000 in 1948, favorable balances to the colonies in each year! Compare these facts with the Anglo-American traffic. In 1938, the U.K. exported to the U.S.A. £20,000,000 of goods; in 1947, £48,-000,000; in 1948, £66,000,000. The U.S.A. exported to the United Kingdom £118,000,000 in 1938; £297,000,000 in 1947; and £148,000,000 in 1948. In passing, note the contraction of American exports in 1948. The deficit each year remains huge. But as the currency of the colonies is geared to sterling, we are informed that the colonial surplus can, by triangular traffic, help the sterling countries in relation to the dollar. That is true enough but the irony of the situation lies in the fact that £46,000,000 out of the £92,000,000 in 1947 and £41,000,000 out of the £106,000,000 in 1948 consists of rubber from Malaya which can be used only by cutting down the production of synthetic rubber in the U.S.A. or in stock piling, the limits of which are quickly reached. And then what?

All these facts must be placed on the background of the cold war, based upon the ideologies of the national states whereby half of Europe and three quarters of Asia have been almost completely cut out of the world market. On that background, which has produced the political unity of two groups of states, the facts enumerated show that the statesmen of the Western Hemisphere have handled the economic problems in a way, that, barring interference, must lead to ruin.

The U.S.A., the richest and the greatest producer of goods the world has yet seen, finances the rehabilitation of the United Kingdom, the commonwealth, and Western Europe, its principal competitors in the world market. Then, at a time when the U.S.A. needs an increasing share in that market, its competitors cease, increasingly, to buy from her, undercut her prices by devaluing their currencies, and simultaneously seek to penetrate her internal market. Were it not for the colossal spending on armaments, a direct product of the ideological warfare between East and West, the productive machinery of the U.S.A. would soon be brought to a standstill. The more steadily and fearlessly these facts are examined the more staggering they appear until one is prone to regard the world as a universal madhouse and statesmen as its principal patients. As the nations of the commonwealth and Western Europe approach the restoration of their full competitive power in multilateral trading, the fundamental contrast between the productive power and market capacity of the Western world becomes increasingly manifest. This attempt to simultaneously develop production and contract the market is both stupid and disastrous.

There are only two courses open. One is for the Western powers, of the dollar and sterling areas, to embark on a war of conquest on the nations guilty of revolution, to transform the *cold war* into a *hot war*, forgetful of fact that the U.S.A. and its British Allies, primarily concerned in such a decision, were themselves born in revolution and grew through revolution and that two world wars have led to the extension of the revolution they are so anxious to avoid. The colossal armament boom, which such a decision would call forth, if embarked upon by every country concerned, could possibly prevent an early slump, although it could not prevent inevitable disaster. It could only postpone the slump by repeating the existing problem and the measures taken already, on a vaster scale. Assuming the physical practicability of such a war and that the peoples of the Western world could be harnessed to such a course, and the Eastern world of social revolution be militarily defeated and their economic and political systems uprooted, what then? No one can contemplate the forces which would be arrayed against each other and the character of that war without realizing that no country could escape ruin and desolation. Instead of Britain, the commonwealth, and the countries of Western Europe requiring *Marshall Aid* from a powerful American productive apparatus, all Europe and all Asia and all the commonwealth countries would require Marshall Aid amidst unspeakable desolation from an America which itself could never again escape her share of destruction in a world at war. Such a course could be adopted only in a world gone mad, although it is the inevitable outcome of cold-war logic.

There is, however, another way still latent within the circumstances of our time. It is the way advocated by every great-power statesman while World War II was raging. They declared that it lay through the *greater synthesis* whereby the three great empires astride the world—the American, Soviet, and British—should lead the United Nations in unison and cooperation. The time has come when the Assembly of the nations must silence the rival propagandists of ideologies, whatever they might be and insist upon the right of every nation to be sovereign in its own house, have its own economy and social set-up, and implement the basic principles upon which the United Nations Organization was founded. For in this organization, and its successful operation, lies the real alternative course from that of disastrous war.

All the facts show clearly that the major problem before the world, and especially the Western Hemisphere, is that of providing an expanding market for rehabilitated and expanding production. That market is located eastward of the Iron Curtain, embraces the Soviet Union, all China, all Asia, the islands of the Pacific, the countries of the Near East, and the African continent. It includes all the vast regions, embracing more than half the human race, waiting to be raised from the level of ancient civilizations to that of the West. To maintain and expand its economy, the United States has reached the stage where its internal market, even when allowance is made for the raising of the standard of life of millions of its inhabitants, is far too small to absorb its total production possibilities. Stock piling cannot go on indefinitely. The vast export of capital during the war in the form of credits, Lend-Lease, and outright gifts, gave all American industry the terrific stimulus that enabled her to reach her present heights of power. By fundamentally the same means, namely, vast credits, loans, grants, investments to the nations on the threshold of industrialization, and the application of Western techniques to production, can the world market be expanded to absorb the increasing productive power of the West. The magnitude of this real market of human need is beyond measure. Such ends cannot be achieved by means of cold war or hot war, but only in the free association of nations acting in unison and abandoning the method of imposing political fetters upon recipients of aid. The political mechanism for this purpose has been created on the initiative of the three great powers upon whom the peace and prosperity of the world depends: the United Nations Organization. Through it, and by these means, the way definitely lies toward a solution of the world's economic problems. In its operation the U.S.A., the Soviet Union, and the British Commonwealth should become three regional organizations in the same free association with each other, and with other groupings of nations, as were those groupings which transformed the British Empire into a Commonwealth of Nations. This is the practical answer to the fear of Communism which flourishes only where other systems fail.

A C K N O W L E D G M E N T S

I HAVE HAD THE BENEFIT OF THE criticism and the advice of a number of persons in obtaining the material and in writing this book. I gratefully acknowledge the assistance of William Clark, Louis Fischer, Joseph Freeman, Lionel Gelber, John Duncan Miller, Madeline Miller, Marcus Sieff, J. T. Murphy and Woodrow Wyatt, M.P. I am equally indebted to the following writers on Commonwealth and British Empire affairs: E. Walker, W. K. Hancock, H. Mansergh, Sir Alfred Zimmern, L. Barnes, B. Keith, C. E. Carrington, G. Palmer, Sir John Seeley, F. Scott, G. Spry, J. A. Hobson, Lord Hailey, Sir Reginald Coupland and, to the following authors of biographies on the various persons dealt with in this volume: R. Jenkins, V. Brome, J. T. Murphy, T. Evans, P. Guedalla, M. Edelman, S. Cloete and J. C. Armstrong. I acknowledge also the use of original writings and speeches by the persons discussed in the book. To Winston Churchill, Herbert Vere Evatt and W. L. Mackenzie King, for the privilege of personal conversations, I wish to add a special word of personal thanks.

While expressing my gratitude for documentary material made available to me and permission granted for publication I must emphasize that the responsibility for all views expressed in this volume are the author's own except what is directly attributable to others by direct quotation.

I N D E X